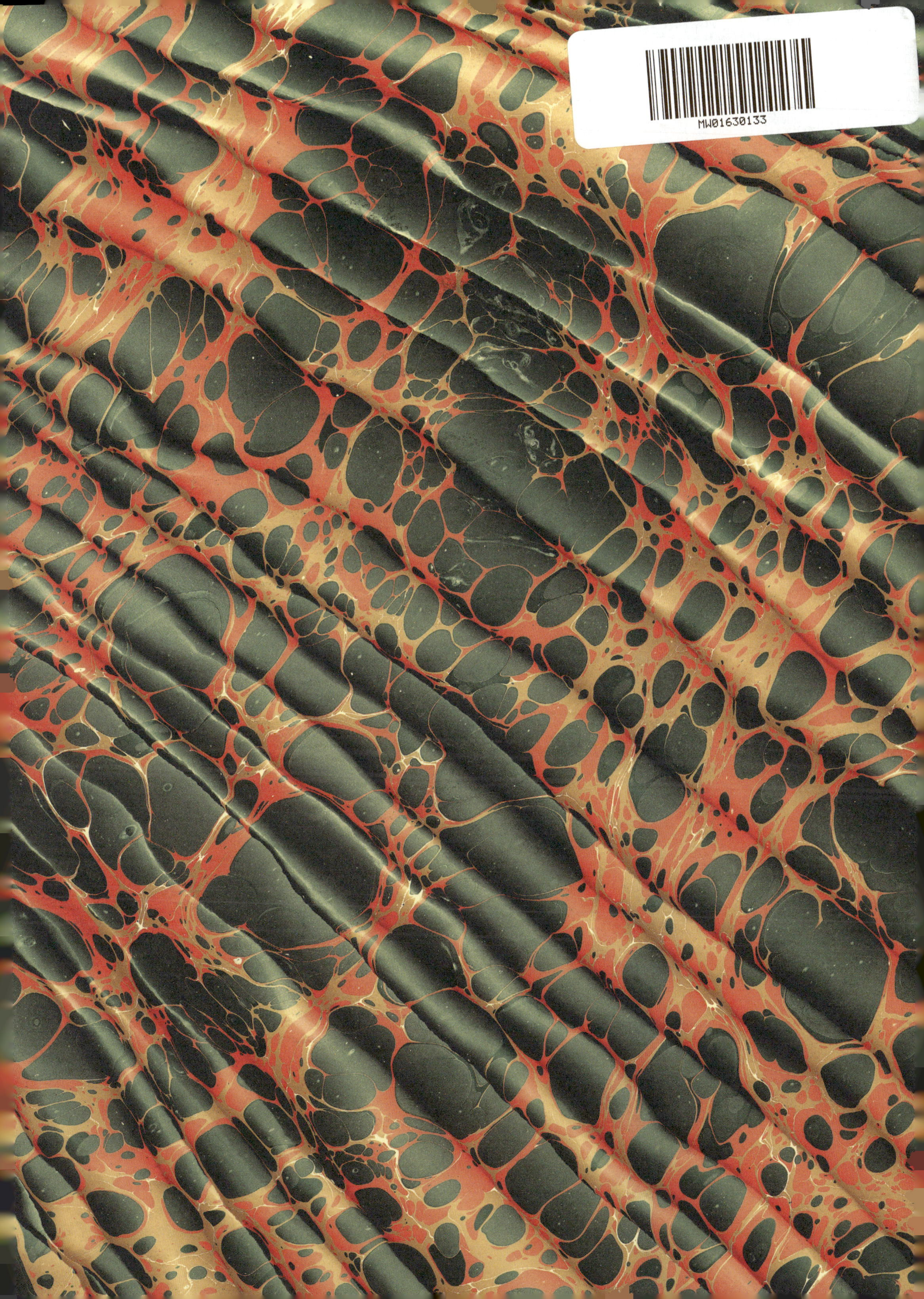
MW01630133

Alexander Lüdeke

TILTROTOR AIRCRAFT
An Illustrated History

Alexander Lüdeke

TILTROTOR AIRCRAFT

An Illustrated History

Schiffer Publishing Ltd

4880 Lower Valley Road • Atglen, PA 19310

Published by Schiffer Publishing Ltd.
4880 Lower Valley Road
Atglen, PA 19310
Phone: (610) 593-1777
FAX: (610) 593-2002
E-mail: Info@schifferbooks.com.
Visit our web site at: www.schifferbooks.com
Please write for a free catalog.
This book may be purchased from the publisher.
Please include $5.00 postage.
Try your bookstore first.

In Europe, Schiffer books are distributed by:
Bushwood Books
6 Marksbury Avenue
Kew Gardens
Surrey TW9 4JF
England
Phone: 44 (0) 20 8392-8585
FAX: 44 (0) 20 8392-9876
E-mail: Info@bushwoodbooks.co.uk.

CONTENTS

FOREWORD AND ACKNOWLEDGEMENTS

Alexander Lüdeke
Dortmund, August 2009

At the time when this book appeared, the U.S. Marines had just successfully completed the Iraq use of the first series-produced tiltrotor airplane in the world, the Bell Boeing MV-22B, and were preparing to transfer it to Afghanistan. At the same time, the prototypes of probably the first civilian tiltrotor airplane to be produced in series, the Bell/Agusta BA609, were flying in the USA and Italy.

Including all prototypes and test models that served to make tiltrotor technology usable and reliable, a total of fifty-one years passed from the first tests of the Transcendental 1-G in 1954 to the approval of series production for the V-22 in 2005. One can imagine what progress the development of conventional winged aircraft made from 1902 to 1954. There, fifty-one years marked the jump from the first flights of the Wright Brothers at Kitty Hawk to supersonic jets. This comparison may offer an impression of what problems and difficulties the development of tiltrotor technology and the related concepts had to fight against. This book portrays the exciting and dramatic development of this revolutionary airplane type and also attempts to offer a look at possible future developments. To illustrate the tremendous variety of solution concepts for one and the same problem, the blending of the best qualities of rotor and propeller aircraft, I have decided to include in this book not only pure tiltrotor planes, but also the related concepts such as tilting propellers and tiltwing craft. The unbelievable variety of studies and projects that never got any farther than the drawing board, though, makes it impossible to treat every design. I also want to indicate that this book was written from the perspective of a historian and not of an engineer. Yet the book that lies before you offers a hitherto unique overview of the history of the origin of this remarkable type of aircraft, which despite everything is surely just at the beginning of its development.

Numerous individuals, companies and institutions have helped in the formation of this book, and my thanks go to all of them.

This applies particularly to the following persons: Gert Dieter Schmidt, Christina Gotzhein (Eurocopter), Hans-Ulrich Willbold (EADS Heritage), Ross Beedle, John Aldaz, Scott Lother (up-ship.com), Tommy H. Thomason (tommythomason.com), Richard Paweling (rp-one.net), Dave Mangham and Kyle Scott.

Special mention is deserved by Herr Jens Baganz, who generously granted me permission to use many of his drawings and obtained hard-to-get information for me. The team at the Helicopter Museum in Bückeburg, namely Messrs. Wolfgang Gastoff, Matthias Stäblein and Roland Oster, are owed my deep gratitude. Their knowledge, readiness to help, and hospitality have made my work much easier.

Not least, my life companion Martina Pohl shall not remain unnamed, for she has read and corrected my manuscripts with great care and patience.

INTRODUCTION

CHAPTER 1

The ability of a helicopter to take off and land vertically and to maintain suspended flight for a long time is of the greatest value in civilian and military action, and modern-day air transport would be unthinkable without it.

To be sure, helicopters must take serious disadvantages in the bargain in return for these abilities. Thus their service flight ceiling is limited to about 6,000 meters as a rule, and only seldom do they attain higher speeds than 350kph. Compared to airplanes with fixed wings, though, helicopters are not deficient in only these realms, as the range and payload of most helicopters are also less than those of fixed-wing planes of the same size. The reason for this is in the construction of the helicopter. Its rotor, of course, allows it to take off and land vertically, but for aerodynamic reasons it also limits its performance.

Thus designers tried early to blend the advantages of both kinds of aircraft. The results are the so-called "vertical takeoff" or VTOL planes. VTOL is the English abbreviation for "vertical takeoff and landing," and since most planes of the type are also capable of short starts and landings, they are often summed up as V/STOL (vertical/short takeoff and landing). The building of a successful VTOL airplane, though, is anything but simple. Such an aircraft must, for one thing, have enough vertically directed thrust or drive to be able to move its weight vertically into the air, and on the other, also enough horizontally directed thrust or drive to be able to move itself. The vertical thrust can be produced in various ways, but basically it is true that an aircraft (that is heavier than air) can only climb vertically when it "thrusts" enough air downward. The takeoff power thus corresponds to the downward-directed motive energy of the air.

An airplane can thus push a little air quickly (jet power) or a lot of air slowly downward (rotor), whereby the latter possibility uses considerably less motive energy. Thus it follows that a rotor that spreads over as large an area as possible (circular

The unique abilities of a helicopter, here an
HH-60G "Pave Hawk" of the USAF before
the background of the Golden Gate Bridge,
make actions possible that would be
unthinkable with conventional fixed-wing
airplanes. *(USAF)*

An AV-8B Harrier of the USMC lands on the
British carrier HMS Illustrious on July 19,
2007. *(DoD)*

A Yakovlev Yak-38 "Forger" on board a Soviet carrier. *(DoD)*

area) is the most effective. The relationship between the circular surface and the flying weight is referred to as circular surface pressure. A meager circular surface pressure is most economical and at the same time creates the least downdraft. This explains why to date only two jet-powered VTOL airplanes have been produced in series, the British Aerospace "Harrier" and the Yakovlev Yak-38, of which only the Harrier can be regarded as a success. The jet engines of the Yakovlev are able to move barely more than the weight of the plane itself, and its performance in hovering flight is marginal.

For this reason, numerous tests have been undertaken to produce not only lift but also forward thrust with the help of a rotor. The idea is old and seems very simple: Why do we not set up the rotor so that its mast can be tipped from the vertical to the horizontal? In this way the rotor would produce lift when taking off and landing, while wings took over this task in conventional flight and the rotor then provided forward thrust.

A real rotor, though, is aerodynamically not ideal for producing forward thrust, for its blades are only slightly twisted in themselves. They also are inclined to flutter in a horizontal position, which can result in dangerous vibrations.

The blades of a propeller, on the other hand, are very strongly twisted in themselves. Since VTOL machines spend only a small part of their flying time in hover-hold, the principle of the tiltrotor was rejected, and machines were built that could tilt their propellers instead of a rotor, and thus are better suited for conventional flight. Thus the difference between propeller and rotor also disappears, for example, as in so-called proprotors.

Both concepts, though, are based on the principle that an airscrew can be tilted so that it produces lift and forward thrust.

This can basically happen in three ways: solely by tilting the airscrew, tilting the powerplant and airscrew, or tilting the wing and airscrew (and powerplant).

To increase the effectiveness of a propeller, many designers equip it with a mantle, but the basic principle remains the same. Tiltrotor, tilting-propeller, tilt-wing and tipping-mantle planes are thus variations on one and the same theme. Thus these four types of VTOL planes all appear together in this book.

Although the idea of tilting the airscrew seems so simple, the problem of VTOL flight just touches on it. Such aircraft must, for example, have an adequate control system, so as to be controllable in hover-hold and slow flight.

A rigid-wing airplane flying level in correct trim generally inclines to turn back to its airplane status on its own, which means that it is stable. The controls must thus try to overcome this "built-in" stability. A rigid-wing airplane must thus try to overcome this "built-in" stability. A rigid-wing airplane accomplishes this mainly with the help of its rudder, ailerons and elevators. Its movement along its longitudinal axis ("rolling") is controlled by the panels on its wings; the side rudder controls the so-called "yawing," the movement along its vertical axis. The height controls steer the plane along its transverse axis ("pitching"). So that these controls can carry out their effectiveness, a certain minimum speed is required. If a VTOL plane flies very slowly or even hovers, this kind of control is ineffective.

A helicopter does not have this problem, as it is controlled by the adjustable angle of its turning rotor blades. The cyclical adjustment is thus responsible for rolling and the collective adjustment for nodding. Movement around the vertical axis ("yawing") is controlled in helicopters with just one rotor mostly by means of the tail rotor.

Vertically starting and landing aircraft must thus be designed so that they can be controlled even in slow or hovering flight. But this task is made harder by the fact that the stability occurring in conventional flight is not present in these types of

The rotor blades of this MH-53 (left) are clearly shaped differently... *(USAF)*

...than the propeller blades of this C-130J (right). *(USAF)*

Conventionally designed helicopters like this Sikorsky R-4 are controlled for their longitudinal and transverse axes by the collective and cyclical adjustment of their rotor blades. Control on the vertical axis is done by the rear rotor. *(NASA)*

flight. This means that the craft does not lie quiet in flight but rather that the pilot (or equivalent automatic controls) must be permanently alert to keep the plane under control. Every tilt, every roll or other movement must be opposed immediately to avoid a crash. But oversteering could have equally fatal results.

To be under control in slow flight or hover-hold, craft with jet engines are equipped with appropriate steering jets, while planes working with tilting airscrews have partially or completely adjustable rotors or propellers. For tiltrotor and tiltwing craft in particular, there must usually be additional steering jets or propellers in use, since their propellers are simply not completely collectively or cyclically controllable.

On the way to the VTOL airplane, the steering problem was a primary problem area. Even experienced pilots were often overwhelmed by these tasks. Only the coming of modern electronic flight and engine controls made successful airplanes of this kind possible. Thus today a tiltrotor airplane, the V-22 "Osprey," is in series production, and it may thus be assumed that a civilian plane, the BA609, will soon follow.

The way to these aircraft was long, full of mistakes and accidents. Remarkably, it began far earlier than one would generally assume.

The Bell Boeing V-22 is the first series-produced tiltrotor airplane in the world. This CV-22B of the 8th SOS of the USAF is taking off from the deck of the USS Bataan (LHD-5) on August 14, 2007. *(USN)*

EARLY PROJECTS AND DESIGNS FROM 1845 TO 1945

CHAPTER 2

In the middle of the 19th century, early air-travel pioneers had already gotten the idea of arranging an airscrew so that it was tiltable on the longitudinal axis. In this way the flying machine was not only to rise vertically, but also to move horizontally through the air without problems. Yet all the designs lacked a suitable power source. Although a suitable powerplant, in the form of the Otto engine, was finally available, the designs of the early 20th century achieved no success. Yet the speedy progress of the fixed-wing airplanes made it clear how much they depended on sufficiently long takeoff and landing runways. Thus many designers were inspired by the progress in the development of the first helicopters and tried to create a link between the two types of aircraft. Most of these craft, though, were the ideas of individual inventors who did not have the means to turn their ideas into deeds.

COSSUS

The first known design of a tiltrotor airplane was made in 1845. The Frenchman Cossus developed the model of a helicopter with three rotors, the largest of which was fixed in the center of the model, while the two smaller ones were mounted beside it and could be tipped. To power his model, Cossus chose a clockwork. Whether this model actually flew cannot be determined.

NELSON

The first patent on an aircraft with a tilting rotor was obtained on June 21, 1861, by the American Mortimer Nelson. In the patent documents the New Yorker stated that his airship ("aerial car") was to be used along with a balloon to allow the latter fast ascent and speedy forward flight. Later, though, Nelson was convinced that his invention was strong enough to stay in the air without a balloon. Nelson's apparatus consisted of a fuselage pointed at the front and rear, a rear rudder and two tilting shafts coming out of the fuselage, each one bearing two rotors. In all, the aerial car thus had four rotors. Nelson was aware that the rotors had to turn in opposite directions to equalize the turning moment. Fuselage, rudder and rotors were to be covered with canvas or silk. Over the fuselage, Nelson planned to install a kind of "sail" of the same material to provide lift. The frame and all the other metal parts were to be made of aluminum, then a new, scarcely known material, in order to save weight.

The aerial car, though, had no adequate power source. Nelson was aware that the steam engines then common were much too big and heavy to drive his invention, so he concentrated on the design of a light combustion engine, for the fuel of which he applied for a further patent, but his aerial car never got beyond the drawing board.

A drawing from the 1861 patent application.

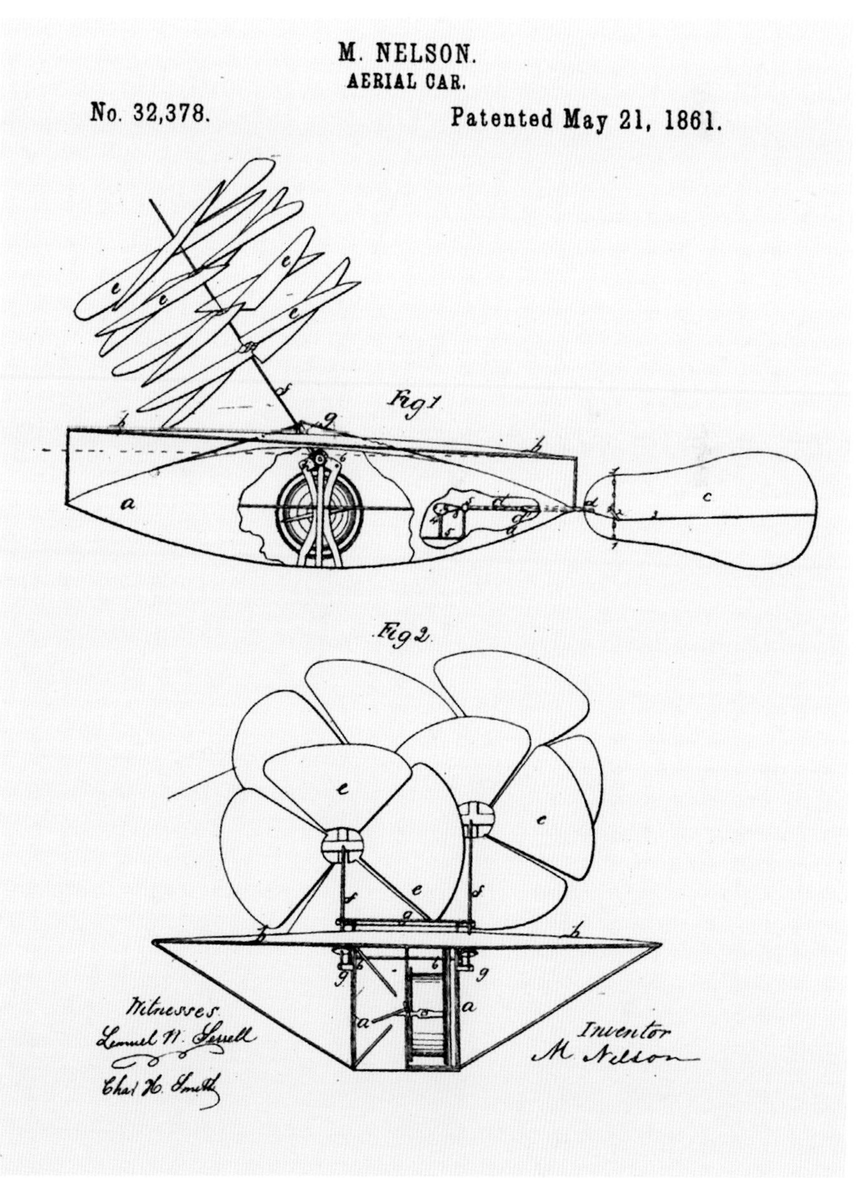

CROWELL

Luther C. Crowell of West Dennis, Massachusetts also received a patent on June 3, 1862, about one year after Nelson, for a flying machine with a tipping rotor. Crowell's design had two opposing airscrews, which were pointed vertically during takeoff and landing but tipped forward for horizontal flight. The fuselage of this flying machine consisted basically of an open frame; Crowell gave no specific information as to its material. Crowell proposed that the wing structure was to consist of wood with oilcloth or silk covering it. A surface thickness of two to three feet (some 61 to 91.4cm) was to allow it to be filled with hydrogen or a similar light gas to support the lift effect. The wings were designed so that they could be folded by hand with the help of a winch for takeoff and landing. Steering the machine was to be done by a vertical and lateral rudder attached to the rear and controlled by cables from the cockpit. Crowell mentioned the installation of a condenser for a steam engine, but gave no further information.

Crowell patented his flying craft during the American Civil War. Thus he also got the idea of wanting to use his craft for bombing attacks.

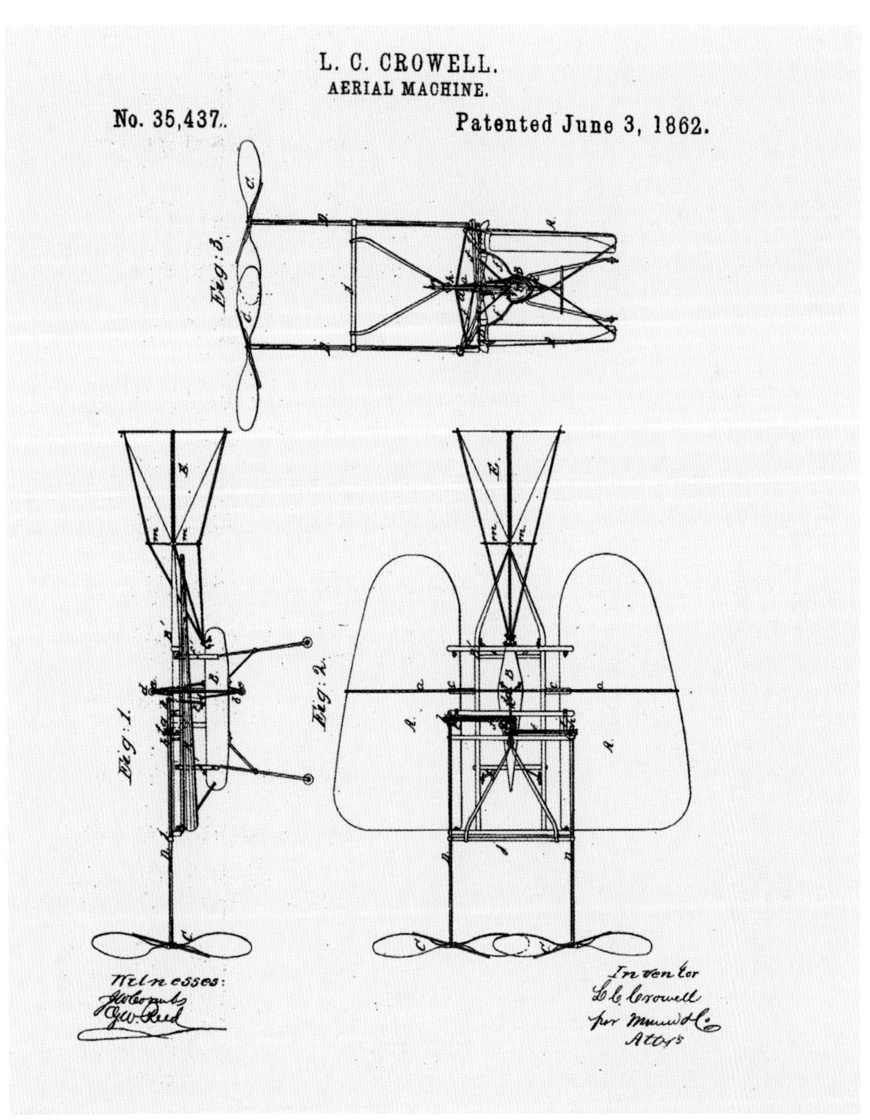

SCHÖRKE

On April 22, 1896, Alexander Schörke of Dresden was issued a patent by the German Reich's patent office for a helicopter with a tilting and swinging rotor on its transverse and longitudinal axes. By the tipping of the "screw wing" in various directions, Schörke thought, no other steering controls would be needed. In the patent papers he described various means and types of power sources, including a model with hand and foot drive, which not unlike a bicycle, had pedals and chains. A version for lifting loads was to be powered by a steam turbine. Schörke suggested leaving this on the ground, since his flying apparatus would only lift loads to a low height. There the turbine was to create electricity by means of generators and, via a cable, load batteries on board the helicopter to run an electric motor. Schörke planned to give his invention steering by electric remote control via cable.

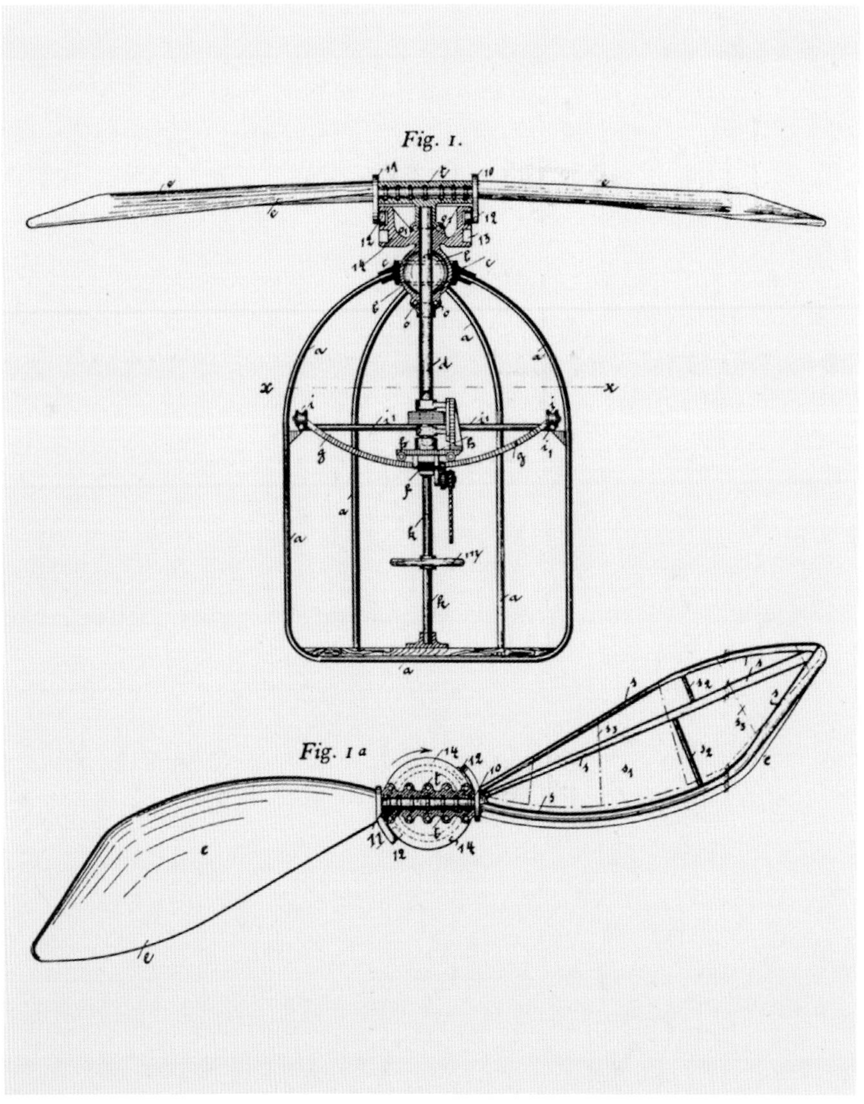

Alexander Schörke's aircraft received Patent No.95 963 from the German Reich on April 22, 1896.

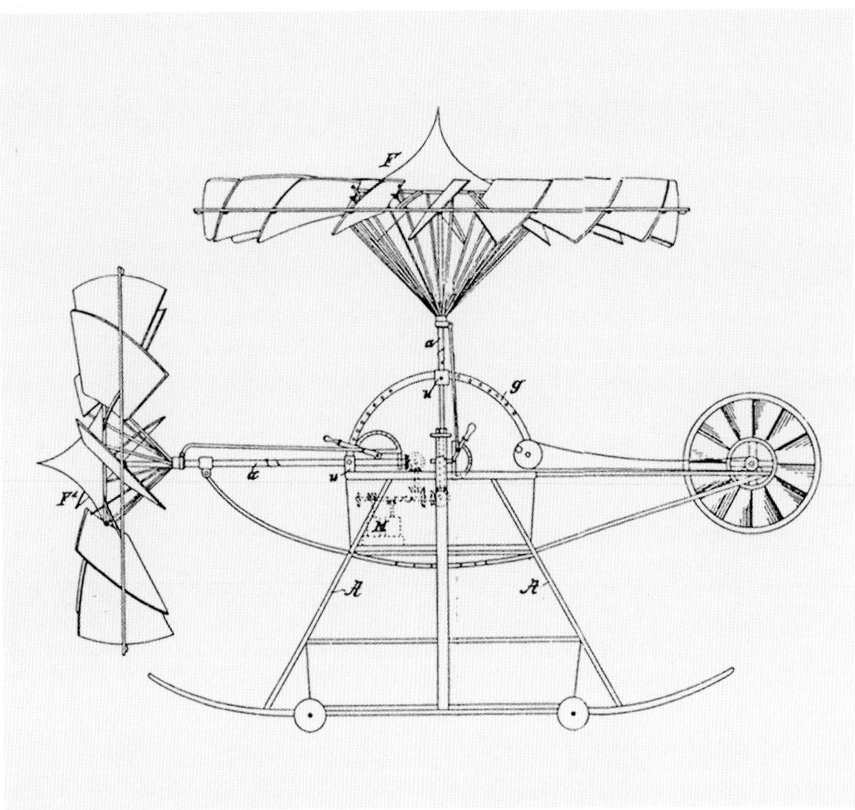

Note the rear rotor, similar to the modern "Fenestron," of Beenen's invention.

BEENEN

Only a few weeks later, on May 6, 1896, another Dresden man, Dr. R. Beenen, received a German Reich patent for a helicopter design with a tilting and swinging main rotor on the transverse and longitudinal axes. When one compares the two designs, Beenen's machine seems to be at first glance to me better developed. Beenen already thought of a rear rotor to equalize the turning moment, even though it was only to be turned by hand. To be sure, he gave no information as to how his flying machine was to be motorized. Beenen's design, though, had landing skids not unlike those of a modern helicopter, plus a main rotor reminiscent of turbine blades. It could be positioned so as to serve, according to Beenen, as a sort of parachute if the motor failed.

DUFAUX

The French Swiss brothers Henri and Armand Dufaux were the first to successfully make a tipping-rotor design fly. The brothers already owned a flourishing company, making motor kits for bicycles and small motorcycles, when they turned to air travel in 1902 and set out to build a flying machine that could take off and land vertically.

At first the brothers built a model for which they adapted their motorcycle motors. Weighing only 4.5 kilograms, it produced 3.1 HP. The model was finally finished in 1904 and had two opposed four-vane rotors, each of two-meter diameter, on two struts. At its introduction in April 1905 in Geneva, this machine was able without problems to lift not only its own weight of 17kg, but also 6.5kg ballast into the air. To be sure, the model had to be steered by means of long ropes, since there was no way to steer the flight movements aerodynamically.

The Dufaux brothers with their tiltrotor model. *(from the Helicopter Museum, Bückeburg-HMB)*

The dragon model during flight at Corsier in 1905. *(from HMB)*

The Dufaux tiltrotor model in the Musée des Arts et Métiers in Paris. *(PHGCOM cc by sa 3.0)*

In May of that year the brothers displayed their design in Paris. Among the excited spectators were aerial pioneers like Louis Blériot, Alberto Santos-Dumont, Clément Ader, Henri Farman and Gabriel Voisin.

Back in Geneva, the brothers began to build a dragon in Hargrave's style around their successful design, to handle lift in level flight. The rotors were mounted between a front and a rear "box" on the dragon and could be tilted upward, downward or backward. The 23kg model rose into the air in the autumn of 1905, but it still was not steerable.

Yet Henri and Armand Dufaux decided to build a manned aircraft. For it they designed a 20-cylinder motor that produced 120 HP but weighed only 85kg. In 1908 the flying machine finally took form. Its structure was reminiscent of the 1905 dragon model. In the center, between the wings, were the motor, the pilot's seat and the struts for the tilting airscrews. The aircraft had a flying weight of 660 kilograms, was nine meters long and had a wing surface of sixty square meters. The airscrews had a diameter of 2.8 meters. But production dragged, for there were problems in the development of the gearbox, the shafts, the powerplant and numerous other details. In a conventional takeoff attempt in August 1909, the plane was badly damaged. The Dufaux brothers, in view of the cost of repairs, decided to give up the project and turn to building conventional airplanes, with which they gained more success.

The Dufaux brothers' helicopter model, along with other renowned historic craft and inventions, has been in the Conservatoire National des Arts et Métiers (CNAM) in Paris since 1911.

CAGE

Early in 1909 the twenty-four-year-old engineer John M. Cage of Denver, Colorado displayed his new type of flying machine. Cage was probably the first who wanted to use tilting mantled propellers and thus preceded designs like the VZ-4 and X-22A, which were to be built some fifty years later.

His flying machine was to consist of a boat-shaped fuselage, across which a rectangular cage of metal pipes, covered with wire, was mounted. Cage planned a cylinder some 1.4 meters long and 1.8 meters in diameter on either side of the fuselage, tilting on the transverse axle. In each cylinder there were to be two coaxial, contra-rotating propellers, which would also rotate counter to their opposite numbers on the other side of the fuselage. It was planned that a steam engine producing 100 HP would drive the four airscrews via a gearbox and shafts at a speed of 3,000rpm. Cage believed he could do without wings in the traditional sense, since he thought the mantled propellers would produce sufficient lift. At the end of the fuselage, though, there would be a conventional elevator of the time, in order to allow the flying machine to make pitching movements. As for how his craft was otherwise to be steered, Cage offered no further data. In the fuselage was an open cockpit for two men. At the sides of the fuselage were two floats, which were to allow the flying machine to take off and land not only on water, but also on land and ice. Cage stated for his invention, minus motor, a net weight of "600 pounds," and "850 pounds" with a motor, being some 272 and 386 kilograms. Tests made with full-size models and mantled propellers promised, according to Cage, that his machine with the projected 100 HP motor could produce enough thrust to lift up to 760kg off the ground. As far as is known, Cage could never realize his project.

A model of Cage's design in the Helicopter Museum, Bückeburg. *(Roland Oster)*

DORNIER

Claudius Dornier, a pioneer in the manufacturing of German metal airplanes, developed the idea shortly after the end of World War I of making the engine or engines of an airplane tiltable around the transverse axis, so that they supplied not only forward propulsion but also lift. But it was not Dornier's goal to create a VTOL machine; he just wanted to improve slow-flight characteristics.

Besides a single-engine plane, its motor in the bow with an airscrew that was to be tilted upward, Dornier also described a tri-motor variant in the patent document. A piston engine with a pulling propeller was to be installed in the nose, not moving, while two motors hung under the wings worked with pushing propellers. In fast flight, all three motors were to remain horizontal, but in slow flight the

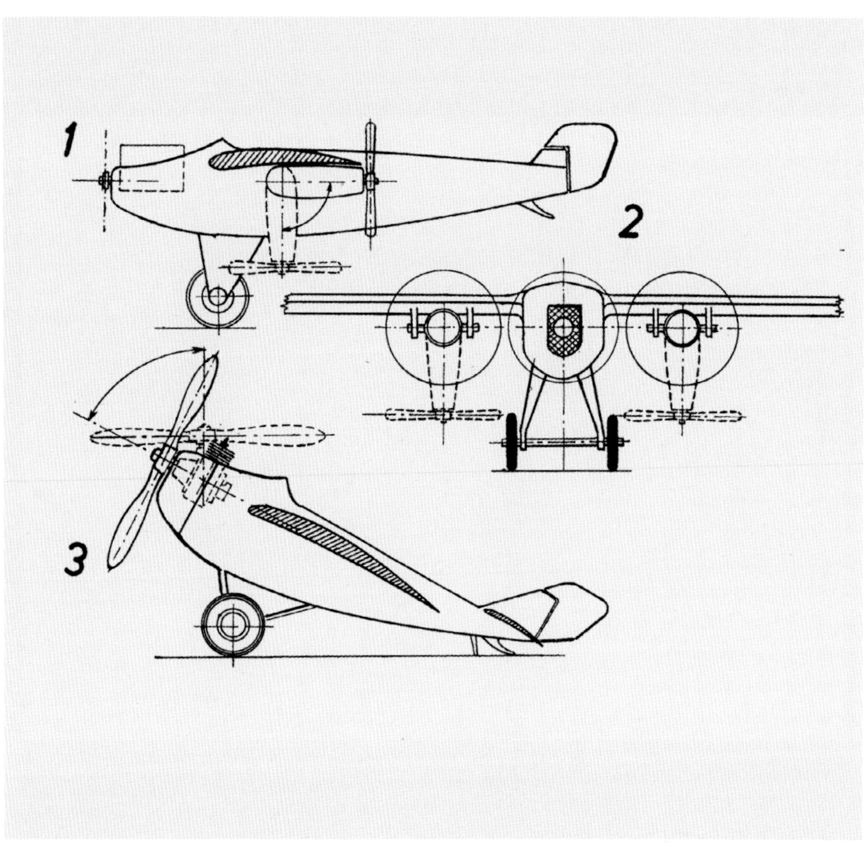

side engines were to be tilted as much as ninety degrees downward, so that the slipstream produced by the propellers could give the plane added lift.

At the end of the 1950s Dornier returned to this concept with the Do 29 test plane.

SCHMIDT

The master painter Ernst Otto Schmidt of Bergen in the Vogtland had already occupied himself intensively with the building of model helicopters since 1908 before, in the years after World War I, developing the concept of a flying machine with two tilting rotors. The contra-rotating rotors were to be attached to side struts and driven via shafts from a combustion engine in the fuselage. Schmidt envisioned that the rotors could be tilted both together synchronically and individually. Above all, the rotors themselves, or "lift screws," as they were called in Schmidt's patent application, were unusual. The two rotor blades of each rotor were very broad and their points were narrowed and angled to the outside. "This edge shall prevent the outward rushing of the air, and thereby improve the effect of the lift screws," Schmidt wrote in his patent application, turned in to the German Reich patent office in 1921. Coverings integrated into the rotor blades were to close the gaps between the blades in case of engine failure, and thus increase the parachute effect of the rotor. This interesting concept was never realized.

Ernst Otto Schmidt received a patent in
1921 for his tilting-rotor design.

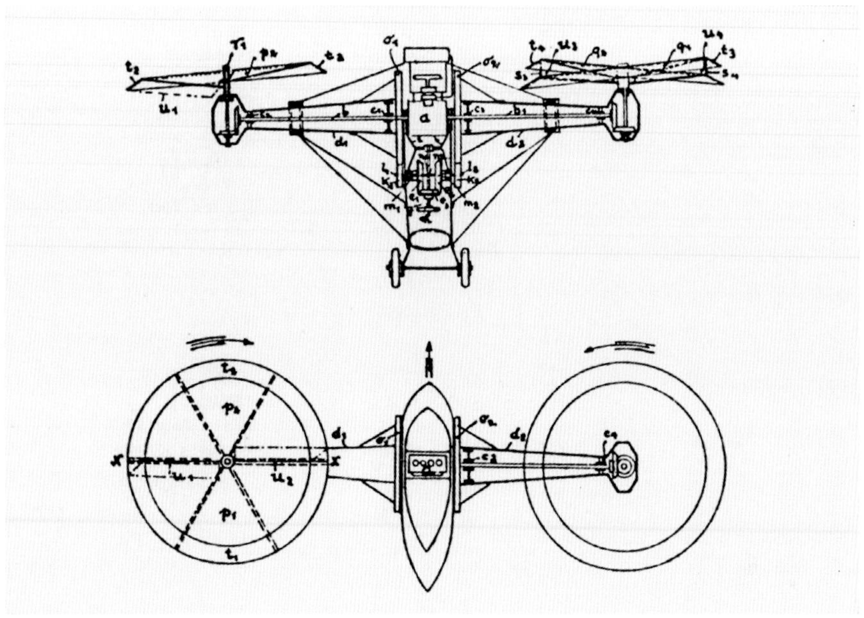

MARGOULIS

W. Margoulis, former director of the Eiffel Laboratory and colleague of Gustave
Eiffel, published the book "Les Helicopters" in 1922. In it he included a suggestion
triple-decker with tilting propellers. Two British Dragonfly radial engines of 320 HP
each, notorious for their unreliability, were to be mounted transversely to the longitudinal axis between the upper wings and drive the propellers from there via a shaft.
The motors were mounted on struts at the ends of the two upper wings, and the
propellers had a diameter of four meters each. When taking off and landing, the propellers were tilted downward; in horizontal flight they worked as puller propellers.
The length of the machine was 7.25 meters, the wingspan (including propellers)
was sixteen meters. Margoulis stated the flying weight as 1,460kg.

If this concept had ever been realized, the
foreseen motor would have proved to be
a bad choice, since the "Dragonfly" was
notorious for its unreliability. *(Jens Banganz)*

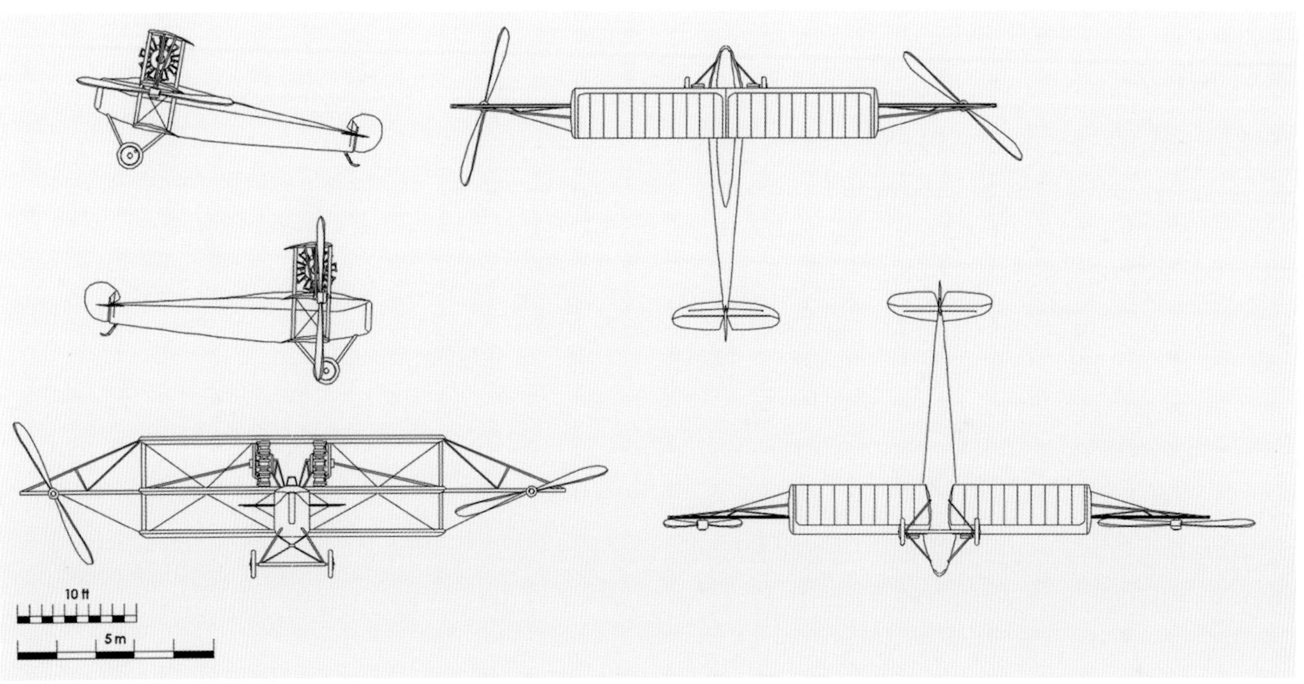

BERLINER HELICOPTER NO.5

Emil Berliner, born in Hannover, emigrated to the USA in 1870 and is best known as the inventor of the shellac phonograph record and the record player. In 1903 he turned to aviation, and by 1910 he had built a series of test helicopters, for which he built his own motors. In 1919 Emil Berliner took up work on helicopters again, but this time as an advisor to his son Henry. After a failed test of a craft with coaxial rotors, they obtained the fuselage of a Nieuport 23 and a 220 HP Bentley motor from military supplies in 1922. The Nieuport was equipped with doubledeck wings, each of which carried a rotor with a 4.57-meter diameter in its outer area. These two contra-rotating rotors could be tilted frontward and backward independently for steering purposes. In horizontal flight the rotors were both tilted forward a few degrees to create forward thrust. Ahead of the lateral controls was a horizontal rotor 76cm in diameter, which served to control pitching. The bow-mounted motor drove all three rotors via a gearbox and long shafts. Under the side rotors were five movable flaps, each 91x20mm. Blown on by the slipstream from the rotors, these flaps were supposed to take over steering along the longitudinal axis. Although it was capable of flight, the plane proved to be scarcely steerable.

At the end of 1923, the Berliners decided to mount a third pair of wings, which was supposed to provide more lift for a safe gliding landing in case of engine failure.

With the help of the third wings, steering improved a little, and Henry Berliner attained, on February 23, 1924, 64kph and an altitude of 4.57 meters with this machine, named No.5 Helicopter. It is true that the flight lasted only one minute and thirty-five seconds. Obviously the rotor performance was too weak to take Berliner's machine out of the realm of ground effects.

Henry and Emil Berliner built a lighter double-decker version in 1925, but it achieved only minimally better results. Frustrated, Henry Berliner gave up helicopters and founded the Berliner Aircraft Company, which designed and produced very successful fixed-wing airplanes. Henry Berliner donated the No.5 Helicopter to the Smithsonian Institution in Washington D.C., but at this time the machine is at the College Park Aviation Museum in College Park, Maryland.

The rotors of the Berliner Helicopter No.5 could be tilted a few degrees forward. *(BA cc by sa 3.0)*

Berliner Helicopter No.5	
Crew	1
Empty weight	748kg
Flying weight	870kg
Length	5,490mm
Height	2,060mm
Wingspan	11,580mm
Powerplant	220 HP Bentley BR-2 radial engine
Top speed	64kph attained
Service ceiling	4.57 meters

Note the flaps on the upper wings of No.5.
(BA cc by sa 3.0)

The Berliner No.5 at the College Park Aviation Museum in Maryland, USA.
(Ralph Ross cc by sa 3.0)

LEHBERGER

George Lehberger's design of an aircraft with tilting rotors and wings was submitted for a patent in May 1929. Over a very conventional fuselage were two coaxial rotors of different diameters.

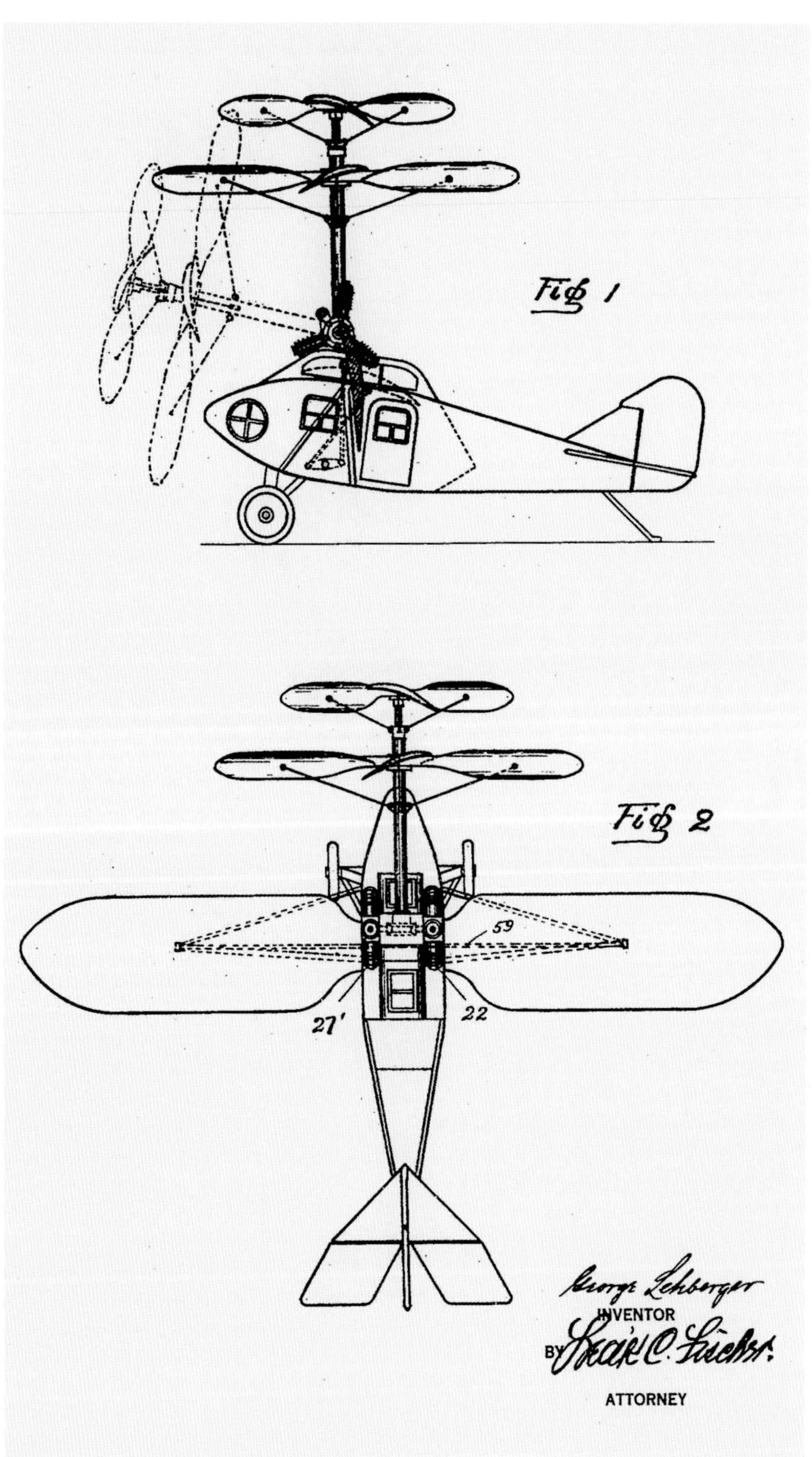

Lehberger's idea of a civilian tiltrotor machine that was to link city centers with each other was decades ahead of its time.

For takeoff and landing, they were to be vertical, while for level flight they were tilted toward a horizontal position and then acted as puller propellers. To be in the way of the downward-directed thrust of the rotors as little as possible, the wings could also be tilted for takeoff and landing. Right at the base of the rotor shaft Lehberger wanted to have two air-cooled radial or rotation motors installed perpendicular to the longitudinal axis of the plane. The tilting itself was to be carried out manually.

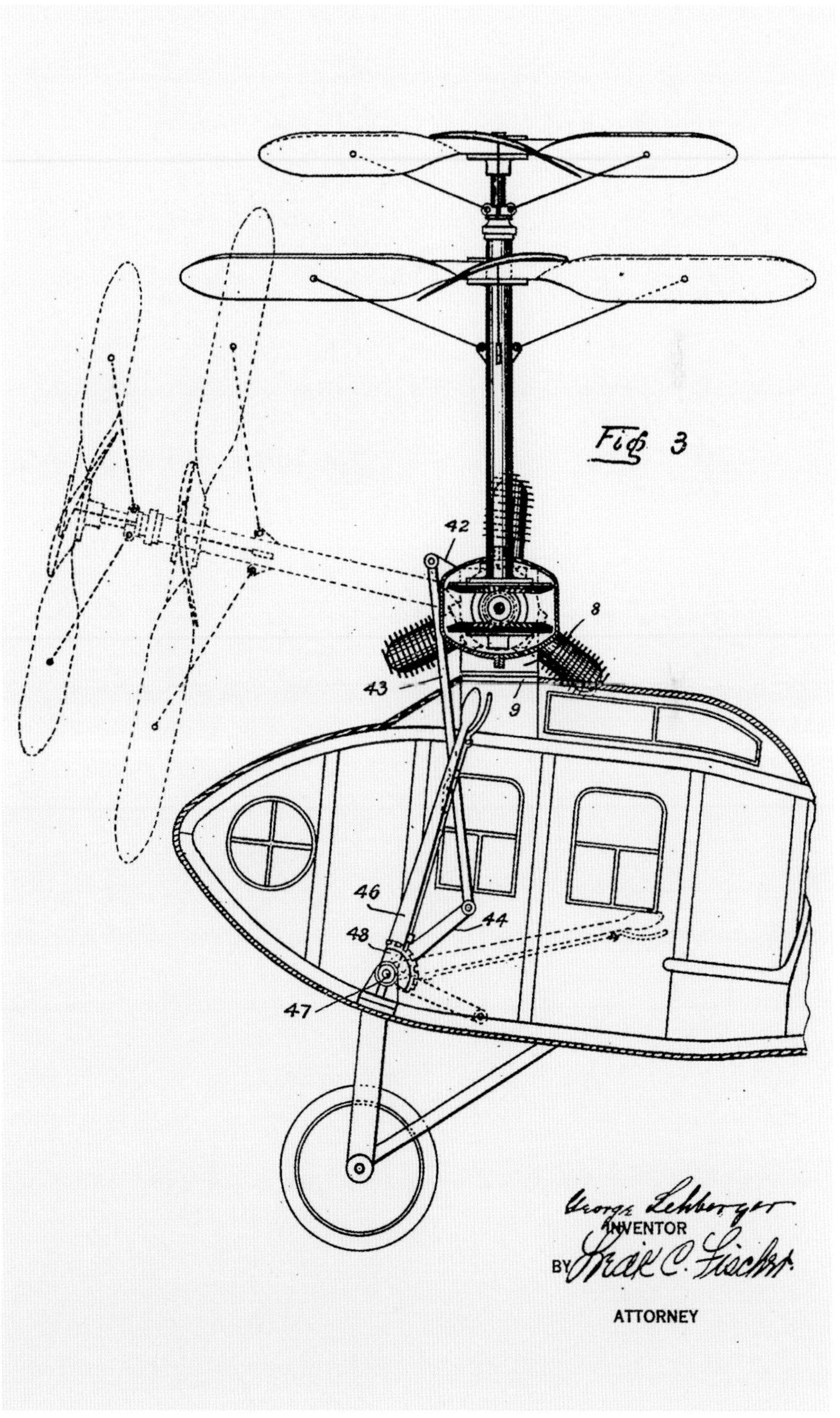

As this detailed view of the front of the fuselage shows, Lehberger planned to have the rotor mast tilt by means of a hand lever.

MARMONIER

On September 24, 1931, Louis Marmonier of Lyons received a French patent, plus a German one on February 13, 1932, for a very unusual-looking tilting-propeller airplane of canard or duck structure, with a double fuselage. These two parallel fuselages carried a large aileron at the front, to which a non-tilting piston motor with a pulling propeller was attached. On the main wings in back was a gondola with the pilot's cockpit. In the rear sections of both fuselages the building of passenger cabins was planned.

Between the two fuselages Marmonier wanted to install tilting propellers at the transverse axis. When these were horizontal, they were to work, depending on their extension, as pulling or pushing propellers. Pointed upward, the propellers were supposed to assure that the plane rose vertically. When the airscrews were pointed downward, Marmonier's machine was supposed to be able to land vertically. In the patent description, different engine configurations were shown. In one drawing, four propellers were mounted in pairs on turning axes, one pair of each to work as pulling and one pair as pushing airscrews. Powerplants are not visible; they were obviously supposed to be mounted in the two fuselages. Another drawing shows two tilting motors, apparently radial, installed between the fuselages.

There was no further development of Marmonier's plans.

Drawing from Marmonier's patent application of 1932. *(from HMB)*

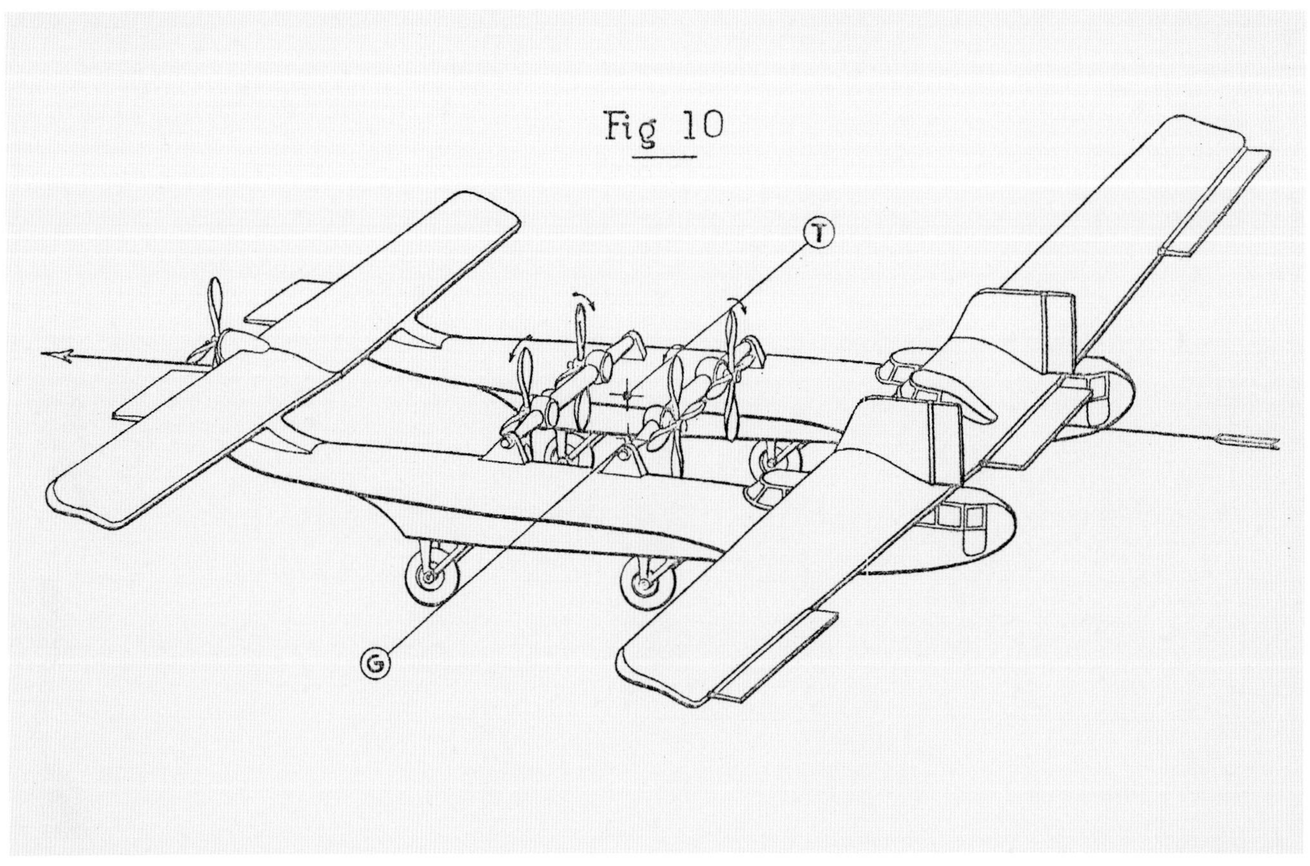

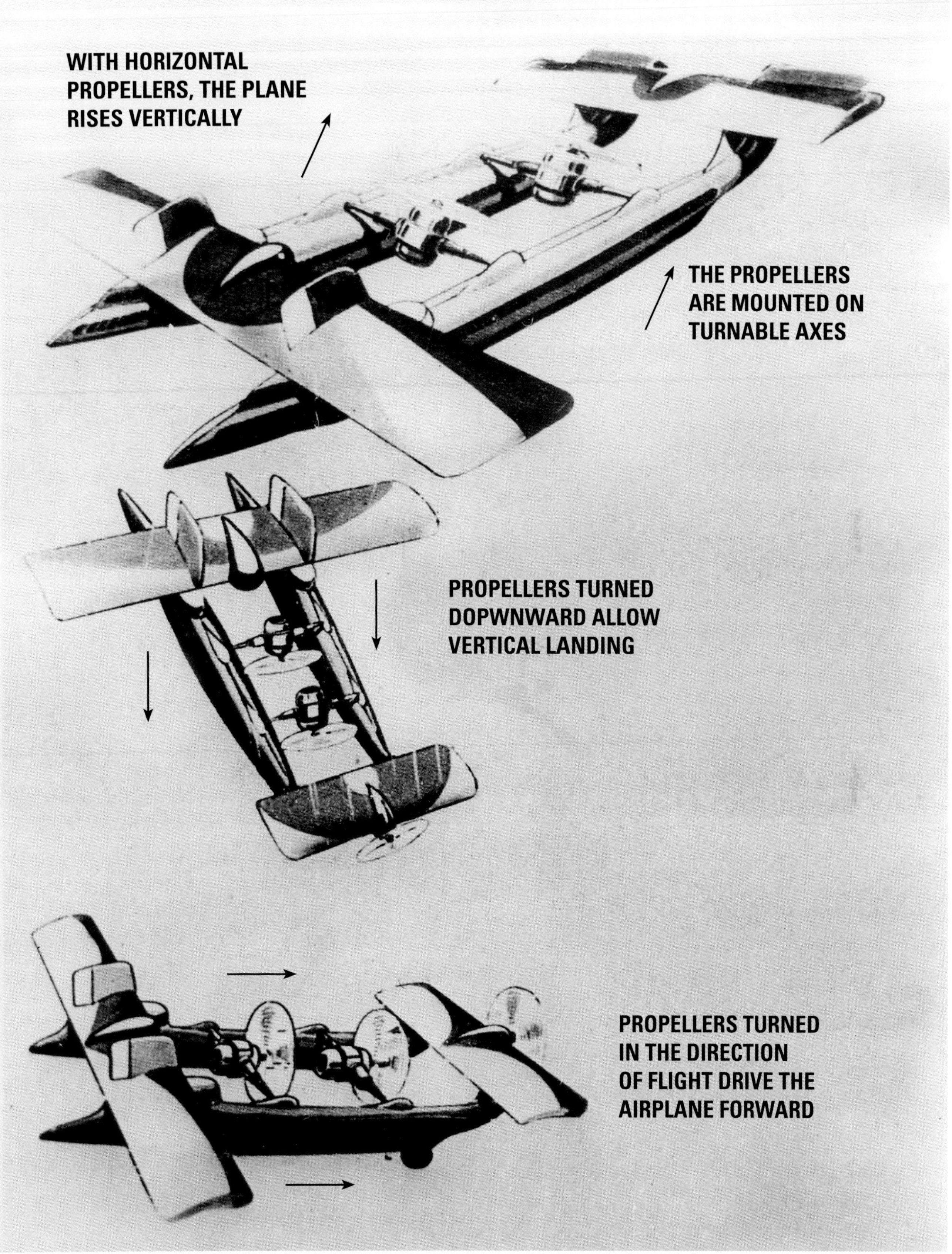

This version of Marmonier's invention shows only two tilting powerplants.
(from HMB)

BLOUNT

The most interesting thing about this design for a tiltwing airplane by Earl E. Blount of Dayton, Ohio, in 1933 is the location of steering surfaces on the rear ends of the engine nacelles. Blount hoped in this way to solve the problem of aircraft control at low speeds and in hover-hold. Since the fully movable rudders were thus constantly in the slipstream of the opposed airscrews, they should also be effective when conventional steering surfaces failed. Therefore the designer did without a conventional elevator.

Blount's design had a teardrop-shaped fuselage and completely retractable landing gear. Besides a single central wheel under the fuselage and a spur wheel on the unmoving rear fin, an additional wheel was attached to each engine nacelle.

The setting angle of the airscrews was to be adjustable according to use and speed. Despite the modern design features and interesting solutions, Blount's design also remained a purely paper project.

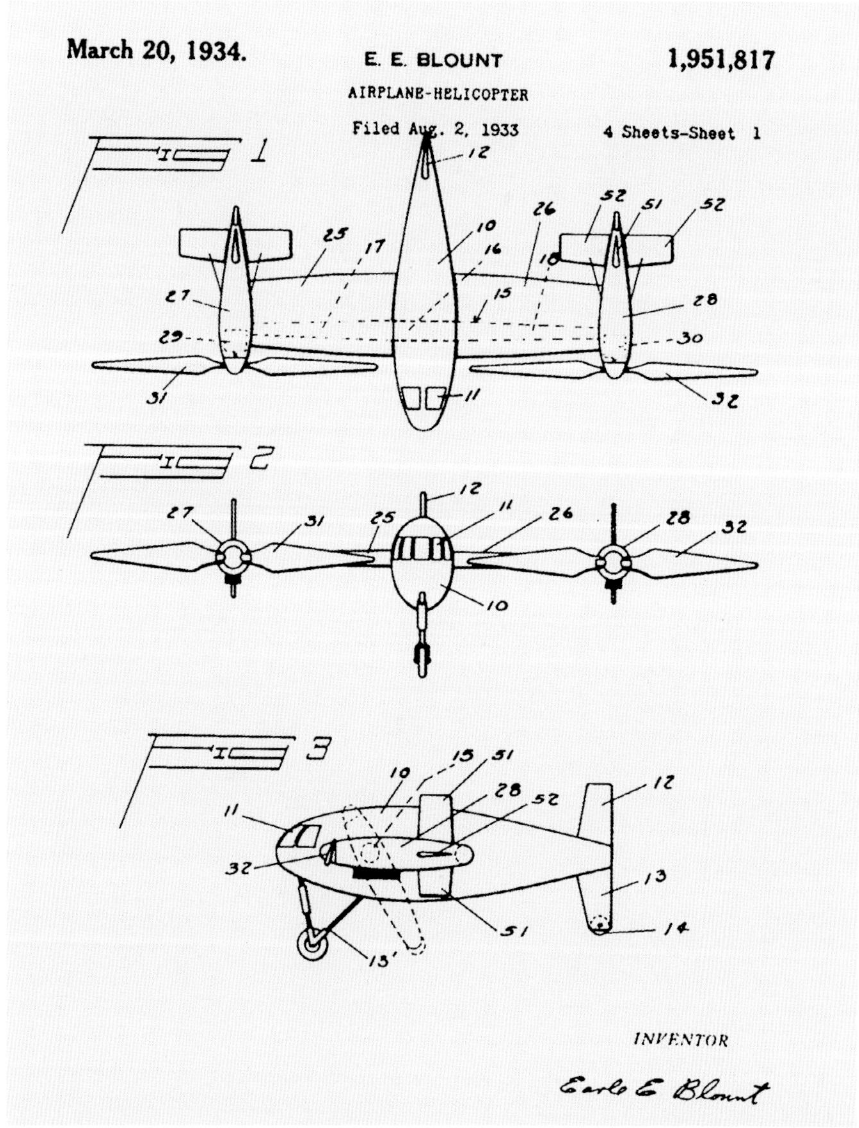

Blount's design from 1933 looks extremely modern for its time.

MAI "SOKOL"

F. Kurochkin, a student at the Moscow State Aeronautical Institution (Moskovsky Aviatsionssiy Institut = MAI), designed in 1935-36, under the direction of Professor B. Yurieva, a fighter plane with tipping propellers. At the end of each wing was a three-bladed propeller four meters in diameter, which could be tilted along with the outer half of the wing for takeoff and landing. Kurochkin wanted thus to minimize the disturbing influence of the wings on the propeller slipstream. Instead of an elevator, there was a horizontally mounted propeller of two-meter diameter at the rear, which steered the plane in hover-hold and slow flight.

Four-side view of the MAI "Sokol."
(*Richard Pawling*)

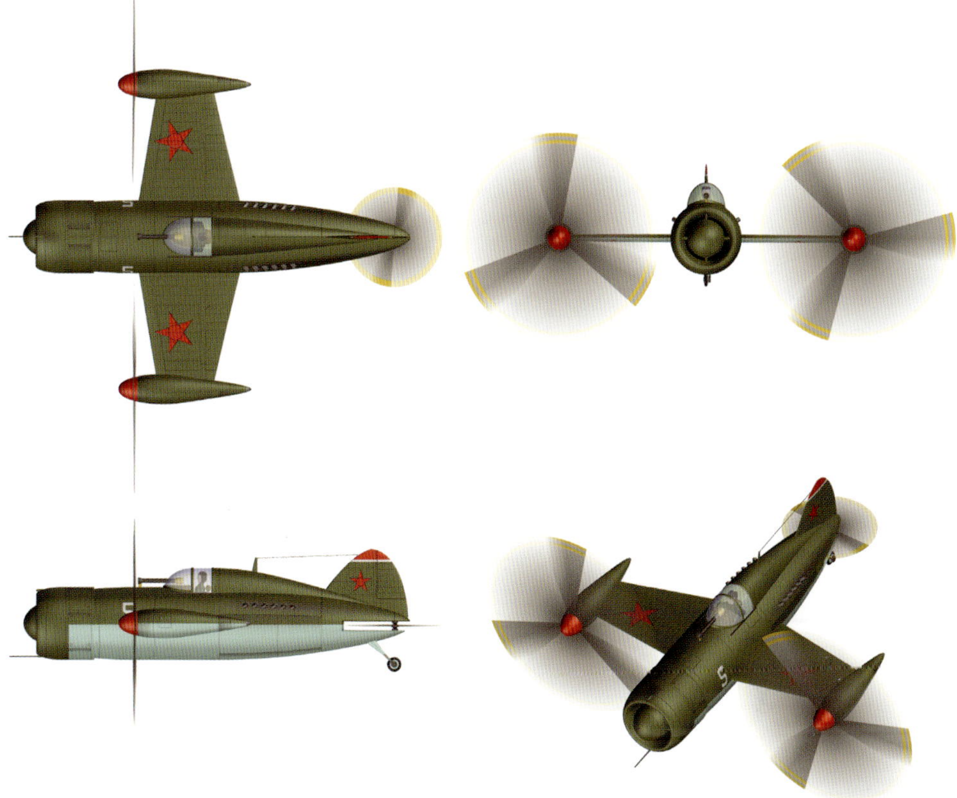

Although the ring-shaped radiator of the "Sokol" suggests a radial engine, the plane was to be driven by a Hispano-Suiza V motor. (*Richard Pawling*)

The landing gear was to consist of a single central wheel that was retracted into the fuselage, a rigid spur wheel, and two small wheels in the rear housings of the tilting propellers. Behind the cockpit was a water-cooled 860 HP Hispano-Suiza V-12 piston engine, which supplied the three propellers with power via shafts and gears. A ring-shaped radiator, reminiscent of a radial engine, and an engine air intake were in the nose of the "Sokol." The installation of one or two machine guns over them was obviously planned. Kurochkin calculated a top speed of 527kph and a flying weight of 1,850 kilograms for his design. Further data for Kurochkin's design are not known. A model of the "Sokol" was definitely built and tested in a wind tunnel, but there was no further development.

LEWIS AMERICAN AIRWAYS

In 1936 the Lewis American Airways firm of Colorado, USA introduced the prototype of a tilting-propeller airplane, of which the magazine "Popular Aviation" stated that it had been flown successfully several times.
The pilot sat in an open cockpit at the bow of the plane and had a good view. Behind him an air-cooled 215 HP Lycoming piston engine was installed, which powered, via gears and shafts, two tilting propellers located at the ends of the wings, with propellers of 2.1-meter diameter. The wings themselves were attached with struts over the fuselage and had a wingspan of some 7.7 meters. The plane had three-piece lateral controls and a rigid spur wheel. The takeoff weight was some 720kg.
For takeoff the propellers were tilted downward, presumably allowing the plane an extremely short takeoff and landing distance.
The builders hoped a more highly developed version with four propellers would have the ability to take off and land vertically, but this version was never built.

MAI "Sokol"	
Crew	1
Empty weight	unknown
Flying weight	1,850kg
Length	7,530mm
Height	unknown
Wingspan	5,800mm (without airscrews)
Powerplant	860 HP Hispano-Suiza V-12 piston engine
Top speed	527kph
Service ceiling	unknown
Range	unknown
Armament	1 or 2 fixed MG in fuselage, aimed forward

According to a contemporary article in "Popular Aviation" magazine, this plane was supposed to have been flown several times in 1936.

AEROSTATOPLAN

The exiled Russian Nikolai Zuchenko, working in Yugoslavia, designed in a single-engine tiltwing airplane in 1937, attracting the attention of the Yugoslavian Air Force. Under an official contract, Zuchenko built a prototype with a Walter Mikron motor producing only 50 HP. The engine was mounted in the fuselage ahead of the cockpit and, via shafts and gears, drove two three-bladed propellers that were mounted outside on the high wings. For takeoff and landing, the wings, along with the propeller, tilted to a vertical position. The length of the Aerostatoplan was 7.3 meters, the wingspan 6.7 meters. After the first limited flight tests had taken place in the summer of 1939, the project was halted after the war broke out in the autumn of that year, since the Yugoslavian Air Force had to use its limited financial means for other things.

The development of the "Aerostatoplan" was halted in the autumn of 1939.
(Vincent Bourguignon)

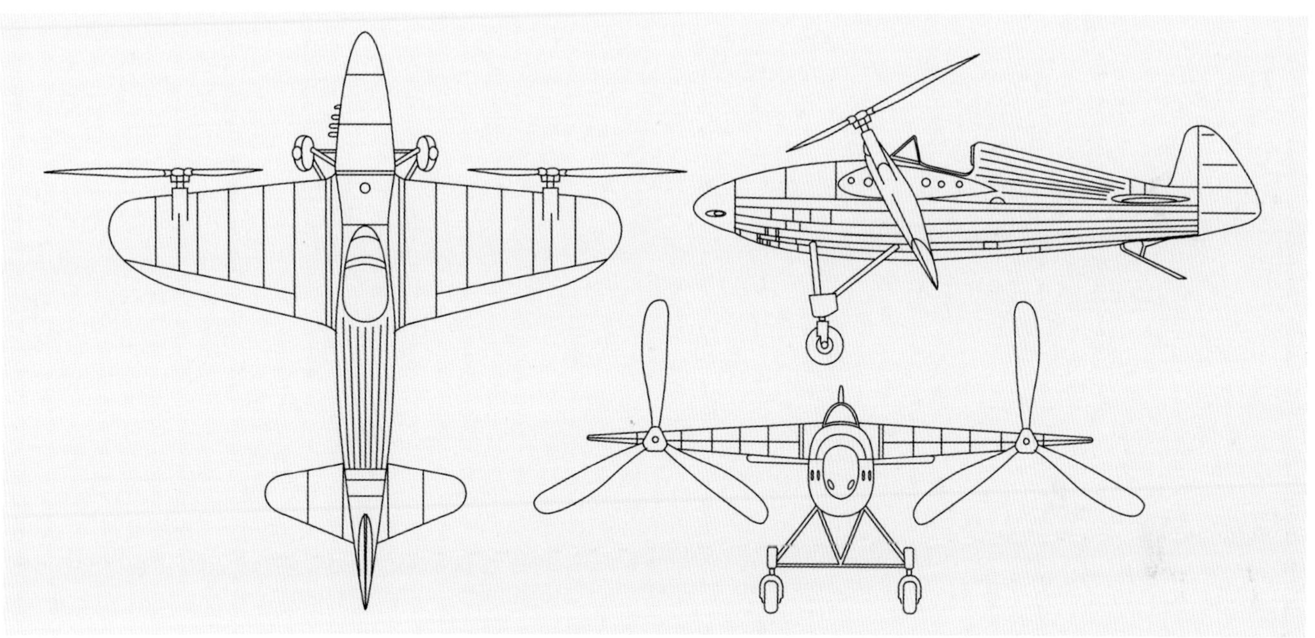

BAYNES "HELIPLANE"

In the years from 1937 to 1939 the British aeronautical engineer Leslie Everett Baynes designed an amphibian fighter and reconnaissance plane with tilting propellers, which he called a "heliplane" because it was supposed to combine the characteristics of a helicopter and a conventional airplane.

Baynes' design had a streamlined fuselage with a full-view cockpit in which two crewmen were to be seated. The middle-deck wings were very short, the wingspan measuring only 6.48 meters. At the wing tips were two nacelles that tilted ninety degrees, with three-bladed propellers of 4.57-meter diameter rotating in opposite directions. In the nacelles were gas turbines, oil tanks and, in back, the wheels of the main landing gear. The gas for the turbines was created by two Pescara free-piston machines located in the fuselage under the wings and ducted to the engines through pipes. Baynes was convinced that this unusual solution saved a considerable amount of weight, so that he could spare gears and long shafts. In addition, the two generators supplied a joint gas line, so that if one Pescara free-piston machine broke down, the other could supply the two turbines with sufficient gas without great effort. If both gas generators failed, Baynes' design was capable of autorotation. As to the engine performance, no information is available, but Baynes calculated a top speed of 587kph.

Since the powerplants were laid out so that they should produce their whole power at about 6,100 meters, one may conclude that the maximum altitude was still higher.

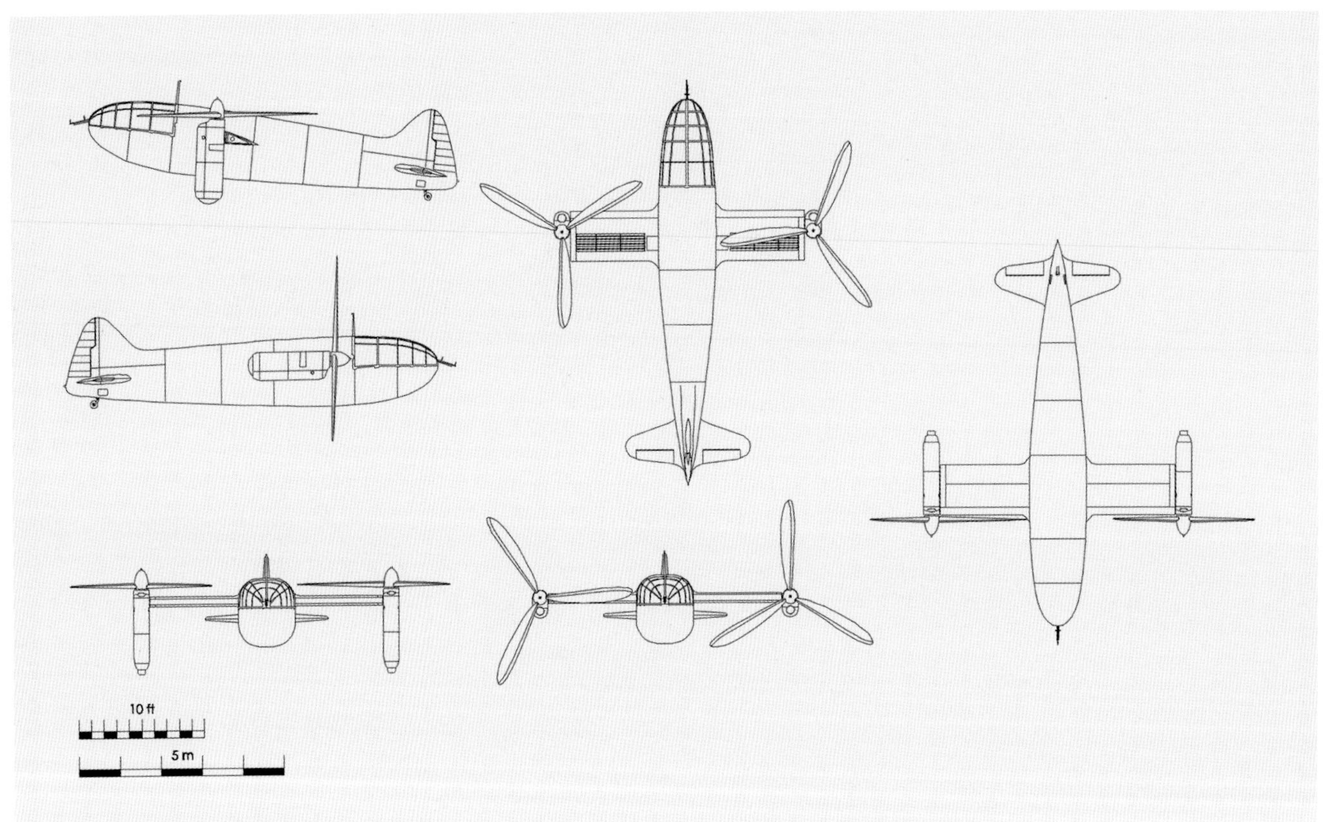

Baynes "Heliplane." *(Jens Baganz)*

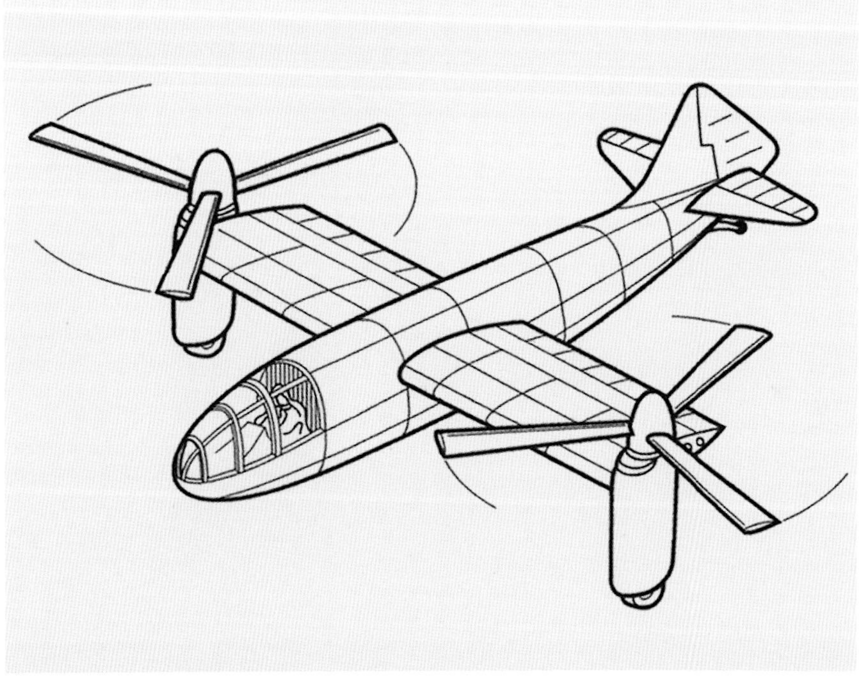

Baynes' design had many interesting features but was rejected by the British Air Ministry. *(NASA)*

Baynes "Heliplane"

Crew	2
Empty weight	1,860kg
Flying weight	2,722kg
Length	9,020mm
Height	2,490mm
Wingspan	6480mm (without airscrews)
Powerplant	2 Pescara free-piston machines of unknown power, as gas producers for 2 gas turbines
Top speed	587kph
Service ceiling	over 6,100 meters
Maximum range	1,600km, 985km with maximum bomb load
Armament	2 20mm MK, 1 7.7mm MG, maximum bomb load 227kg

The steering in helicopter flight was to be done by the tiltable propellers plus the independent tilting of the propeller axes. The propellers were designed so that the angles of the blades automatically suited the flight situation. The tilting process of the nacelles was done hydraulically. To save space, the propeller blades could be folded manually when at rest.

As already described, the wheels of the main landing gear were in the rear parts of the nacelles. At the tail the "Heliplane" had a retractable spur wheel. Baynes designed his aircraft so that the lower fuselage was watertight. Since the propellers would be vertical for takeoff and landing, vertical descent to and liftoff from the water had to be possible. In this way it was also possible to omit the "step" in the fuselage floor, otherwise needed in seaplanes. The two nacelles were also made watertight and stabilized the "Heliplane."

As armament, Baynes foresaw a movable 7.7mm MG of unknown type in the nose of the fuselage, to be operated by the observer-radioman. There were also two rigid forward-firing 20mm MK mounted in the fuselage. No information exists as to the planned ammunition supply, but the "Heliplane" was to be capable of carrying up to 227kg of bombs. Baynes stated its range without a bomb load as some 1,600km, and with a maximum load as 985km.

Although Baynes patented his invention successfully in Britain and the USA, it was not recognized by the British Air Ministry. Thus further development of his private design never took place.

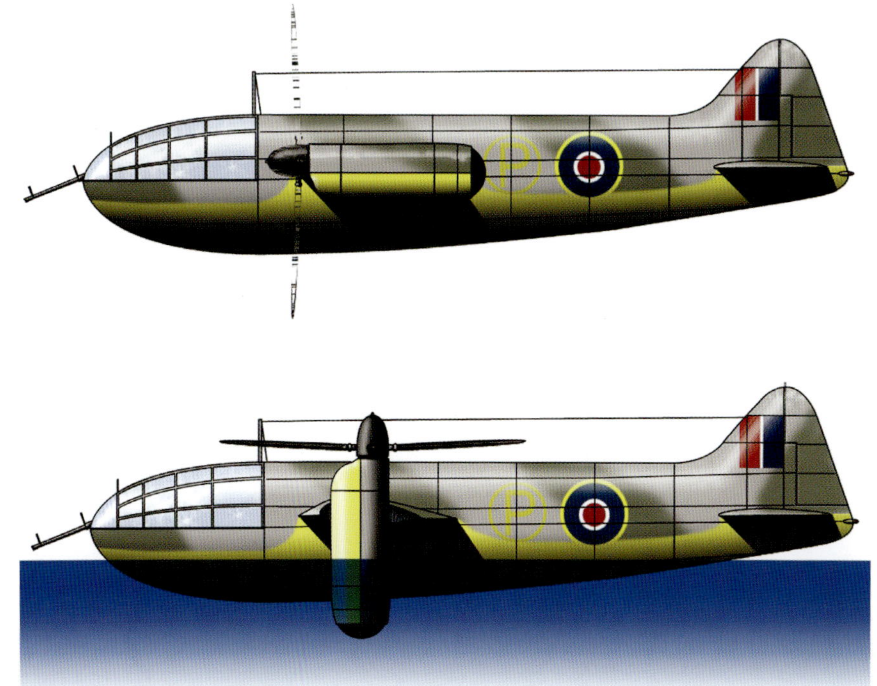

The "Heliplane" in the prewar colors of the RAF. (Vincent Bourguignon)

WESER-FLUGZEUGBAU P 1003/1

The Weser-Flugzeugbau GmbH (Weserflug) of Lemwerder near Bremen was a branch founded by the Deutsche Schiff- und Maschinenbau AG (DeSchiMAG) in 1934. In the same year Weserflug obtained the Rohrbach Metallflugzeugbau GmbH of Berlin, and Adolf Rohrbach became the technical director of Weserflug. Probably with Rohrbach's help, Dipl.-Ing. Simon designed an airplane at the beginning of 1938 with two large airscrews, of four-meter diameter, that tipped ninety degrees. Otherwise the structure of the airplane looked very conventional. The two-man crew was to sit under a large glassed canopy at the bow, with a 900 HP engine, probably a Daimler-Benz DB 600, installed behind them. The cooling air for the engine was taken in through a shaft under the nose. It was planned that the motor, via long shafts, would also drive the two propellers at the ends of the wings. The P 1003/1 was planned as a shoulder-decker to give the airscrews as much ground clearance as possible. The main landing gear was to be retracted toward the back of the fuselage, likewise the spur wheel. The outer halves of the wings tipped upward with the propellers for takeoff and landing to minimize the disturbing effect of the wings. Only after a speed of 76m/s (about 275kph) did the wings create enough lift to keep the P 1003/1 in the air; thus under this value the tilted airscrews had to provide lift. Since the conventional steering was ineffective during hover-hold, the propellers were to take on this task via thrust changing and blade adjustment. The steering surface was large, so as to be fully effective at speeds over 275kph; at higher speeds it was overly large.

Simon planned on the use of his design as a fast reconnaissance plane, but nothing is known of planned armament or other military equipment.

Although the Reich Patent Office issued a secret patent on September 19, 1940, for a "vertically ascent-capable airplane with tilting airscrews," Weserflug did not follow up the P 1003/1 project. Nothing is known of the building of models, wind-tunnel tests or the like.

Factory drawing of the P1003/1.
(EADS via HMB)

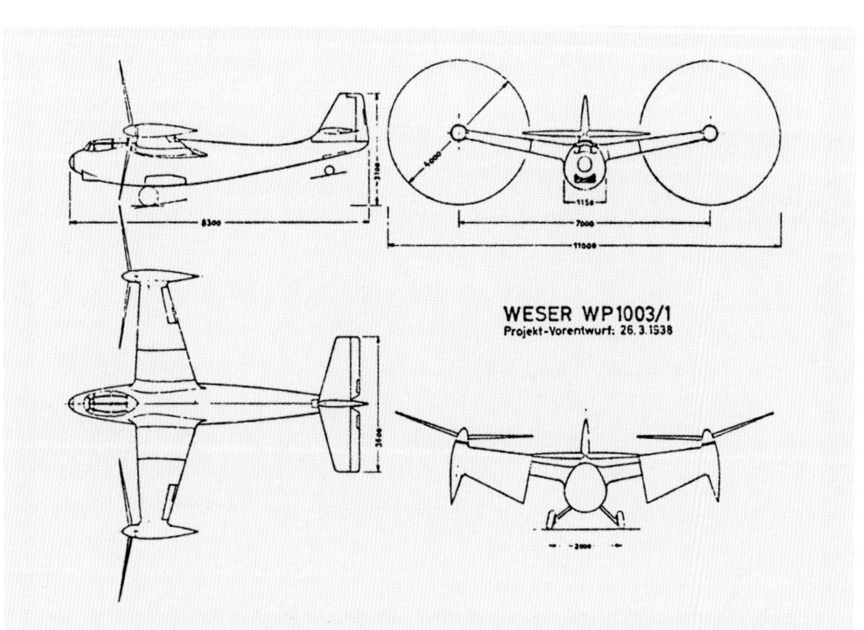

Weserflug P 1003/1

Crew	2
Empty weight	unknown
Flying weight	2,000kg
Length	8,300mm
Height	3,100mm
Wingspan	7,000mm (without airscrews)
Powerplant	900 HP piston engine (DB 600?)
Top speed	665kph
Service ceiling	unknown
Range	unknown
Armament	unknown

An artist's conception of the P 1003/1 in
Luftwaffe colors. *(Kyle Scott)*

FOCKE-ACHGELIS FA 269

Focke-Achgelis had already begun in 1939 to develop a fighter plane that was supposed to combine the vertical takeoff and landing characteristics of a helicopter with the speed of a fixed-wing airplane. Dipl.-Ing. Klages thus developed a free-bearing middle-decker, called the Fa 269, which was unusual in that the airscrews were tilted not upward but downward.

On about half of the wingspan breadth, the Fa 269 had two three-bladed propellers of 4.6-meter diameter, which could be tilted downward eighty degrees for takeoff and landing. In horizontal flight they were brought back to their normal position and functioned as pressure screws. A BMW 801 radial engine mounted in the middle of the fuselage, with air-cooling and producing 1,660 HP, was to drive both propellers over a system of gears and shafts, and to move the Fa 269 at 4,100 meters at a speed of 570kph. The arrangement of the airscrews made high-kneed, telescopically extendable tail-wheel running gear that could be pulled into the fuselage toward the tail necessary. The one-man crew was to be kept forward in the bow under a large glassed canopy. Viewing windows in the cockpit floor allowed the pilot good downward visibility. The Fa 269 was to be built completely of duraluminum (Dural), with only the rudders covered with cloth.

The steering of the machine in helicopter flight was to be done, for one thing, by adjusting the airscrew blades, and for another, by the blown-on elevators. The cooling air of the powerplant passed out through the rear angle of the elevators and streamed over the control surfaces.

The propellers of the Fa 269 were supposed to have the ability to autorotate in case of emergency; theoretically, though, it was also supposed to be possible to move the propellers to a horizontal position in case of damage and to land the plane by gliding. To prevent the plane from turning over, the landing would then have been made with retracted running gear. The empty weight of the Fa 269 was to be 2,700kg, and the flying weight 2,888kg.

This data, though, is based only on the so-called test plane; the actual fighter planes were to have an empty weight of 3,000kg and a flying weight of 3,760kg. In addition, Focke-Achgelis considered installing an unnamed radial engine of the 2,700 HP class, with which the production planes could reach up to 600kph and climb to 5,000 meters in 7.5 minutes.

Original March 1940 documents from the Focke-Achgelis works list the armament of the Fa 269 as two 7.92mm MG 17, each with 750 rounds, mounted on the sides of the fuselage, and one 15mm MG 151 with 250 rounds, mounted under the cockpit. In the literature, though, it is generally stated that the planned armament consisted of two side-mounted 30mm MK 108 guns. Sometimes a 20mm MG 151/20 under the fuselage is also listed. Nothing is known of the intended supply of ammunition in this configuration.

Besides its use as a fighter, Focke-Achgelis also considered using the Fa 269 for reconnaissance because of its ability to hover and its large glass windows.

At Focke-Achgelis, inclusive design and development work were begun, including those on the subjects of gears, shafts and tipping mechanisms for the propellers.

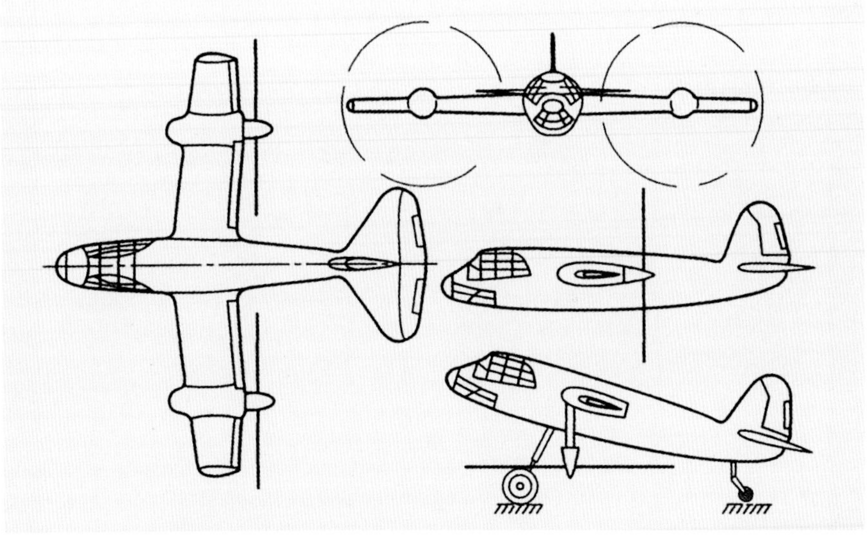

Schematic drawing of the Fa 269. *(NASA)*

A conception of the Fa 269 that came from Focke-Achgelis. Note the air inlets for motor cooling at the roots of the wings. *(from HMB)*

As this Focke-Achgelis works drawing shows, the propellers of the Fa 269, when tipped downward, required very high-legged running gear. *(from HMB)*

Besides a full-scale model that was subjected to intensive tests in a wind tunnel, the firm also built a mockup of the Fa 269 in full scale. Both models were examined several times by RLM officials. On the night of June 4-5, 1942, in an Allied bomb attack on the Focke-Achgelis works in Hoyenkamp, practically all designs, data, and the two models of the Fa 269 were destroyed. Because of the extensive work on gears and shafts, as well as other research, the designers had already reckoned before the raid on an extent of some five years until a flyable prototype could be finished. But in view of the war, the bomb raid meant the end for the Fa 269.

Planned Fa 269/V1 Test Plane

Crew	1
Empty weight	2,700kg
Flying weight	2,888kg
Length	8,930mm
Height	3,250mm
Wingspan	10,000mm (without airscrews)
Powerplant	1,660 HP BMW 801 radial engine
Top speed	570kph at 4100 meters, 540kph at 0 meters, 30kph backward
Service ceiling	9,550 meters (fixed wings), 4,300 meters (tipping rotors)
Range	unknown
Armament	none

Planned Fa 269 Production Plane

(as of March 1940)

Crew	1
Empty weight	3,000kg
Flying weight	3,760kg
Length	8,930mm
Height	3,250mm
Wingspan	10,000mm (without airscrews)
Powerplant	2,000 HP radial engine, type unknown
Top speed	600kph at 4100 meters, 570kph at 0 meters, 30kph backward
Service ceiling	9,050 meters (fixed wings), 1,800 meters (tipping rotors)
Range	unknown
Armament	2 7.92mm MG 17 and 1 15mm MG 151, rigid, pointing forward from fuselage

Intensive wind-tunnel tests were made on models of the Fa 269. *(via HMB)*

An artist's conception of a Fa 269 in hovering flight. *(Kyle Scott)*

MILITARY PROJECTS IN THE USA AFTER 1945

CHAPTER 3

All service arms of the USA used great numbers of helicopters after 1945 and soon recognized the tactical advantages of these aircraft. The Army, Air Force, Marines and Navy also recognized, though, that the capabilities of their helicopters quickly reached their limits. In search of an aircraft that united the advantages of the helicopter and airplane, the Pentagon, since the early-1950s, financed a series of developments, all of which failed to go beyond the prototype stage.

TRANSCENDENTAL 1-G

Robert Lichten, who had formerly worked as an engineer for the Platt-LePage firm and collaborated on a tiltrotor project there, founded along with Mario A. Guerrieri, who came from Kellet, the Transcendental Aircraft Corporation in 1947. The firm began to develop a tiltrotor airplane with private means and to carry out groundbreaking mechanical and aerodynamic tests. Robert Lichten left Transcendental, though, in 1948 to go to Bell Helicopter, where he continued his work and later played a leading role in designing the Bell XV-3.

A first prototype was badly damaged by massive vibrations during ground tests in 1951. Transcendental had to realize that design errors had been the cause of this accident, and they began anew with essential tests of the behavior of a tilting rotor. In the meantime, the U.S. military's interest had been awakened, so that the development and design of a model called 1-G, beginning in 1952, could be carried out with the financial help of the U.S. Air Force.

Works photo of the Transcendental 1-G
during ground testing. *(from HMB)*

The small size of the Transcendental 1-G
becomes apparent in this works photo. *(from HBM)*

The Transcendental 1-G in hovering flight.
(NASA via HBM)

The Transcendental 1-G had a short fuselage with high-set wings, on each end of which a rotor of 5.2 meter diameter, capable of tilting eighty-two degrees, was mounted. In horizontal flight the rotors were also supposed to be tilted six degrees upward. The rotors opposed each other to equalize the turning moment.

The pilot sat in a partly open cockpit, and a Lycoming O-290-A six-cylinder piston engine producing 160 HP was mounted in the fuselage, transmitting its power to the rotors by a two-stage gearbox. These gears made sure that the rotors turned at 240rpm in helicopter mode and 633rpm in horizontal position.

The Transcendental 1-G was supposed to be steered during helicopter flight by its collective and cyclical blade adjustment, and in airplane mode by conventional rudders. The flight-testing of the 1-G began (depending on the source) on June 15 or July 6, 1954. At first, though, it was limited to hover-hold; only on December 13, 1943 did the first forward flight begin, though with its rotors not yet tilted. As of December 17, 1954, they began to tilt the rotors into a horizontal position, step by step. By April 1955 an angle of thirty-five degrees out of the vertical was reached, and finally it was possible many times to tilt the rotors to an angle of seventy degrees, whereby the wings created over 90% of the lift. On July 20, 1955, after an almost complete transition, there was a mechanical error in the rotor steering, which resulted in a forced landing in the Delaware River. Although the 1-G tipped over and could not be repaired, the pilot was only slightly injured and reached the shore under his own power.

In its short career, the 1-G made more than 100 flights, was in the air over twenty hours, and reached a height of 1,066 meters. It proved to be quite steerable and showed no vibration problems worth noting. Although it never made 100% transition, the 1-G is classed today as the first actually flown manned tiltrotor airplane in the world.

TRANSCENDENTAL 2

Shortly after the crash of 1-G, Transcendental began to design a larger and more powerful successor type. Its development as of March 1956 was financed to a great extent by the U.S. Air Force. In October 1956 the airplane, called Transcendental 2, was already finished. The fuselage and cockpit were closed and looked much more conventional than 1-G. The two-man crew sat side by side in the bow of the fuselage. To keep the rotors as far from the ground as possible, the wings were mounted at the very top of the fuselage. At their ends were three-bladed rotors with a diameter of 6.26 meters, driven via gears and shafts by a 250 HP six-cylinder piston engine mounted vertically in the fuselage and turning in opposed directions. The motors were tilted smoothly by electric motors between 90 and 0 degrees. In a vertical takeoff the maximum load was about 300kg, but when Transcendental 2 made a rolling start with its rotors tilted a few degrees, the load could increase considerably.

Like Transcendental 1-G, this craft, in helicopter flight, could be steered via the collective and cyclical blade settings, and in airplane mode by conventional rudders.

Transcendental 2 was subjected first to ground tests, and also seems to have been flown, but in 1957 the U.S. Air Force halted their financial support in order to concentrate on the Bell XV-3, and the project had to be ended. A further design, the turbine-powered Transcendental 3, was never realized.

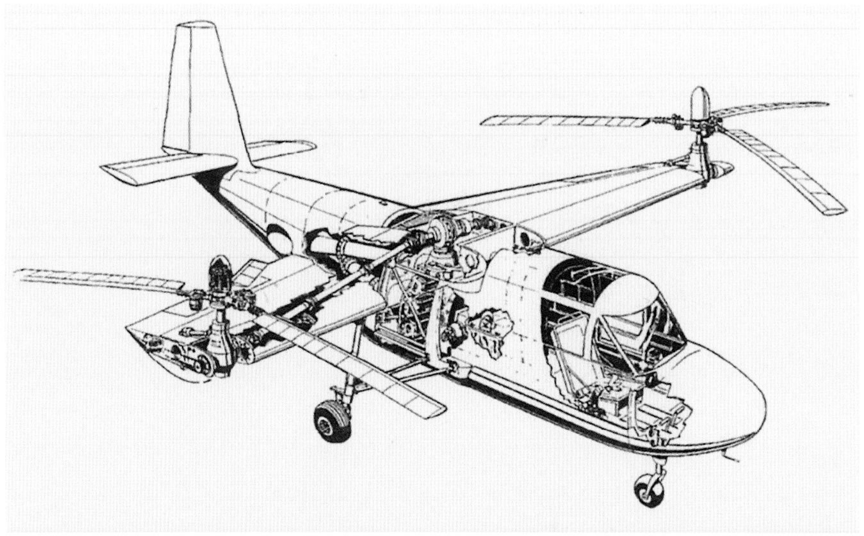

Cutaway drawing of Transcendental 2.
(NASA)

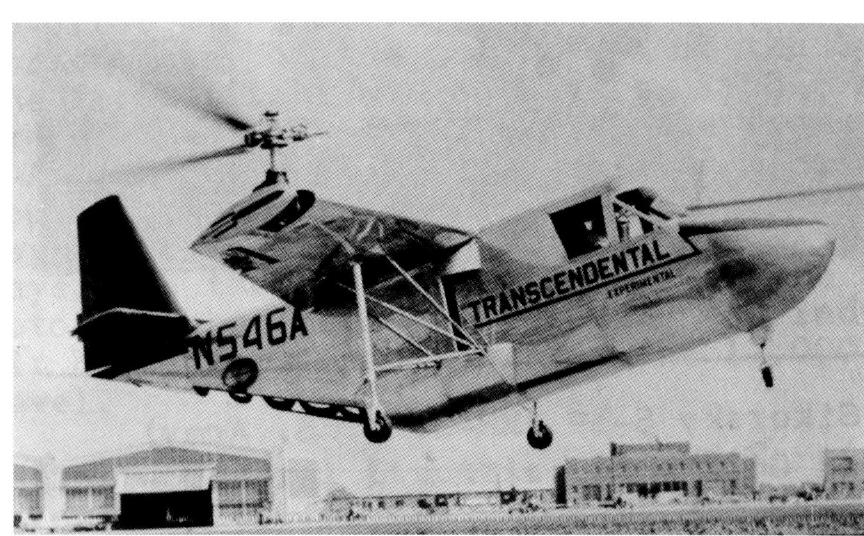

Transcendental 2 in hovering flight.
(Works photo from HMB)

Transcendental 2

Crew	2
Empty weight	719kg
Takeoff weight	1021kg
Length	6,730mm
Height	2,845mm
Wingspan	6,934mm (without rotors), 11,887mm (with rotors)
Powerplant	1 Lycoming O-435-23 6-cylinder piston engine, 250 HP
Top speed	256kph (as helicopter 196kph)
Service ceiling	unknown
Range	unknown

BELL XV-3

In 1941 the Bell Aircraft Corporation was already beginning to develop helicopters, and it made helicopter history on March 8, 1946, when the Bell 47 became the first helicopter to gain a civilian permit.

Long before Transcendental began to develop the 1-G, the first considerations and preliminary work on a tiltrotor aircraft were beginning at Bell. Robert Lichten, who moved from Transcendental to Bell in 1948, gained the opportunity there to direct the development of a tiltrotor concept with the research and development possibilities of one of the leading U.S. helicopter producers.

In August 1950 the U.S. Army and Air Force published a joint description of a changing airplane ("Convertiplane"), which was to fulfill the following criteria: capability for extended hovering flight, high maneuverability, high agility, higher speed and range than helicopters of the time, and a moderate rotor slipstream, to enable safe rescue actions to be made under the craft. This "Convertible Aircraft Program Request for Proposal" (RFP) description resulted in seventeen U.S. firms submitting nineteen different suggestions for such a changeable aircraft.

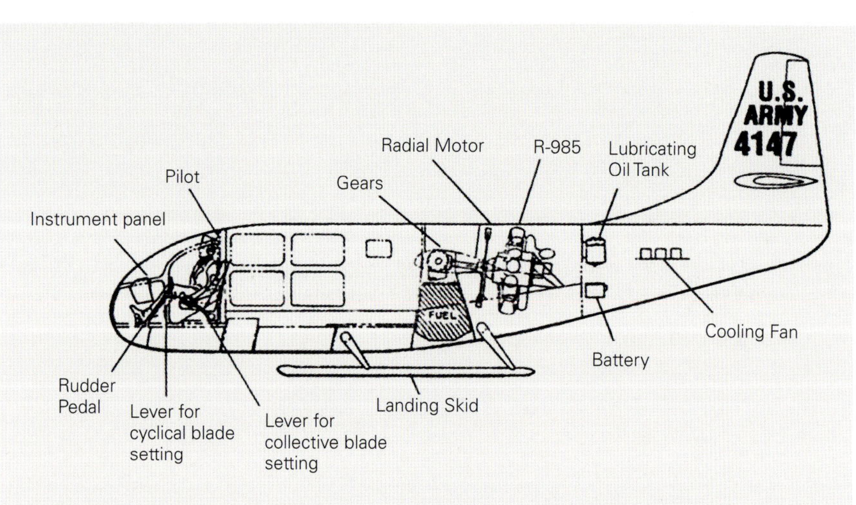

Cutaway drawing of the XV-3. *(NASA)*

The XV-1 cooperative helicopter was McDonnell's contribution to the U.S. Army's "Convertible Aircraft Program."

The first prototype of the XV-3 (4147)
during the individual steps of transition.
(Bell Helicopter)

Finally three drawings made it to the narrower choice: the McDonnell Model 82 (XV-1), the Sikorsky S-57 (XV-2), and the Bell Model 200 (XV-3), with "X" standing for "Experimental" and "V" for "Vertical." While the XV-1, equipped with blade-tip drive, auxiliary wings and a pusher propeller, was actually built and tested, the XV-2, equipped with a retractable rotor, did not get beyond wind-tunnel tests. In October 1953 Bell received a contract to build two test machines of the XV-3 type. Craft No.1 (tail number 4147) was finished at the Bell works in Forth Worth, Texas at the end of 1954, and had its "roll-out" on February 10, 1955.

The XV-3 had a full-sight cabin with two seats, one behind the other, for the pilot and co-pilot/observer. The powerplant, an air-cooled radial engine of Pratt & Whitney Type R-985-AN-1 that produced 450 HP, was located in the central fuselage behind the cockpit. Although a more powerful motor would have been desirable, the Pratt & Whitney "Wasp Junior" was decided on because of its reliability. A fuselage tank under the wings held a maximum of 378 liters of fuel. The rear cockpit resembled that of a conventional airplane with rudder and elevators. Under the fuselage were two long landing skids with hydraulic shock absorbers; later wheels were integrated into the skids to make rolling starts possible for XV-3. At the end of each wing, in aerodynamically shaped nacelles, were the tipping mechanism, steering rods and mount for a rotor with a diameter of 7.62 meters. The helicopter-type rotor at first had three blades, which were attached to the rotor disk by striking and swinging links, and whose setting angle for vertical or horizontal use could be adjusted suitably. The tilting process was carried out by electric motors, which were capable of moving the rotor a full ninety degrees in ten to fifteen seconds. The rotors could also be held at any angle setting between 0 and 90 degrees, or tipped back in them. The powerplant sent its power to the rotor by means of a two-speed gearbox and long shafts. In helicopter flight the XV-3 was steered by adjusting the rotor blades; in horizontal flight, conventional steering was used.

After its "roll-out" XV-3 was subjected to intensive ground tests. For this, a special frame was built, which allowed XV-3 to tilt its rotors forward while on the ground.

After a successful conclusion of the ground tests, XV-3 (4147) lifted off on its first test flight on August 11, 1955. After an initially problem-free flight in helicopter mode, test pilot Floyd Carlson observed strong vibrations during hovering. On a later flight on August 18, there were stability problems with the rotor. The plane landed roughly and was slightly damaged. Bell then carried out extensive examinations to find the reason for these problems. The team around Robert Lichten had the rotor rods strengthened, the wings braced with double struts to the fuselage, and big flaps provided at the rear, which inclined downward in hover-hold, to minimize the disturbing effect of the wings. With the large flaps, the transitional speed in horizontal flight was reduced to 157kph, which allowed transitions at lower speeds.

The flight program was taken up again at the end of March 1956 and at first proceeded without problems; thus tilting the rotors forward step by step was begun. On July 11 the rotors were tilted five degrees for the first time, and on July 25 an angle of seventy-five degrees and a speed of 148kph were attained. In this test, though, there was instability in the rotors again. Thus Bell began a new series of ground tests and investigations, and modified the rotor system again.

The first XV-3 (4147) in flight. To improve
motor cooling, parts of the fuselage skin
were removed. *(USAF)*

The second XV-3 prototype (4148) in flight.
The additional lower tailfin has not yet
been mounted. Note the cooling air intake
on the top of the fuselage.

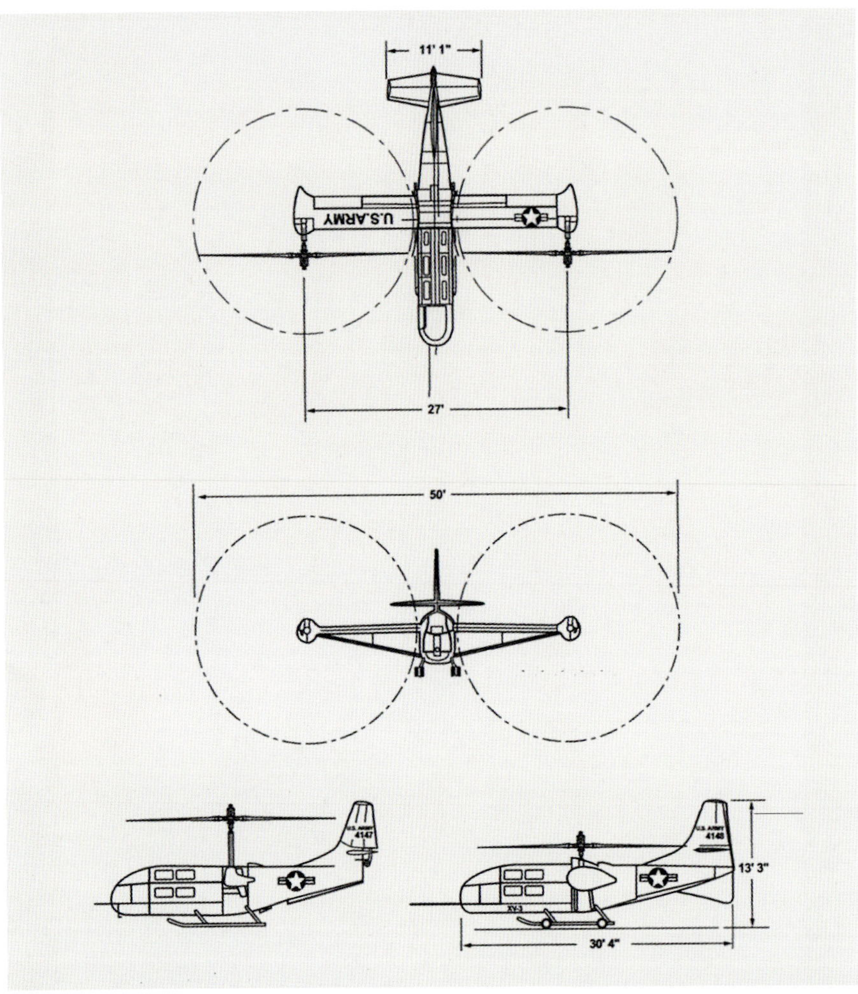

This drawing shows clearly the differences between the first (lower left) and second XV-3 (lower right). *(NASA)*

Prototype No.2 (4148) taking off in Ames, Iowa. *(NASA)*

When Bell's test pilot Dick Stansbury tilted the rotors seventeen degrees forward, a strong instability beset the rotors again, which led to the XV-3 being shaken by massive vibrations. Stansbury lost control of the craft and crashed. He was badly injured in the crash, and the XV-3 was so badly damaged that repairs were deemed pointless.

The lost of the No.1 (4147) craft almost meant the end of the XV-3 test program. Obviously, Bell alone was not in a position to solve the instability problem and the involved vibrations. Although the negative voices were increasing in the Department of Defense, those who favored tiltrotor technology prevailed and Bell received a contract to test the second prototype (4148) in the wind tunnel of the NASA Research Center in Ames (north of San Francisco).

After these tests, carried out in September and October 1957, it was decided to replace the three-bladed rotor with striking and swinging links with a semi-fixed model with two blades. This rotor had a diameter of 7.32 meters, a newly reinforced steering rod, and a shorter rotor mast. The wings of 4148 were also supported by doubled struts, and the motor cooling was improved by an air intake on the top of the fuselage. After thorough tests in the wind tunnel at Ames, which made further detail modifications necessary, the flight testing of 4148 began on January 21, 1958, and ran almost without incident at first.

In all, the craft showed very satisfactory characteristics in helicopter flight and proved that it was capable of autorotation. On May 6, 1958, though, there was another incident. At a rotor-tilting angle of forty degrees, strong vibrations began again, so that the test flights were broken off again and Bell agreed with the U.S. Army and NASA to test the flying characteristics in the wind tunnel again. The result of these tests, carried out in the autumn of 1958, was a renewed reinforcement of the steering rod, the attachment of counterweights to the steering mechanism of the collective blade adjustment, and a change in the rotor-blade adjustment.

After the resumption of flights on December 11, 1958, a full transition finally took place on December 18. The XV-3 at first flew in helicopter mode at 166kph and then tilted the rotors step by step until at a setting of ninety degrees in airplane mode a speed of 212kph was reached. A full tilting of the rotors on the next day also took place without any special incidents. Only the directional stability left a little to be desired, so a wooden fin was attached under the back of the fuselage.

Now Bell modified the struts of the wings so that their supporting effect during flight could be removed to determine whether the wings had actually contributed to the earlier problems. As of January 16, 1959, completed flights confirmed that the struts were no longer needed, so that on January 22 they were finally removed. In this form 4148 attained a straight flight speed of 222kph with rotors tilted fifty degrees forward.

By the installation of small wheels to the landing skids in April 1959, rolling starts became possible, in which 4148 lifted off after less than sixty meters with rotors tilted ten degrees forward and only 66% of its engine power.

Encouraged by these experiences, a flying transition was made for the first time during a flight on April 14, 1959, in which the engine speed and the resulting vibrations could be reduced. The gear change itself was as difficult as before and demanded more or less simultaneous activation of the clutch, the blade setting and the coordination of the engine speed by the pilot.

Bell XV-3 (4148)

Crew	1
Empty weight	1,910kg
Takeoff weight	2,134kg (planned), 2,220kg (real)
Length	9,246mm
Height	4,037mm
Wingspan	9,496mm (without rotors), 15,240mm (with rotors)
Powerplant	1 Pratt & Whitney R-985-AN-1 9-cylinder radial engine, 450 HP
Top speed	287kph
Service ceiling	over 3,650 meters (in theory over 4,500 meters)
Range	maximum flight time 2 hours

In mid-May 1959, almost four years after its first flight, the official flight-testing of the Bell XV-3 by a joint commission of the U.S. Army and Air Force took place at Edwards Air Force Base in California. In the course of these tests, 4148 made thirty-eight flights adding up to almost thirty hours, reached heights of over 3,650 meters, and completed forty transitions and twenty gear changes during flight. The XV-3 successfully demonstrated that it could also return to the vertical even after engine failure in horizontal flight with the rotors tilted completely forward and could land by autorotation. After the tests were finished in July 1959, the Army and Air Force experts were of the opinion that the tiltrotor concept was, to be sure, basically practicable and opened very promising possibilities for the future, but that XV-3 itself showed basic problems. They included inadequate powerplant performance and directional stability in hover-hold, the occurrence of massive rotor fluttering during certain maneuvers in horizontal flight, and sensitivity to strong wind. The Army and Air Force also pointed out that the XV-3 had not met the prescribed flight performance and had exceeded its specified weight.

After the testing, 4148 was flown aboard a USAF Lockheed C-130 "Hercules" to Ames, where flight-testing was continued until July 1962. Further modifications to the rotors finally allowed speeds of up to 287kph. Although the craft was never again to fly after the end of these tests, it was still tested several times in the wind tunnel. In May 1966 the XV-3 was tested in the Ames wind tunnel at a speed of 385kph, the highest possible speed in the wind tunnel.

On May 20, 1966, though, both rotors came loose in such a test, damaged the fuselage, and finally ended the XV-3's test program.

The Bell XV-3 had been flown 270 times during its testing, had attained a total flight time of 125 hours, and had carried out 110 complete transitions.

The main problem of the XV-3 was its large rotor, plus the lack of knowledge of the transitional effects that occur when such a rotor is used as a propeller. At that time the computers needed to approach this problem theoretically simply did not exist, so that Bell had to use the laborious process of trial and error.

Today the 4148 is found in restored condition at the Museum of the U.S. Air Force in Dayton, Ohio.

The XV-3 (4148) in the NASA Research
Center's wind tunnel at Ames on
May 12, 1966. *(NASA)*

The second XV-3 in flight. *(NASA)*

Today XV-3 is in the museum of the U.S. Air Force in Dayton, Ohio. *(USAF)*

VERTOL VZ-2A

Frank Piasecki built and flew in 1943 what was, after the Sikorsky VS-300, the second most successful helicopter in the USA. Later the Piasecki Helicopter Company was best known for helicopters with tandem rotors, like the H-21 "Flying Banana." Frank Piasecki himself left the firm in 1955, and a short time later the company renamed itself Vertol (from "vertical takeoff and landing").

On April 15, 1956, Vertol received a joint contract from the U.S. Army and Navy to develop and build a research airplane with tilting wings, which was to have the official designation VZ-2A. The Vertol Model 76, as it was called at the works, looked quite improvised and fragile at first glance, but proved itself to be a very successful test craft.

The VZ-2A had a large bubble-like pilot's compartment in front, reminiscent of a helicopter and offering space for two people side by side. The fuselage itself consisted of uncovered steel and aluminum tubes, with the rear part later being given a covering for aerodynamic reasons. On the fuselage a Lycoming YT-53-L-1 turbine was mounted, driving the two propellers, which were attached to the wings, via gears and shafts. These propellers had very wide blades and a diameter of 2.9 meters. The turbine exhaust gases were ducted out through a large pipe and ejected to the left before the elevators. Via a shaft, the turbine also drove two mantle screws located in the rudder and elevators. They served to provide steering along the vertical and transverse axes in hover-hold and slow flight.

The VZ-2A taking off. *(NASA)*

VZ-2A

Crew	1-2
Empty weight	1,130kg
Takeoff weight	1,450kg
Length	8,052mm
Height	4,570mm
Wingspan	7,595mm
Powerplant	1 Lycoming YT-53-L-1 turbine, 860 HP
Top speed	340kph
Service ceiling	4,205 meters
Range	210km

Control on the longitudinal axis was maintained with the help of various adjusting angles of the propeller blades. As soon as VZ-2A went over to horizontal flight, conventional rudders took over the steering.

The wings were mounted in shoulder configuration behind the cockpit and tilted one-third of the profile depth. The running gear of the VZ-2A was rigid and consisted of two main wheels, a small rear wheel, and later another small wheel under the cockpit to avoid damage better.

The ground tests of the VZ-2A began early in April 1957, and on April 13 the machine first lifted off vertically from the ground. On January 7, 1958, the first horizontal flight took place, and the first transition was carried out on July 15, 1958. During the testing of the VZ-2A only a few problems were found. The changes to the craft mainly concerned a stronger arching of the leading wing edges, to deal with the problem of slipstream shear in the transition from hovering to horizontal flight. For the same reason, additional flaps were installed on the rear parts of the wings, which increased the lift with partially tipped wings.

After the end of flight training by the U.S. Army, the VZ-2A was turned over to NASA, which carried out numerous further test flights. In all, the VZ-2A made 450 flights with thirty-four complete and 240 partial transitions during its long career, and showed that the tipping-wing concept was practicable. Finally VZ-2A was turned over to the Smithsonian Institution in Washington D.C., where it is now on display.

Testing of the VZ-2A took place without serious problems. *(NASA)*

November 15, 1962: VZ-2A shortly before
taking off. *(NASA)*

DOAK VZ-4DA

Edmond R. Doak founded the Doak Aircraft Company in Torrance, California. He had formerly worked for the aircraft constructor Douglas and experimented with mantled propellers since the mid-1930s. In 1950 Doak had already suggested a VTOL craft with tilting mantled propellers to the U.S. military, but could turn his ideas into deeds only when, on April 10, 1956, he was given a contract by the U.S. Army to develop a single research plane on this principle. The official military designation of the factory's Model 16 was VZ-4DA. The craft, finished at the end of 1957, had a slim fuselage with a tandem cockpit at the front and conventional control surfaces.

The fuselage was made of welded steel tubes, which were uncovered in the first tests. Later the fuselage was covered at the front with fiberglass-reinforced plastic (GFK) and at the rear with aluminum to make the craft more streamlined. The wings and control surfaces were made completely of metal.

To build as financially economical a place as possible, Doak turned to already available elements. The landing gear came from a Cessna 182, the motors of the tilting mechanism originally operated the landing flaps of a Lockheed T-33, and the seats came from a P-51 Mustang.

The most notable features of the VZ-4 were the tilting mantled propellers attached to the ends of the wings. Their diameter was 1.5 meters outside and 1.2 meters inside. Inside the mantling, which was made of aluminum and GFK and measured 0.8 meter in length, eight-bladed propellers made of GFK turned at speeds up to 4,800rpm. In front of the propellers were fourteen adjustable inlet flaps of GFK, with the help of which the thrust created by the propeller was regulated, so that the steering along the longitudinal axis could be regulated in hover-hold. Behind the propellers were nine steel panels that made sure the airstream was directed out of the mantling. The mantled propellers were put in horizontal position for conventional flight, but tilted ninety-two degrees for vertical flight. Since the exit of the turbine exhaust gas at the rear produced additional thrust, the propellers were tilted two degrees beyond the vertical.

A Lycoming YT-53-L-1 turbine producing 840 HP was mounted in the fuselage ad transmitted its power to the two mantled propellers via a gearbox and shafts. The exhaust gases were led to the rear end of the fuselage through a long steel tube, where they met a cross-shaped ducting panel of steel. Depending on the position of the panel, the pitching and yawing movement of the VZ-4 could be steered in hover-hold. In conventional flight the usual flaps and rudder rook over this task.

Early in February 1958 Doak began the testing of VZ-4 on the ground and in tethered flight. The first free hover-hold too place on February 25. After extensive testing by Doak, the plane was taken to Edwards AFB on October 1958, where it was tested intensively in a fifty-hour flight program. It carried out numerous complete transitions, some of them at altitudes of over 1,900 meters, steered and landed vertically and made short starts with partly tilted mantled propellers. In September 1959 the plane was turned over to NASA, which carried out further tests. In 1975 NASA turned it over to the U.S. Army Transportation Command Museum at Fort Eustis, in Newport News, Virginia, where it can still be seen today.

In the testing of VZ-4 a few negative flying characteristics appeared. In hover-hold and transition, the craft tended to hold its nose up too high, and its short starting and landing qualities were worse than expected. But these problems were not regarded as insoluble, and in any case the plane had shown that the concept of using mantled propellers worked.

VZ-4DA	
Crew	1-2
Empty weight	1,043kg
Takeoff weight	1,443kg
Length	9,750mm
Height	3,048mm
Wingspan	7,770mm
Powerplant	1 Lycoming YT-53-L-1 turbine, 840 HP
Top speed	370kph
Service ceiling	over 1,900 meters
Range	370km

A works photo of the still unbodied Doak VZ-4DA. *(Doak works photo via HMB)*

The Doak VZ-4DA in hover-hold. *(Doak works photo via HMB)*

Although the Doak proved to be a very successful test craft, there was no further development. *(Doak works photo via HMB)*

Patent drawings for the Doak Model 20.

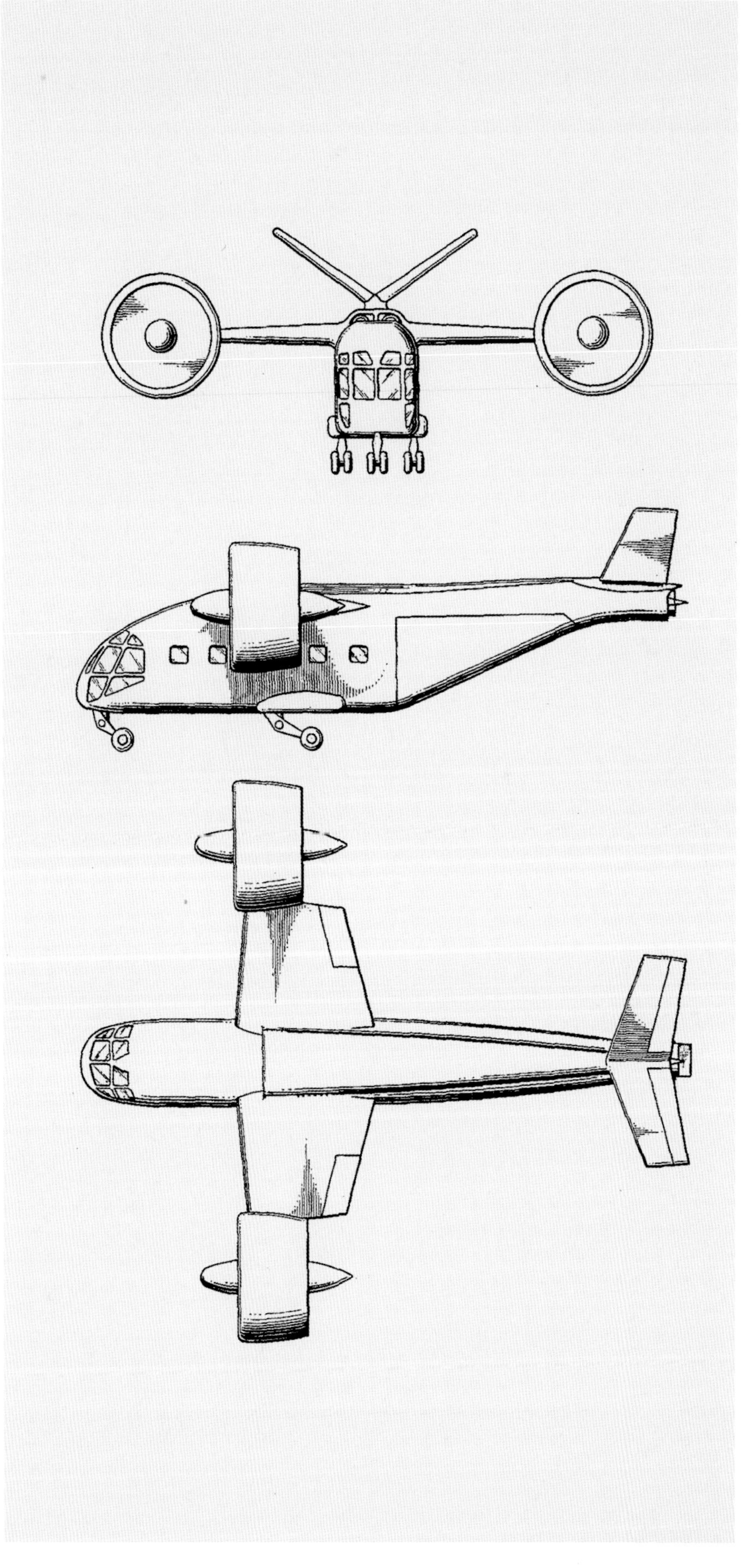

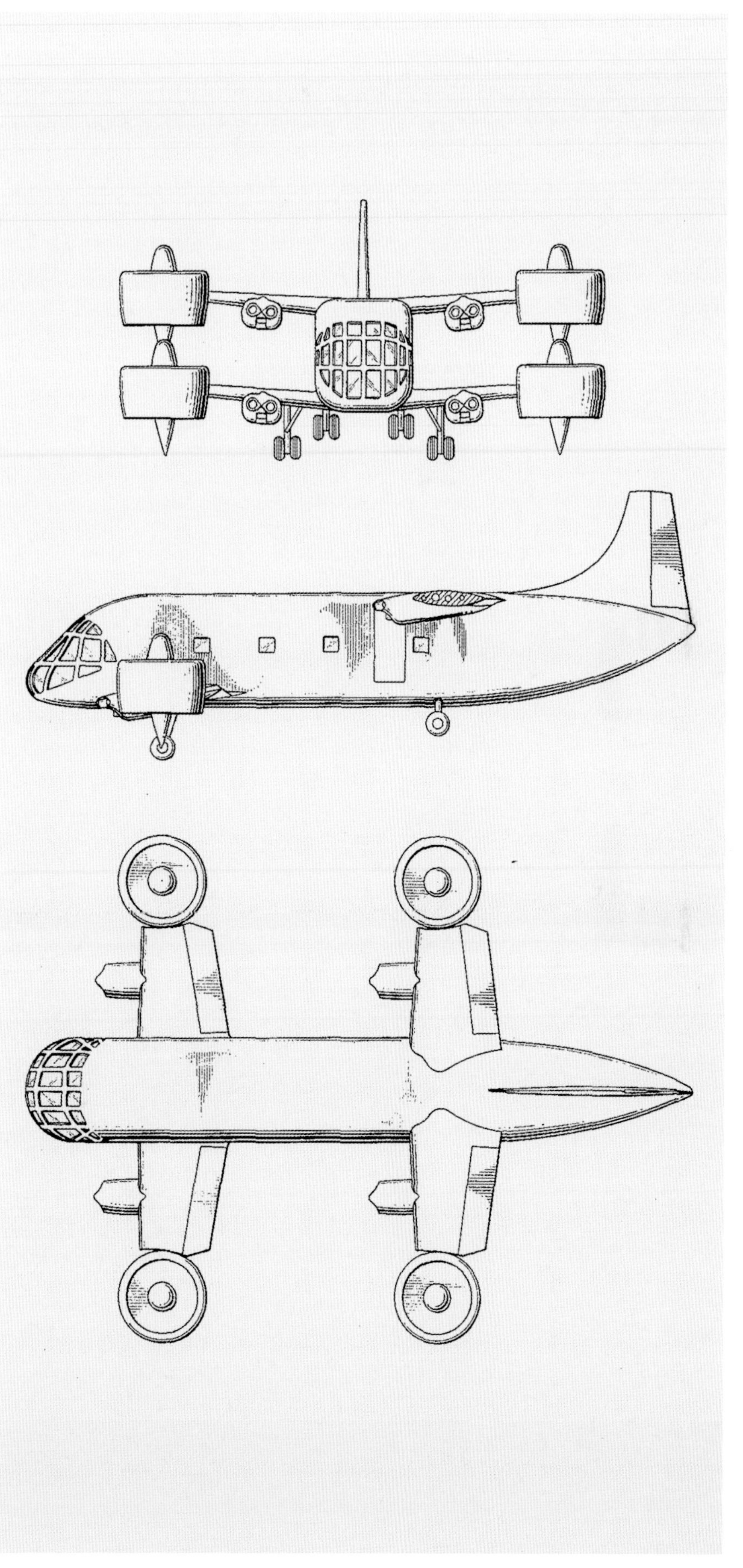

DOAK-DOUGLAS PROJECTS

In the late-1950s, Doak examined various designs with two, four and eight mantled propellers, but very little is known of them. The design work for two transport planes, Models 20 and 22, seem to have progressed the farthest. The Doak Model 20 had a conventional airplane fuselage, a rear flap and a butterfly control surface. Over the high-mounted wings was a separated air intake for two turbines located in the upper fuselage, which drove tilting mantled propellers mounted at the ends of the wings. The exhaust gases that exited at the rear of the fuselage were obviously used, as in VZ-4, for steering in hover-hold. The tripod landing gear was retractable, two aerodynamically sheathed bulges on the sides of the fuselage took in the main landing gear.

The Doak Model 22 had a considerably larger fuselage and a conventional lateral rudder, but no elevators. Instead, Model 22 had two pairs of tandem wings, mounted low on the fuselage in front and high at the rear. At the end of each wing was a tilting mantled propeller. The eight turbine engines were mounted in pairs in nacelles under the wings. Steering in hover-hold was probably done by different adjustments of the four mantled propellers.

Because of financial difficulties, the Doak Aircraft Company had to report bankruptcy in 1961, and transferred its patents, drawings and data to Douglas. Several Doak engineers also moved to Douglas. Douglas then suggested an improved version of Doak 16 to the U.S. Army, but could not get a contract.

The suggestion submitted by Douglas for the design of a test craft with four tilting mantled propellers, for the competition described by the U.S. Air Force and Navy, was also unsuccessful. The Douglas design was based for the most part on the Doak Model 22.

A certain similarity of the Douglas design to the Bell X-22A cannot be denied.

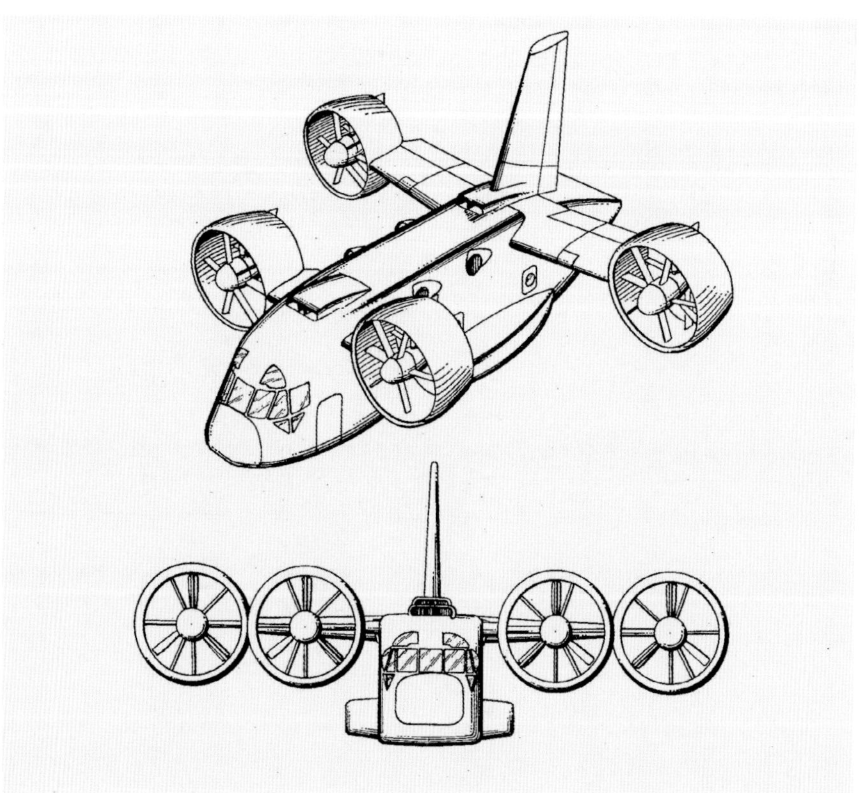

VERTOL TIPPING-WING WIND-TUNNEL MODEL

At the beginning of 1959 Vertol finished a wind-tunnel model built under contract from the U.S. Army. It was to be used for testing whether this technology would also be usable on larger transport planes. The appropriate series of tests were made in the NASA wind tunnel at the Langley Research Center in Virginia under Army contract. The model itself resembled a transport plane in shape, was some 8.23 meters long, had a wingspan of some 10.67 meters and weighed 6,350 kilograms. Its wings were fitted with six relatively small propellers powered by a 1,000 HP electric motor in the fuselage. The wings could be tilted ninety degrees and had large flaps along their entire length, which served to direct the propeller slipstream downward. The outer wings, including the two outer propellers, could be removed very easily so the model could be tested with only four propellers.

In 1959 Vertol designed this wind-tunnel model with tilting wings under U.S. Army contract. It was tested intensively at the NASA Langley Research Center. *(NASA)*

CURTISS-WRIGHT X-100

During World War II Curtiss-Wright was the USA's largest producer of aircraft and propellers. After the war it was not able to convert to civilian production or secure military contracts, so the firm's aircraft-building branch disappeared into insignificance within a few years of the war's end. But then as before, Curtiss-Wright was one of the world's leading producers of propellers. Its works research had shown that properly formed propellers produced a power vertical to the propeller axis, the so-called "radial lift component." The wings could be kept smaller, thus making the craft lighter. The firm's engineers had also calculated that these special propeller blades would produce enough energy to let a plane lift off and land vertically.

To prove this theory, Curtiss-Wright designed a test machine, the X-100, in 1958, with a length of only 8.64 meters and a wingspan of just 4.9 meters. The fuselage consisted of welded steel tubes and was sheathed in front with aluminum and in back with cloth. The cockpit had seats for two persons sitting side by side and was located ahead of an air intake on top of the fuselage for a Lycoming YT-53-L-1 turbine producing 825 HP and mounted in the fuselage. Via gears and shafts, it supplied not only the propellers with power, but its exhaust gases also steered the pitching and yawing movements in hover-hold and slow flight. The gases were ducted to the rear of the X-100, where a system of panels (called "jetivators" by Curtiss-Wright) caused them to be directed in the right direction. With full turbine performance, a thrust of 64kp for movements around the transverse axis (pitching) and 18kp for movement around the vertical axis (yawing) could be produced – too little, as it later turned out. Movement around the longitudinal axis (rolling) was controlled by changing the propeller blade angles. In horizontal flight conventional rudder and flaps handled the steering.

At the ends of the wings were contra-rotating propellers 3.05 meters in diameter, each with three wide shovel-shaped blades, which showed a strong twisting and, except for a steel core, were made completely of plastic. The two propeller nacelles could be tilted from the vertical to a position of twelve degrees over horizontal. Their setting was done in steps of ten degrees, in which it was to be observed that the craft gained some 32kph in horizontal speed for every ten-degree step.

The X-100 had only small wings, since its strongly twisted propellers produced a large part of the lift. *(Curtiss-Wright via HMB)*

The X-100 in flight. *(Smithsonian Institution)*

To avoid the danger that the X-100 might land first on its nose, two wheels were mounted under the bow during testing.
(Curtiss-Wright via HMB)

Curtiss-Wright X-100

Crew	1-2
Empty Weight	1,481kg
Takeoff weight	1,691kg
Length	8,640mm
Height	3,280mm
Wingspan	4,900mm
Powerplant	1 Lycoming YT-53-L-1 turbine, 825 HP
Top speed	290kph
Service ceiling	unknown
Range	unknown

For the designing and building of the X-100, Curtiss-Wright needed only ten months, from February 20 to December 22, 1958. The X-100 made its first tethered flight on April 20, 1959. Its first free flight took place on September 12, 1959; the first conventional takeoff on March 29, 1960. On April 13 of that year the X-100 finally made its first and only complete transition. After the plane's flight-testing was finished in the autumn of 1960, Curtiss-Wright evaluated the program as a success. The plane took off from the ground with no problems, the propellers produced the calculated lift, and, unlike the Bell XV-3, there were no unwanted, uncontrollable vibrations. In horizontal flight, at speeds over 112kph, the X-100 proved to steer well and be stable. In hover-hold and slow flight, though, this was absolutely not the case. The "jetivator" at the rear proved to be especially problematic, simply not producing enough thrust to steer the X-100 effectively. The throttling of the turbine necessary for landing made this condition even worse, so that there was danger of the tail suddenly pancaking. If the pilot steered against it, there was danger that it would do too much good and raise the X-100's nose. Thus two more wheels were mounted under the bow during testing.

The X-100 was also problematic in safety aspects. Its propellers were not big enough to allow a safe return to earth by autorotation in case of engine failure. The same applied to conventional gliding flight because of the small wings.

In October 1960 Curtiss-Wright turned the craft over to the NASA Research Center at Langley, where there was much interest in further research in the VTOL realm. There the X-100 made bound flights the following year, in which the effect and rear slipstreaming of the propeller air on various ground surfaces such as grass, snow, mud or stone were tested. On October 5, 1961, there was an accident, which damaged the X-100 only moderately but meant the end of the test program. In all, the X-100 had spent only fourteen hours in free flight in its career. The X-100 was then returned to Curtiss-Wright by NASA. The firm finally donated the plane to the National Air and Space Museum in Washington D.C., where it can still be seen today.

HILLER X-18

After the U.S. Army and Navy had tested a tiltwing plane, the V2A, the Air Force also issued a contract for the designing and building of such a test plane. In February 1957 the U.S. Air Force and Hiller Helicopters made a contract to build a craft with tipping wings. It was to have two motors, a top speed of ca.740kph, the ability to take off and land vertically, and excellent short takeoff and landing capability. During 1957 the U.S. Navy also granted its support for the test program.

Hiller Helicopters, founded by Stanley Hiller in 1942, was one of the first U.S. firms that only built helicopters. In 1953-54 Hiller had already made studies for a series of tiltwing craft. Among them was Model 1048A, which resembled in size and appearance a C-130 with tilting wings. In 1954-55 Hiller began the first design work on a plane to test the tipping-wing principle. Since at the time it did not look as if Hiller alone could cover the resulting costs alone, the engineers fell back on already available parts, wherever they could be found. The fuselage and control surfaces of the X-18 came from the Chase YC-122 "Avitruc," a transport plane of which a small pre-series had been built for the USAF in the late-1940s.

The propellers and powerplants of the X-18 came from the rear-takeoff program of the U.S. Navy (Convair XFY-1 "Pogo" and Lockheed XFGV-1 "Salmon"). Other parts of the Convair R3Y "Tradewind" flying boat were also used. The wing with its 14.8-meter wingspan was designed new by Hiller; it could be tilted ninety degrees by two hydraulic cylinders in six seconds and had forewings and rudder

The fuselage of the Hiller X-18 came from the Chase YC-122 "Avitruc" built at the end of the 1940s. *(USAF)*

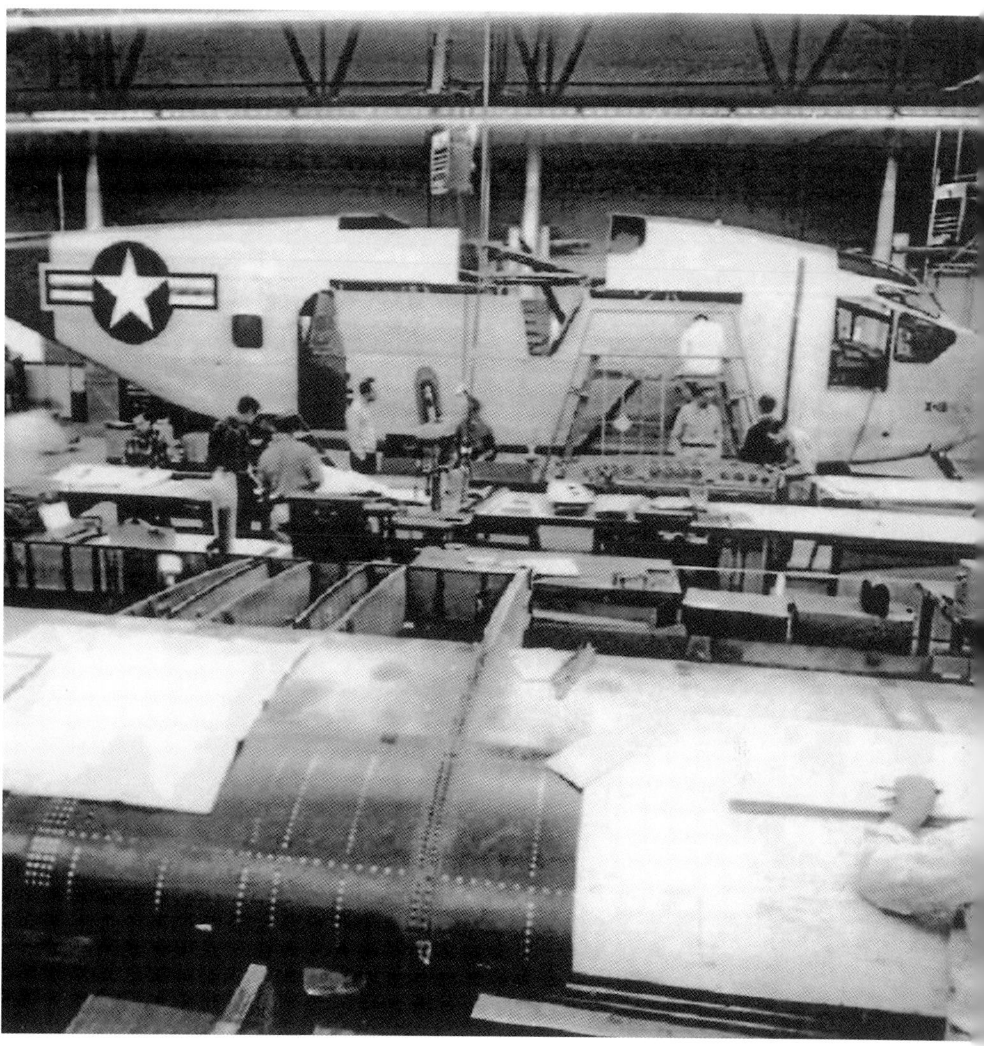

but no landing flaps. To keep the costs low and the design effort modest, the X-18 had rigid landing gear.

The X-18 was a considerably larger airplane than any previous VTOL craft. With a fuselage length of 19.20 meters, it weighed 12,230kg empty and 14,970kg ready to take off. Thus it was some ten times heavier than the VZ-2A. Each of the two Allison T-40-A-14 double engines consisted of two coupled T-38 turbines, producing 5,932 HP, and drove coaxial, contra-rotating three-bladed propellers 4.9 meters in diameter. This powerplant had already proved to be problematic, for all prototypes equipped with these turbines, such as the Douglas A2D "Skyshark" or the Convair R3Y "Tradewind," suffered from their unreliability and high vibra-

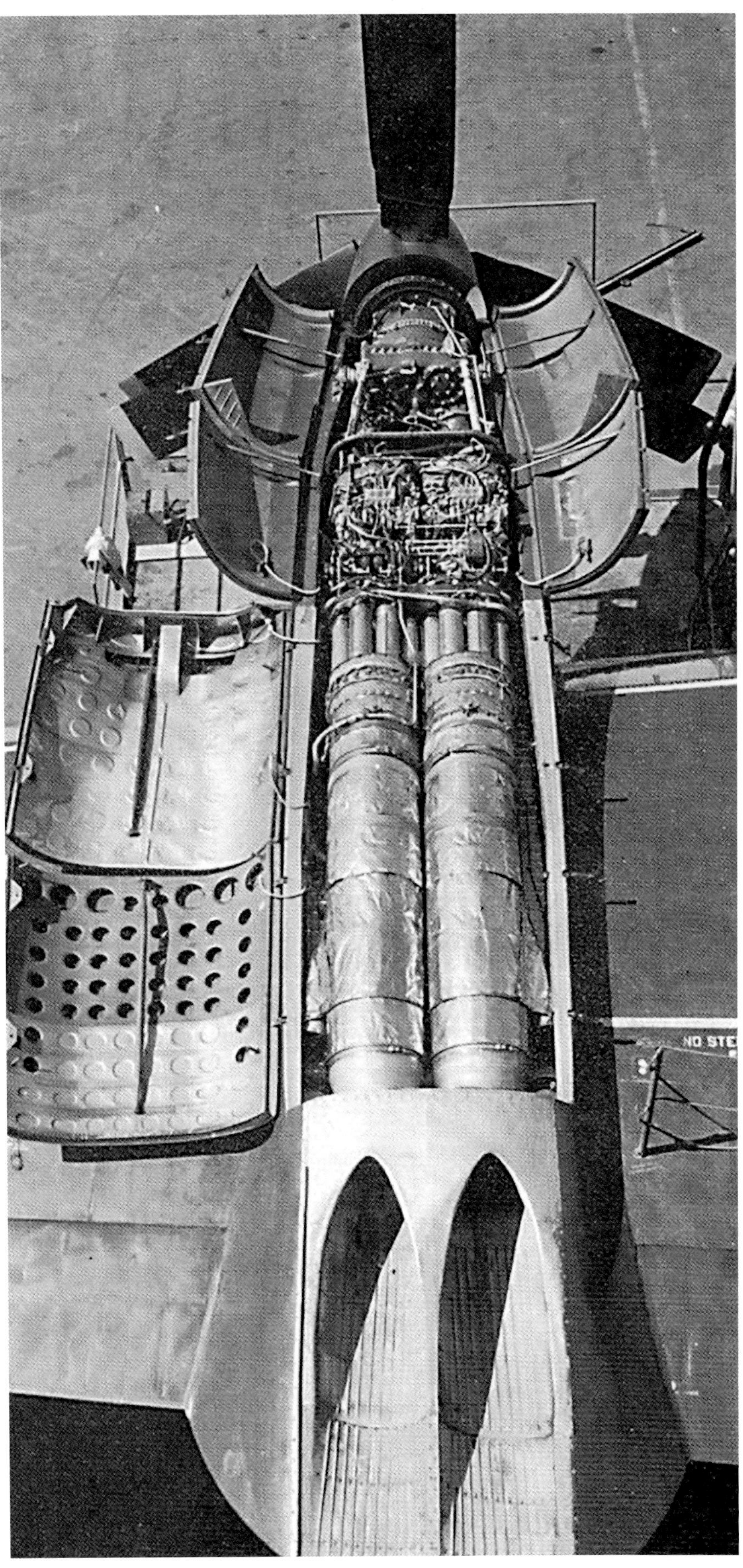

The Allison T-40-A-14 double powerplant of the X-18. *(USAF)*

Note the steel tube of the Westinghouse J34 jet engine installed in the fuselage of the X-18. Its exhaust gases were used to steer the pitching movements in hover-hold. *(USAF)*

tion levels. Unlike practically all other craft of this type, the engines of the X-18 were not connected by a cross shaft, to be sure that if one of them failed, the propeller would still be supplied with power.

A Westinghouse J34 jet engine giving 15,542kp of thrust was mounted in the fuselage. Its exhaust gases were ducted to the rear of the plane, where they, as needed, streamed out upward or downward to steer the craft on its transverse axis during hover-hold and transitional flight.

Steering on the longitudinal axis was done by adjusting the propeller setting; that on the vertical axis by the elevators. After a transition, steering was automatically taken over by the conventional rudders.

In December 1958 the building of the X-18 was ended, and after that the plane was at first subjected to intensive tests at Moffett Field (near Palo Alto, California), including those to make sure there were no unwanted vibrations of the powerplant. After that the X-18 was taken to the USAF's Edwards Air Base,

Complete transitions were made by the X-18 pilots only on the ground. *(USAF)*

Hiller X-18

Crew	2
Empty weight	12,230kg
Takeoff weight	14,970kg (VTOL), 16,012kg (STOL)
Length	19,200mm
Height	7,490mm
Wingspan	14,630mm
Powerplant	2 Allison T-40-A-14 propeller turbines, 5,932 HP each; 1 Westinghouse J34 jet engine with 1,542kp thrust
Top speed	402kph
Service ceiling	unknown
Range	360km

where it made its first flight on November 24, 1959. In the following months the X-18 made a total of twenty flights, in which the test pilots slowly worked up to a complete tilting of the wings and thus reached an angle of thirty-three degrees. Since the nose of the X-18 also rose seventeen degrees because of the resulting aerodynamic forces, the two movements added up to a tilting angle of fifty degrees. In this tilting angle the conventional flight steering was already partly ineffective, thus the hover-hold steering was to take over its task, which it did not do sufficiently. Above all, the electric setting of the propeller blades proved to be problematic, in that it reacted too slowly and thus made control on the longitudinal axis difficult. During its twentieth flight, in July 1961, problems with the propeller setting resulted in the craft getting into a spin. Only the fact that this happened at a height of 3,000 meters and the pilot had time to straighten out the X-18 prevented a crash. Yet this incident led to a flight ban, and the X-18 was never again to lift off the ground. To be sure, extended ground tests were made with it at Edwards Air Force Base from 1962 to 1964, in which the thrust produced by the propellers with tilted wings and its distribution were tested especially.

In these tests a test rig collapsed in 1964, and the X-18 was severely damaged. Since repairs did not seem worth the cost, the plane was scrapped shortly thereafter.

Although the X-18 flew only a few times and never made a single hover-hold, valuable experience and data for the later XC-142 program were gained with its help. During the program, Hiller suggested various further developments of the X-18, including two slightly differing transports and a search-and-rescue plane. With the ending of the official test program, though, the work on these projects also ended.

The X-18 in ground testing at Edwards AFB.
(USAF)

KAMAN K-16B

The Kaman Aerospace Company, founded in 1945 by helicopter pioneer Charles H. Kaman, became known for a series of helicopters with coordinated rotors, such as the H-43 "Husky" and the "K-Max." Although the U.S. Navy was already participating in the X-18 program, it issued in 1959 or 1960, depending on the source, a contract to Kaman to build another tipping-wing craft, the K-16B.

This aircraft was also similar to the X-18 in being built in part of already available parts. The fuselage of the K-16B came from an amphibian flying boat built in the 1940s, the Grumman JRF-5 "Goose." The most noticeable difference from the original was that the wings, spanning 10.36 meters and tilting some fifty degrees, were designed and built by Kaman. Large flaps, extending over the entire trailing edge of the wings, made sure that the propeller slipstream was directed vertically downward. Also of significance were the two massive engine nacelles, each holding a GE T58-GE-2A propeller turbine (by works sources, also GE YT58-GE-6), which drove three-bladed opposed propellers of 4.57-meter diameter. To supply both propellers with power, even in case of an engine failure, the turbines were linked via gears and a cross shaft.

Front view of the K-16B. Note the wide blades of the propellers. *(USN)*

The K-16B was based on the Grumman JRF-5 "Goose" of the 1940s. *(USN)*

Kaman K-16B

Crew	2
Empty weight	unknown
Takeoff weight	unknown
Length	11,680mm
Height	5,867mm
Wingspan	10,360mm
Powerplant	2 General Electric T58-GE-2A propeller turbines, each 1,024 HP
Top speed	320kph
Service ceiling	4,870 meters
Range	325km

The propellers of the K-16B were unique in that their wide blades had small, steerable flaps and cyclical adjustment, so they could operate effectively as rotors. Cyclical longitudinal adjustment helped to control yawing movement, a change in the adjusting angle regulated their rolling movements. This system of "rotoprops" was also supposed to make the craft steerable in hover-hold and slow flight in the realm of up to 80kph if the normal rudder and flaps showed no effect.

Kaman had developed this system already in the mid-1950s and designed a test craft, designated K-16, but no prototype had been built. Only when the U.S. Navy wanted to investigate the possibility of a high-sea-capable VTOL flying boat for submarine warfare did Kaman rework the original design as the K-16B.

The K-16B was finished in 1960 and subjected to intensive ground testing, and was also tested by NASA during 1962, among other things, in the Ames wind tunnel. Several problems that would have to be solved before the flight tests began appeared clearly. The Navy canceled the program. Whether the craft made tethered flights during the test program is not clear. The only K-16B is now on display at the New England Air Museum in Windsor Locks, Connecticut.

The wings of the K-16B tilted only fifty degrees, Large flaps on the trailing edges directed the propeller slipstream vertically downward. *(USN)*

In 1962 the K-16B was studied exhaustively by NASA. *(NASA)*

CURTISS-WRIGHT X-19

After the X-100 had shown that the theory of radial lift components was correct, the firm planned a commercial use of the principle. For this purpose the Curtiss-Wright engineers designed a fast commercial passenger airplane with VTOL capability for four passengers in a pressurized cabin, the X-200 or Model 200. This design was to have a range of 1,500 to 1,700km at a speed of some 740kph and a height of 5,000 meters.

The X-200 had a slim fuselage in metallic half-shell design and two pairs of tandem wings high up on the fuselage. At the end of each wing was a small tilting nacelle, each holding one of the three-bladed propellers. As in the X-100, the propellers, made mostly of plastic, had a very deep profile and were strongly coordinated. The diameter of the airscrews was 3.96 meters. For the takeoff and landing phase, they were vertical; for traveling flight they were moved to the horizontal. The front nacelles were tilted somewhat above the vertical (ninety-seven degrees), meaning they pointed slightly backward. The rear propellers, unlike them, were tilted only eighty-two degrees, so that they pointed slightly forward.

On the fuselage was a divided air intake for the two Lycoming T-55-5 propeller turbines, each producing 2,230 HP, but the literature also gives a partial statement that T-55-7 turbines, each with 2,650 HP, were installed. The two turbines

Three-side drawing of the X-19 from an old Curtiss-Wright brochure.
(Curtiss-Wright via HMB)

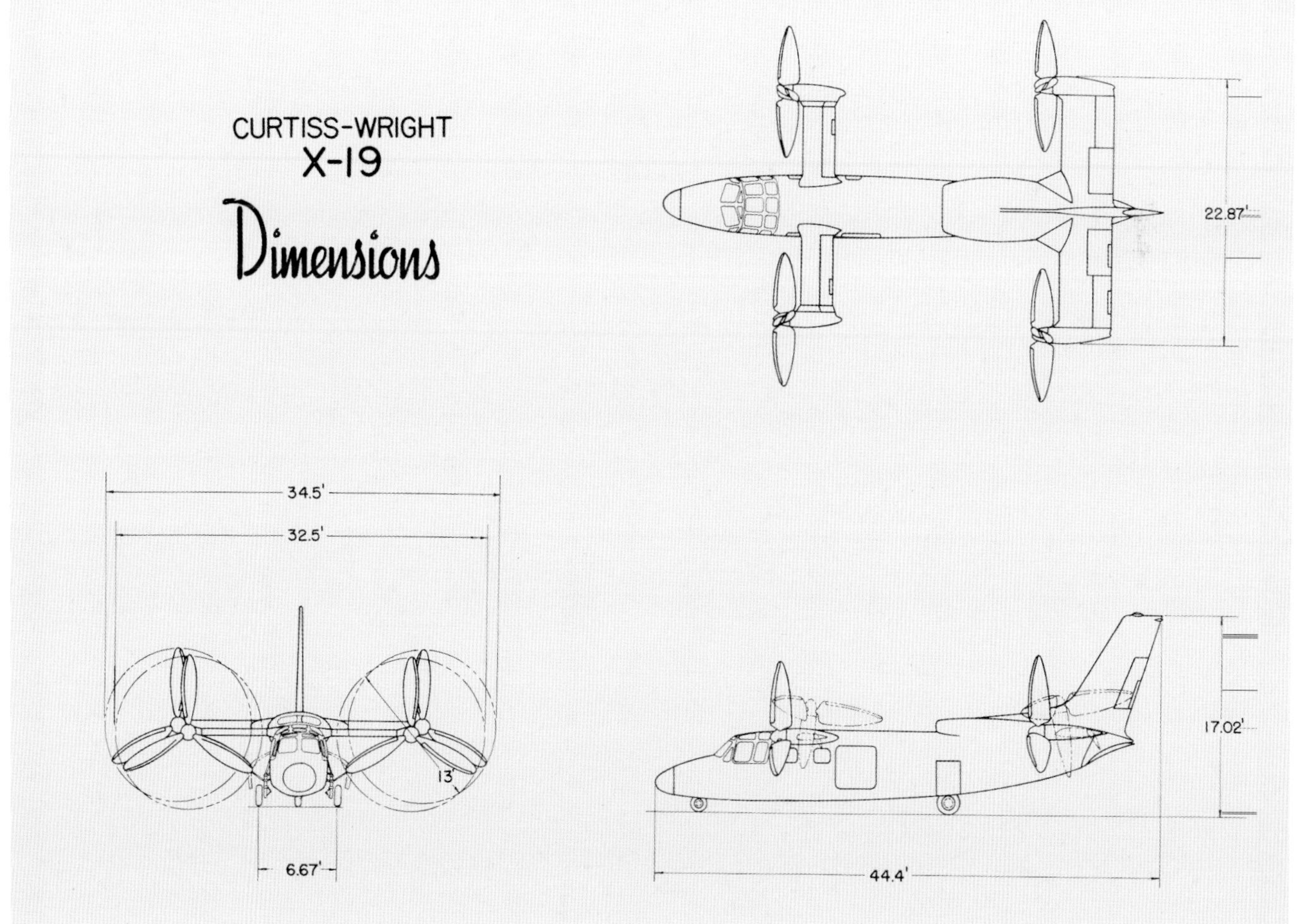

were linked with the propellers by gears and shafts, so that each one could run all four propellers alone in an emergency (or to save fuel). The turbines were geared down so that the propeller tips turned at a maximum of 250m/sec and thus made relatively little noise.

Interestingly, Curtiss-Wright had originally planned to use four Wankel circular-piston motors of 580 HP each for power. Since the company wanted to produce these motors itself and sell them not only in North America but worldwide, they could not agree with the inventor as to the licensing fees, so that the two propeller turbines were finally chosen.

The X-200, because of its tandem wings, had no conventional elevators, but could not do without a rudder for reasons of stability. The front wings had a wingspan of some 6.1 meters and were very narrow; the rear wings measured 6.4 meters and had a greater profile depth. The front pair of wings had landing flaps along their full length, while the rear wings had lateral flaps inside and height flaps outside. In hover-hold all the flaps and rudders were lowered sixty degrees to disturb the propeller slipstream as little as possible.

The steering of the plane on its transverse axis was to be done by adjusting the blade-angle settings between the front and rear propellers. For steering on the longitudinal axis of the plane, the blade-angle settings between the propellers on the left or right side were to be changed, and for steering on the vertical axis, those of the diagonal propellers would be adjusted.

The four broad propellers of the X-19 are clearly visible in this image. *(USAF)*

For takeoffs and landings, all the flaps and rudders of the X-19 were inclined sixty degrees to disturb the propeller slipstream as little as possible. *(USAF)*

Schematic drawing of steering for the X-19. *(Curtiss-Wright via HMB)*

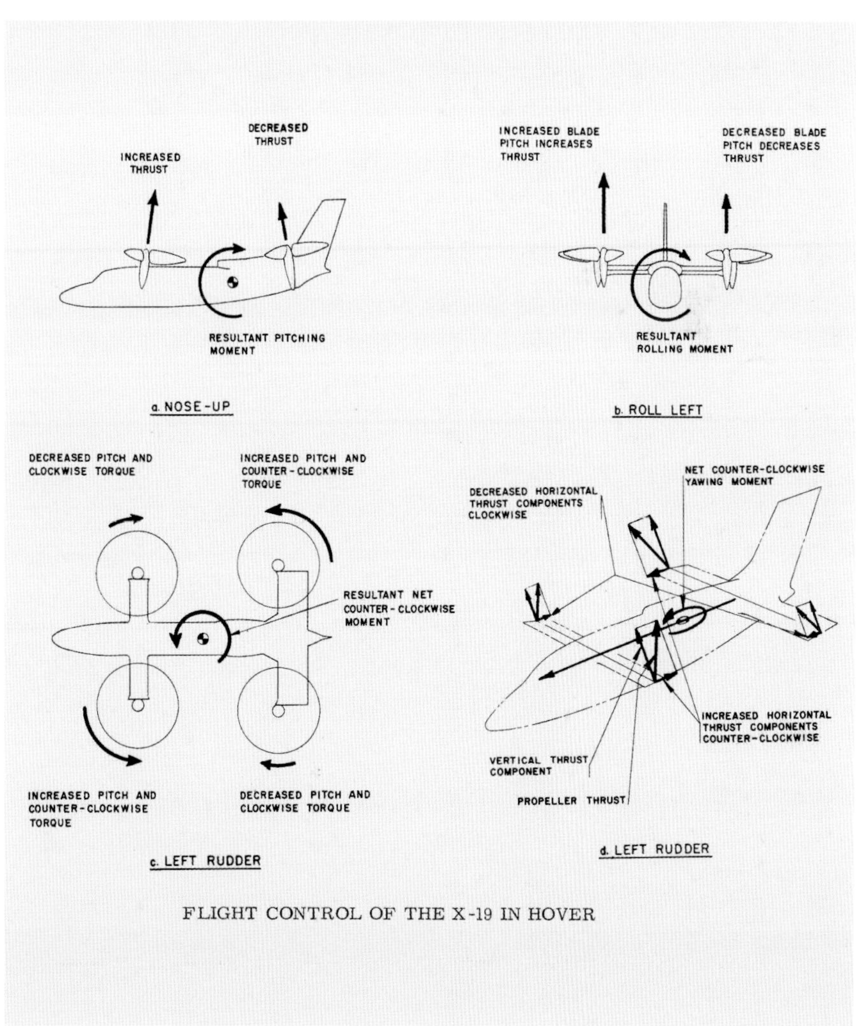

The tripod running gear was quite low and could be retracted into the fuselage. The cabin in its original layout had a height of only 1.22 meters, a width of 1.35 meters and a length of 2.44 meters. The entire rear area of the fuselage, which was originally 12.5 meters long, was taken up by the shaft of the main engine, three fuel tanks holding a total of 2,720 liters, the two turbines and the gears. The empty weight of the planned civilian version was to be about 3,600kg, while the takeoff weight was suggested as ca.5,580kg.

The X-200 was at first a purely private program, financed by Curtiss-Wright itself, but the firm's interest in the project faded because of the ever-higher costs in the course of development. Thus the management decided to offer the two prototypes then being built to the U.S. Air Force, in the framework of the Tri-Service VTOL research program of the Army, Navy and Air Force. After negotiations that covered over eighteen months, the USAF finally agreed to buy the two X-200s.

So that consideration could be given to the requirements of the military, several changes had to be made to the airplanes. They included the lengthening of the cabin to offer space for six passengers, which increased the fuselage length to 13.51 meters. In addition, the cabin door had to be widened to 107cm and a rescue winch installed over it. The USAF insisted on two zero-zero ejection seats

The X-19 was first designed as a private program of the Curtiss-Wright firm; only later did the U.S. Air Force finance the plane's testing.

being installed in the cockpit, to allow the pilot and co-pilot, sitting side by side, a safe exit, even at zero altitude and zero speed. The second prototype was modified in the same way, but was also given new instruments, improved devices for registering flight data, and a mockup of a midair fueling sonde. All of this made the empty weight of the plane, now designated X-19, increase to 4,846kg and the takeoff weight to 6,200kg.

The first X-19 was displayed to the public on July 23, 1963. After extensive ground tests, it was planned to have the plane flown first by Curtiss-Wright test pilots, who were to make sure that the X-19 was capable of hover-hold and transitions. Then the flight-testing would be taken over by a team from the Tri-Service Program.

The first flight of X-19 on November 20, 1963, ended with an accident. The plane arose only briefly, rocked and landed hard. Only the landing gear was damaged, but flight-testing could be continued only in the summer of 1964. On June 25, 1964 the X-19 lifted off the ground for the second time and then made numerous test flights, but without making a transition. The plane did prove its ability to hover backward and turn in place, but could be steered by the pilot only with difficulty and highest concentration. In horizontal flight, though, it proved to be stable and flew at over 160kph. After the automatic flight-position steering was put into service, the steering problem improved in hover-hold, but it was still present.

On December 4 of that year, X-19 was damaged by loose stones on a freshly paved runway. All four propellers and both turbines were involved. When a propeller failed on January 31, 1965, this meant another interruption, of some six months, in the flight program.

All the tests to date had taken place at the Curtiss-Wright factory airfield in Caldwell, New Jersey. Now it was decided to continue the testing at a U.S. Air Flight Department (NAFEC) facility near Atlantic City, New Jersey, where a U.S. Air Force team was to be brought into the testing. After the X-19 had been repaired, it undertook a short hovering flight on July 31, 1965, and was then shipped to Atlantic City by truck. The Air Force technicians quickly learned that the control problems in hover-hold were caused by a poorly tuned steering system, and these could be cleared up only after great expense. In August the X-19 made several flights and tilted its propellers more and more toward the horizontal. Finally, on August 24, 1965, during the fiftieth flight, the first complete transition was to be made. While the plane was some 400 meters up with the propellers tipped sixty-five degrees, warning signals showed malfunctions in parts of the gearing, warning the crew to return to the base. The position did not seem so dramatic for the pilots and ground crews to have considered an emergency landing necessary, so they decided on a normal approach to the airfield. Suddenly there were strong vibrations and a partial loss of steering ability. Since the X-19 was flying toward a patch of woods and the pilots feared they would hit the treetops, they flew the plane upward at full power. The pilot could not regain control over the plane at first. Then at a height of some 120 meters, the left rear propeller came loose, followed by the others shortly thereafter, so the crew catapulted out on their ejection seats. Shortly afterward X-19 crashed and was fully destroyed. The two pilots survived the accident with only minor injuries. The X-19 had been tested on the ground over 129 hours, but in its fifty flights it had spent only three hours and fifty-one minutes in the air.

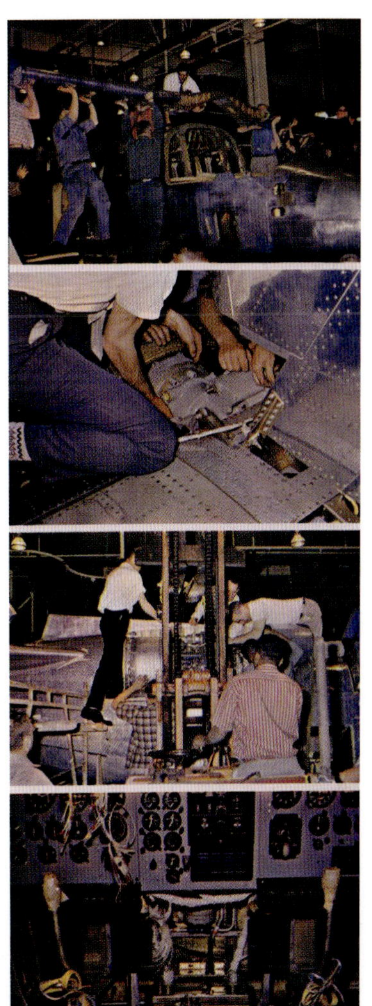

The X-19 under construction – pictures from a sales brochure of Curtiss-Wright. *(Curtiss-Wright via HMB)*

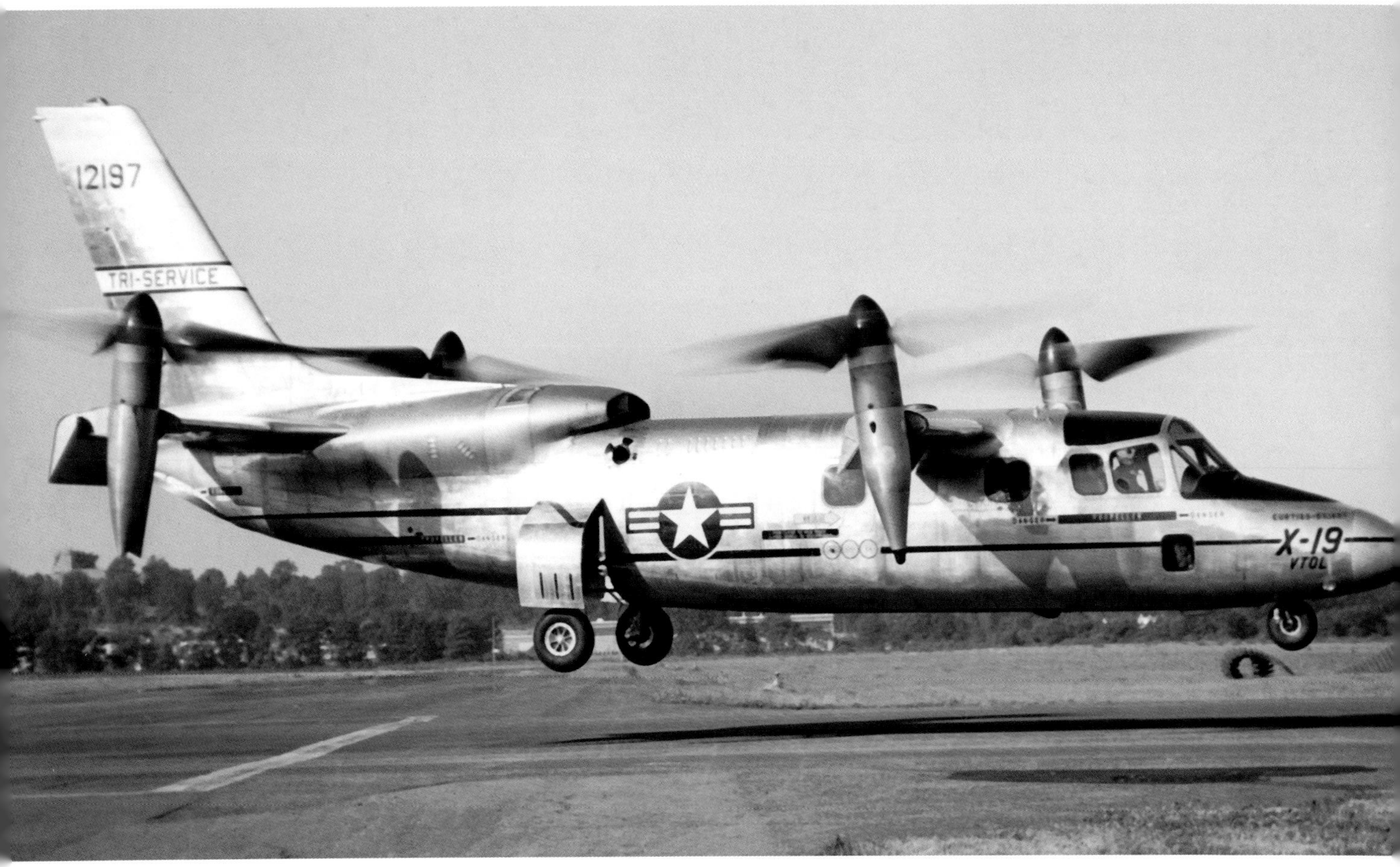
12197
TRI-SERVICE
X-19
VTOL

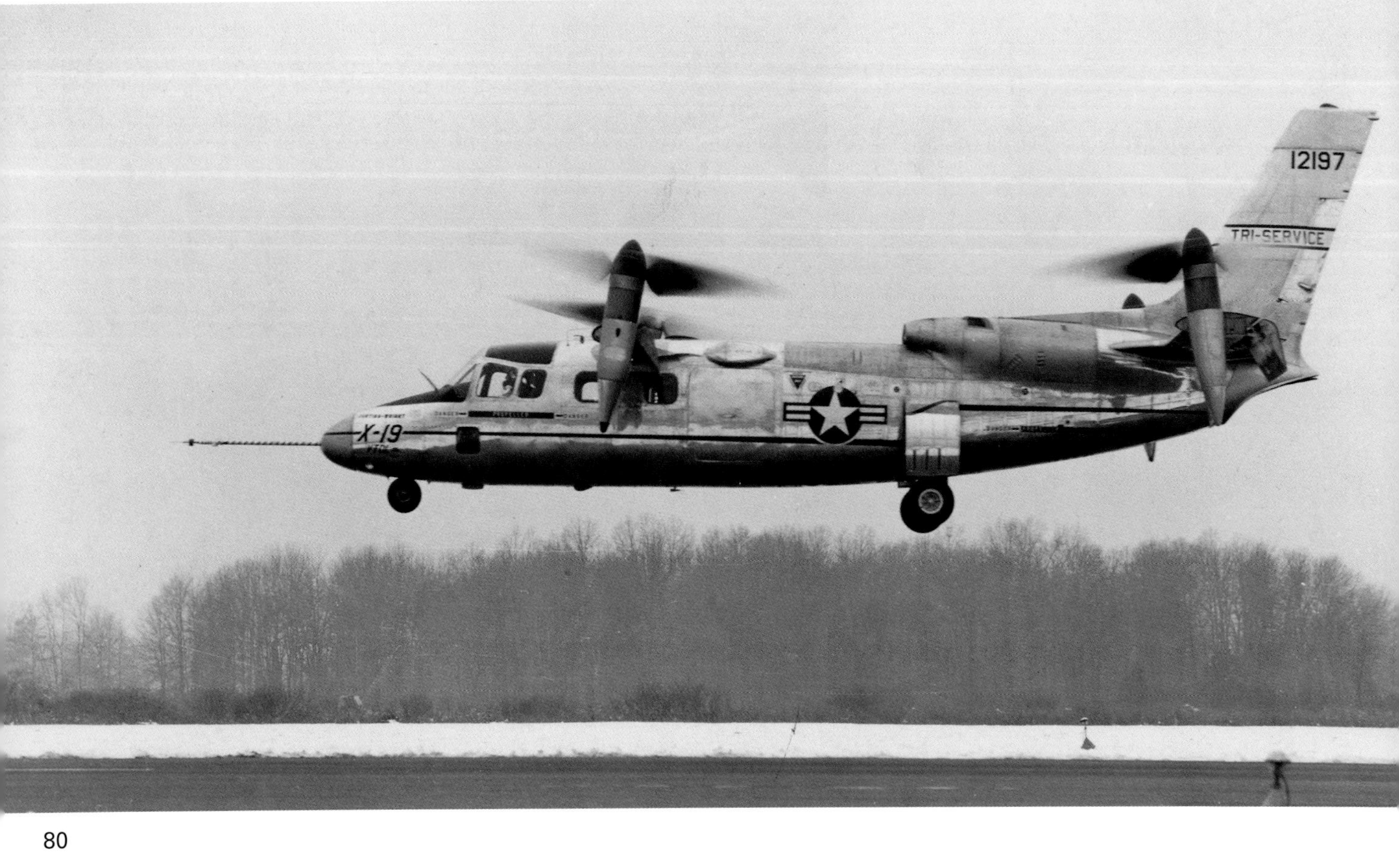
12197
TRI-SERVICE
X-19

A later investigation showed that the cause of the crash was the steep ascent under full power made by the pilot, which had overstressed the gears. The gears had originally been removed to take up and exceed the performance, which required a takeoff weight of 5,580kg for lifting off. The plane's takeoff weight, though, had increased in the course of development to 6,200kg. In addition, the pressure limit of the gearbox part that coupled the two turbines was at most 2,900 HP. The full power of the two 2,230 HP engines had to result in serious gearbox damage.

Despite this design error and the resulting accident, the USAF wanted to continue testing the X-19 with the second prototype. To be sure, there was disagreement at Curtiss-Wright as to further financing, which finally led to the halting of the X-19 program at the end of 1965. The second plane was stored at first and is now (2009) being restored at the USAF Museum in Dayton, Ohio.

Although Curtiss-Wright had quickly lost interest in commercial marketing of the original X-200, and was not ready later to bear part of the financial risk of the X-19 program, the firm projected a whole series of variants of the type. Its use was suggested as a search-and-rescue plane, submarine fighter, and a light transport plane, for police and surveillance tasks and special actions. But the end of the X-19 program meant the end of all these projects.

An artistic conception of some uses of
the X-19 suggested by Curtiss-Wright.
(Curtiss-Wright via HMB)

Curtiss-Wright X-19

Crew	2
Empty weight	4,846mm
Takeoff weight	6,200kg
Length	11,680mm
Height	5,867mm
Wingspan	6,096mm (front), 6,400mm (rear)
Powerplant	2 Lycoming T-55-5 propeller turbines, 2,230 HP each
Top speed	740kph
Service ceiling	over 6,100 meters
Range	788km

CURTISS-WRIGHT TILT-PROPELLER PROJECTS

When the U.S. Army established the AAFSS (Advanced Aerial Fire Support System in 1964-65, Curtiss-Wright took part with a slightly modified version of the X-19, the Model 90.
The most striking feature of this type was the newly designed tandem cockpit in the style of a combat helicopter. Although the power transmission system had been improved from that of the X-19, the design could not succeed in the AAFSS competition. This competition was finally won by the Lockheed AH-56 "Cheyenne."
On the basis of Model 90, Curtiss Wright also conceived a light transport craft, which used the wings, powerplants and power train of the Model 90 but had a new fuselage. This design was offered to the U.S. Army in the parameters of their search for a light tactical multi-purpose and transport aircraft (Army Utility Tactical Light Transport) but could not find acceptance.

In 1965 Curtiss-Wright sent a modified X-19, the Model 90, into the running for the U.S. Army's AAFSS competition. *(Curtiss-Wright via HMB)*

Curtiss-Wright's concept of a light tactical transport plane. *(Curtiss-Wright via HMB)*

Left | This study of a transport plane was considerably larger than the X-19/Model 90. *(Curtiss-Wright via HMB)*

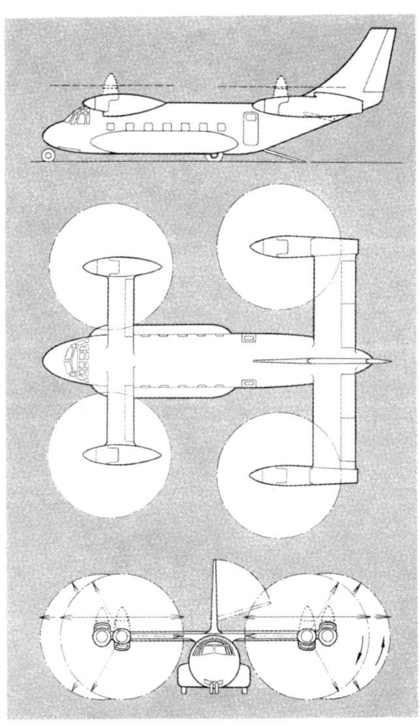

Finally Curtiss-Wright suggested a military and civilian transport version considerably enlarged from the X-19/Model 90. It was to carry a payload of five to ten tons or thirty-five to fifty passengers. The plane, some nineteen meters long, was to be powered by four propeller turbines in tilting nacelles on the tandem wings.

LTV-HILLER-RYAN XC-142A

In view of the numerous different military VTOL programs of the fifties, the three service arms of the USA (Army, Navy and Air Force) began in 1959 to coordinate their information on this subject to have a prototype developed that would be right for their jointly formulated requirements. A VTOL war-zone transporter was sought to complement the heavy transport helicopters of the three service arms and finally to replace them. After a successful testing, the design was supposed to be built in full scale and large series. In January 1961 the Army, Navy and Air Force jointly published a description that, because of the fact that all three branches of the U.S. military wrote the description jointly, was called the "Tri-Service Competition." Although the costs were born in equal shares, the U.S. Air Force was to lead the program.

In September 1961 the V-447 design of a consortium composed of LTV, Hiller and Ryan was declared the winner over the entries of Boeing-Vertol, North American Aviation, Grumman and Bell/Lockheed and Bell Helicopter. At the beginning of 1962 a contract for the building of five prototypes was issued, calling for the first flight in July 1964.

The main contractee was Vought Aeronautics; Ryan Aeronautical took on the design and building of the controls, the rear fuselage, the engine nacelles and wings, while Hiller Aircraft accepted responsibility for the gearing plus the flaps and rudders.

The joint design was designated XC-142A, which was to mean that it was not a pure research aircraft (V classification), but the prototype of a series-produced transport plain (C = cargo). The XC-142A, although it seemed quite compact, was a large airplane. Its length was 17.71 meters, its wingspan some 20.57 meters, and its normal takeoff weight was a good seventeen tons. For VTOL action a payload of 3,629kg was possible. For short takeoffs (STOL) it rose to 5,443kg. The fuselage was box-shaped and had an almost square cross-section with just slightly rounded angles. In front was the well-glassed cockpit for two pilots sitting side by side; behind was a cargo space for thirty-two soldiers, 9.14 meters long, 2.29 meters wide and 2.13 meters high, with a lowering loading ramp at the rear. The crew included not only the two pilots but also a loadmaster.

The bow wheel was retracted into the fuselage and the two main landing-gear legs into housings on the sides. The wings were set high up on the fuselage and tilted hydraulically 100 degrees, so that the XC-142A could hover problem-free even in a tailwind. As its power source there were four T64-GE01 propeller turbines, each producing 3,080 HP; they were located so that their propeller slipstream blew on the entire wing, to improve the short-takeoff characteristics. The turbines, though, did not drive the airscrews directly, but gave their power to a joint gearbox that used a complex system of shafts and reduction gears to assure that all four propellers would be driven if one or even two powerplants failed. In addition, a long shaft to the tail drove a three-bladed propeller at the rear, which took over the steering on the transverse axis and was blocked for direct flight.

The milestones of XC-142A development are shown in a sales brochure from Vought. *(Vought via HMB)*

Prototype No.3 of the VC-142A. *(USAF)*

Right: In hover-hold and landing flight the elevators of the XC-142A were also tilted. *(Vought)*

To save cargo space, this propeller was hinged. The four-bladed propellers made by Hamilton Standard consisted of GFK and had a diameter of 4.75 meters each. By adjusting their setting angles, they served in hover-hold to control movement along the longitudinal axis. Steering on the vertical axis was done by the rudder, which lay in the propeller slipstream. During hover-hold and the transition to horizontal flight, an automatic system regulated the coordination of the individual steering elements before the conventional flaps and rudders took control. The elevators were fully movable, and large landing flaps (the two outer ones on each wing also served as rudders) and forewings could be set so that they prevented slipstream shear during transition.

After a first mockup was finished in July 1962, the first plane that could fly was displayed to the public on June 17, 1964. A good three months later, on September 29, it made its first flight. The first hover-hold followed shortly before the end of that year, and on January 11, 1965, the XC-142A carried out its first complete transition. After intensive tests by Vought, the first XC-142A was turned over to the USAF for testing in July 1965. The last of the five planes to be built was delivered in August 1966.

The Air Force tested the planes intensively in the following months, making not only transport flights with full payloads but also freight drops and rescue missions in hover-hold. The XC-142A proved that it could carry armed Jeeps, light trucks with 3/4-ton loads, 10.5cm howitzers and freight containers on board and take off vertically. The XC-142A was also tested under desert conditions and successfully on board an aircraft carrier. Plane No.5 made forty-four short takeoffs and landings plus six vertical takeoffs and landings on the deck of the carrier USS Bennington. All in all, the type showed satisfactory characteristics, its main problem being the high surface pressure of 278 kilograms per square meter. Although the four propellers together swept a total surface area of sixty-five square meters, this was only a fraction of the complete surface that the rotor of a comparable heavy helicopter sweeps. Thus the turbines of the XC-142A had to run with high power in hover-hold and made so much noise in the process that this influenced the crew's work, to say nothing of its influence on the surroundings. Beyond that, the high engine speeds led to strong vibrations, resulting in premature metal fatigue as well as an added burden for the crew. A further factor that burdened the crews was the high cockpit temperature. The large glass panels let the temperatures on some flights rise over sixty-eight degrees Celsius because of solar radiation, so that the crews had to wear special cooling suits. Later part of the upper cockpit window was covered to decrease solar radiation.

Positive factors were the maneuverability of the XC-142A, which was able to fly up to 37kph backward and 75kph sideways. Its climbing performance, thanks to its strong engines, was around 1,150 meters per minute, even with only three turbines; with all four turbines, it was even some 2,070 m/min. The STOL capability of the XC-142A was slightly short of expectations, but the type was capable of overcoming a fifteen-meter-high obstacle after a takeoff run of only 120 meters with a payload of over 4,500 kilograms. But the cruising speed and the thrust produced by the propellers did not correspond with the calculated values. In addition, the stability in hover-hold near the ground was unsatisfactory with the wings set between thirty-five and eighty degrees, and the steering demanded high concentration despite the automatic system,

An airplane the size of the XC-142A must be a breathtaking sight in hover-hold, to say nothing of ear-splitting noise. *(Vought)*

Below | An XC-142A flying low over the desert. Note what a lot of dust is raised in the process. *(USAF)*

XC-142A
XC-142A
NASA
UNITED STATES

The XC-142A being tested by NASA at Langley, January 17, 1969. *(NASA)*

The shafts and gears also showed that they were not equal to the developing pressures, especially shear pressure during the tilting process. Along with pilot errors, this led during the course of testing to a series of accidents in which all five planes were more or less badly damaged. In May 1967 one of these accidents ended fatally for three crewmen. In a simulated rescue action near the Vought factory airfield outside Dallas, Texas, the tail propeller failed because of a break in its driveshaft. Plane No.1 thus went out of control, crashed in a heavily wooded area and burned out. The crew had no chance to save themselves.

In August 1967 the testing by the Tri-Service test team was ended. In all, the five planes had made 515 flights by then, put in 420 hours of flight time, and had been flown by twenty-one civilian and eighteen military pilots. Because of the occurring problems, the performance slightly under what was stated, requirement changess, in addition to financial and political reasons, the U.S. forces decided against having the model go into series production.

Although the XC-142A also attracted international attention, and one plane crossed the Atlantic aboard the carrier USS Saratoga in May 1967 to take part in the air show at Le Bourget, no offers to build the type came in from outside the country either.

On the morning of May 10, 1967, an XC-142A prepares to take off in the direction of Frankfurt from the deck of USS Saratoga. This plane later took part in the air show at Le Bourget. *(Ross Beedle)*

If it had gone into series production, this version would have differed from the prototypes in several points. The boxy shape of the XC-142A was based mainly on requirements of the U.S. Navy, which had insisted that the plane had to fit on the elevators of its carriers. The original requirement for retractable landing gear had been dropped for the prototypes, because the complexity of the design was already great enough. Since the Navy had withdrawn from the program during the testing, the U.S. Air Force requested that Vought design a production model that no longer had to match the Navy's requirements.

The XC-142B (or C-0142) model was practically identical to the prototypes technically, but showed a few significant external differences. The XC-142B was not only longer and higher than the prototypes, but had stronger powerplants, each producing 3,400 HP, and a completely redesigned bow and cockpit area.

An XC-142A still flew for NASA as a research craft until 1970 and provided valuable data. Looking back, it seems that the problems of XC-142A were not insoluble and the model certainly could have become ready for action. The last plane still in existence, No.2, is today at the U.S. Air Force Museum in Dayton, Ohio.

Artistic conception of the possible production version, XC-142B (or C-142).
(Vought, via Scott Lother)

Vought-Ryan-Hiller XC-142A

Crew	2-3
Empty weight	10,850kg
Takeoff weight	17,013kg (VTOL),
	18,659kg (STOL)
Length	11,680mm
Height	7,955mm
Wingspan	20,570mm
Powerplant	4 General Electric
	T64-GE-1 propeller turbines,
	3,080 HP each
Top speed	657kph at 0 meters,
	693kph at 6,100 meters
Service ceiling	7,620 meters
Range	1,385km

BELL X-22A

In 1960 Bell was bought by the Textron firm. The aircraft branch, located in Buffalo, New York, continued in business under the name of Bell Aerosystems and took part along with Lockheed in the Tri-Service competition proclaimed by the U.S. forces in 1961. The Bell/Lockheed suggestion was a design, designated D-2064, of a very bizarre-looking transport plane with four tilting mantled propellers and a voluminous fuselage. It was based primarily on Bell Aerosystems studies.

The D-2064 was to gain no success in the original competition, but Bell Aerosystems was issued a forty-two-month contract on November 30, 1962, to build two smaller test planes, and thus prevailed against a very similar design by Douglas.

Although this contract was part of a "Tri-Service Competition," it came primarily on the urging of the U.S. Navy, which placed particularly value on limited space needs for their planes, and was also convinced that mantled propellers offered a certain safety advantage on the narrow decks of their carriers. In February 1963, Bell began wind-tunnel tests with models of the type known at the works as D-2127. The first of the two prototypes was displayed to the public on May 25, 1965. The X-22A, its official military designation, was 12.06 meters long and has a largely glassed cockpit in helicopter style, in which the two crewmen sat side by side on zero-zero ejection seats. The cargo or passenger space behind the cockpit had room for 545 kilograms of freight or six persons. The maximum takeoff weight was 7,582 kilograms. The X-22A had tandem wings, the front one with a wingspan of 7.01 meters and the rear one of 11.89 meters.

The front wings and the outer sections of the rear ones were surrounded by four big mantled propellers that could tilt ninety-five degrees. The three-bladed propellers themselves had a diameter of 2.13 meters and consisted of GFK over a steel core. Movable flaps at the rear of each mantle housing served as combined vertical and lateral rudders. Along with the adjustment of the setting angles of the propellers, they took over the steering of the X-22A in all phases of flight. Each of the four-mantled propellers had its own tilting mechanism, but could only be tipped together. Setting the tilting angle of a single mantle housing was not possible. In horizontal flight the front mantle housings were tilted at three degrees over, and the rear ones at two degrees under the horizontal line.

Left | The D-2064 was Bell's candidate for the Tri-Service competition.
(Bell via Scott Lother)

Right | *An early design of the Bell X-22A.*
(Bell via HMB)

The first prototype (1520) of the X-22A. Note the huge propeller mantles. *(USAF)*

Below: The flaps at the ends of each mantle housing served as combined vertical and lateral rudders. *(USAF)*

Four General Electric YT58-GE-8D turbines, each producing 1,250 HP, supplied the driving power. The powerplants were housed in aerodynamic nacelles on the roots of the hindwings and passed their power to a cross shaft running through the wing. It led to a central gearbox in the rear of the fuselage, which shared the power with the four mantled propellers. Thus it was assured that the propellers would be driven evenly even if one or more powerplants failed.

The great power of the four turbines assured that the X-22A could also take off with only three powerplants, stay in the air with two, and land safely with one. Along with vertical takeoffs and landings, the Bell X-22A was also able to make short take-offs and landings. For this purpose the mantled propellers were tipped at 30 to 45 degrees, so that the plane could lift off after a short run on the runway.

On May 25, 1965, the first of the two prototypes was presented officially; the second followed on October 30 of that year. Before the first X-22A (tail number 1520) lifted off for its ten-minute maiden flight on March 17, 1966, it had already been through intensive ground tests. The 1520 proved to be easy to steer and made the test flights without problems at first.

Schematic drawing of the drive elements of the X-22A. *(Bell via HMB)*

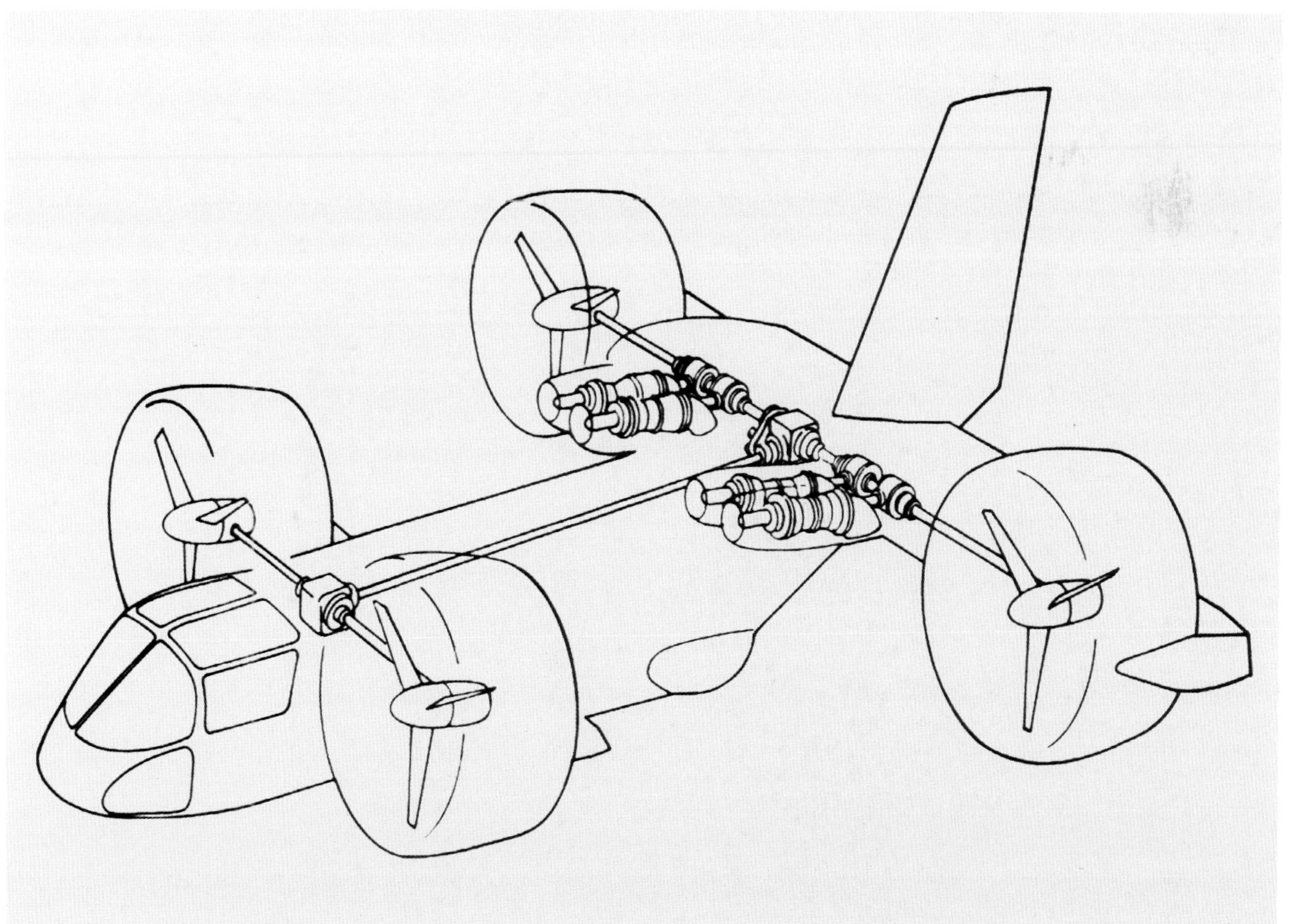

1521
TRI-SERVICE
X-22A

The second prototype (1521) in hover-hold. *(USAF)*

Below | The second prototype (1521) during a transition. The "ba" on the tailfin stands for "Bell Aerosystems." *(USAF)*

On August 8, 1966, on its fifteenth flight, heavy vibrations resulted in double failure of an actually redundant hydraulic tube. The plane landed so hard that the fuselage broke into two pieces. Fortunately, both pilots came through the accident uninjured. The 1520 was scrapped and usable components were stored as replacement parts for the second X-22A (tail number 1521), while the front part of the fuselage was used to build a flight simulator. To prevent another accident of this kind, the hydraulic tubes of the combined lateral and vertical rudders, previously made of aluminum, were replaced by those of stainless steel and secured with extra clamps against vibration.

Thus 1521 made its first flight only on January 26, 1967 and carried out its first full transition on March 3. Shortly afterward the X-22A was fitted with an automatic Variable Stability System (VSS) developed by Cornell Aeronautical Laboratory (now Calspan Corporation). It made the pilot's work much easier. The system could also be programmed so that the plane simulated the flight characteristics of any other VTOL airplane. By January 1971, 1521 had been flown by pilots from the manufacturer, NASA and the three service arms, and in 228 flights it attained a total flight time of 125 hours. The plane made over 400 vertical and over 200 shorts takeoffs, plus over 250 full transitions, without problems. X-22A performed hovering flights at over 2,400 meters and reached speeds of 507kph in horizontal flight. The entire testing was evaluated as a success, and the plane had proven that it was simple to handle and the problems that occurred during the test flights could be solved with no difficulty.

Yet there was no further development of the X-22A, although Bell Aerosystems made various suggestions in that direction. They included a slightly enlarged multipurpose plane with 1,400 HP T58-GE-5 powerplants (X-22B), an enlarged transport variant with a rear-loading ramp, which was to be powered by 2,650 HP turbines of the T55-L-7 type (X-022C), plus an armed combat version with a new tandem cockpit (X-22A-1 or X-22D) and 1,680-kilogram weapon load.

In connection with the Tri-Service testing, X-22A was turned over to the Calspan Corporation, which made numerous further test flights with 1521 under contract from the U.S. Navy without having any problems. By 1980, though, the Navy's interest in a VTOL plane had practically died out, and X-22A was turned over to the Naval Test Pilot School in Patuxent River, Maryland, where 1521 made several flights as a demonstration object until October 1984. Then nobody was really interested in this onetime airplane any more, and it was stored at Calspan until the newly founded Niagara Aerospace Museum obtained the plane in 1998. It is still on display there today.

Bell X-22A

Crew	2
Empty weight	4,763kg
Takeoff weight	7,582kg (VTOL)
Length	12,060mm
Height	6,310mm
Wingspan	7,010mm (front), 11,890mm (rear)
Powerplant	4 General Electric YT-GE-8D Turbines, 1,250 HP each
Top speed	507kph
Service ceiling	unknown
Range	716km

The Bell X-22A in hover-hold. The small propeller on the tailfin served to regulate the speed. *(USAF)*

Although X-22A was one of the most successful VTOL research airplanes, there was no further development of this interesting concept. *(USAF)*

BELL TIPPING MANTLE PROJECTS OF THE 1950s AND 1960s

At the beginning of the 1950s, Bell was already beginning to do studies on the use of mantled propellers for VTOL airplanes. Various ideas for possible test, transport, reconnaissance, multipurpose and rescue planes came up. One of these studies concerned a transporter (D-181) with four tilting-mantle propellers, another treated two variants of a research plane (D-182A and C), which had two propellers of that type. The longest of them, though, was the D-190 project, which was first initiated by Bell itself, and carried on as of 1957 with support from the USAF. Bell suggested many variants of the D-190, depending on whether the plane should be used as a search-and-rescue, observation and communication, or light transport plane. The D-190 was to be flown by a two-man crew and have a takeoff weight of about 5,900 kilograms.

Of particular interest is a version of D-190 that was to take off and land alone but be carried to its destination under the fuselage of a C-130 "Hercules," to carry out rescue missions and pick up as many as five people before returning to the C-130. The U.S. Air Force called this concept "Mother and Daughter" and hoped to be able to carry out search-and-rescue missions that way worldwide soon. Bell carried out intensive studies and wind-tunnel tests on the D-190 and even built a full-size mockup before the project was halted in 1960.

In 1957, the U.S. Navy awarded a contract to Bell to make a study of a transport plane with tilting-mantle propellers for the U.S. Marine Corps. Bell then planned the D-2005, which was offered to the Marine Corps and the Army in slightly changed form in 1960. The D-2022 was to be equipped with four Lycoming T55-L-5 turbines of 2,200 HP each, have a takeoff weight of some 13,000 kilograms, and transport up to thirty soldiers and a two-man crew. Designated as D-2020 and D-2021A, smaller designs of this project were also made for civilian purposes.

The D-2005/D-2022 was modified into the D-2064 in 1961. With it Bell, in conjunction with Lockheed, took part in the Tri-Service competition (see Bell V-22A).

Bell suggested numerous roles for the D-190, including use as a rescue plane that was to be carried by a C-130 to the scene of the action. *(Bell)*

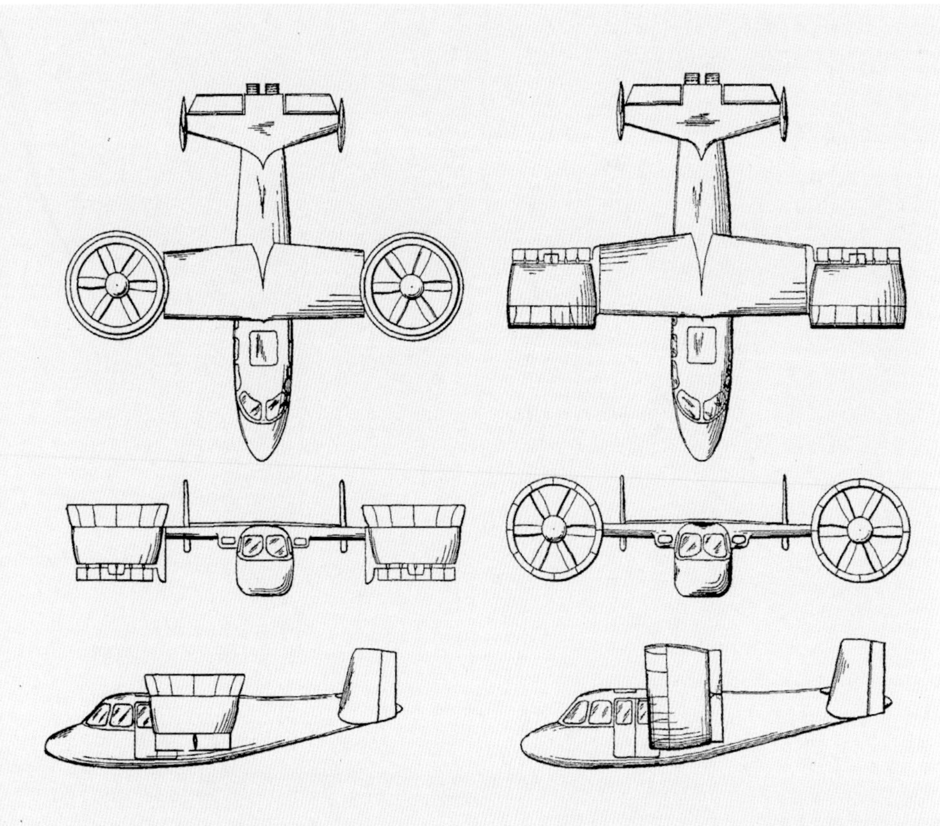

Patent drawings of the D-190.

Left | Bell offered the D-2202 to the USMC and U.S. Army in 1960 as a transport plane, but had no success. *(Bell via HMB)*

Above | Cutaway drawing of the D-2064. *(Bell via Scott Lother)*

BELL TILTROTOR PROJECTS
OF THE 1950s AND 1960s

Countless concepts and projects for tiltrotor airplanes arose at Bell Helicopter since 1953, and could fill a whole book. Thus only a few of these designs can be treated briefly here.

The D-223 of 1956 with its tilting engine nacelles and three-bladed rotors was very similar to the present-day V-22. The main landing gear was retracted into side pods on the fuselage, and there was a lowering rear flap planned for unwieldy cargoes. It was to be powered by four General Electric XT58 turbines.

The D-246 of 1960 was unusual in that its four Lycoming T55-L-5 engines, each with 2,200 HP, were mounted in nacelles under the wings and thus made the plane look like a jet. Although the fuselage of the D-246 was very similar to that of the D-223, the main landing gear could be retracted into the engine nacelles, and the rotors were not on the wing tips but attached about 4/5 of the way out. The outer parts of the wings tilted along with the rotor nacelles.

Bell's suggestion for the Tri-Service competition of 1961 was the D-252 design, which was to have two T64 powerplants, each producing about 3,000 HP, but it could not find acceptance. The planned takeoff weight was some 14,664kg, the payload about 4,613kg. With a maximum load the radius of action was to be up to 480km, the one-way range was circa 4,180km, and the top speed was envisioned as 480 to 640kph.

Bell D-246 *(Bell via HMB)*

The D-252 was Bell's contribution
to the 1961 Tri-Service competition.
(Tommy H. Thomason Collection)

The design of the D-252 as a deep-decker was very unusual for a plane with tilting rotors. Bell had given great care to the design, making it simple to maintain and (probably with the Navy in mind) able to be parked in a minimum of space. Slightly modified (D-252A), the design also took part in the NATO NBMR 4 competition but could not find acceptance.

MAINTENANCE AND ACCESSIBILITY

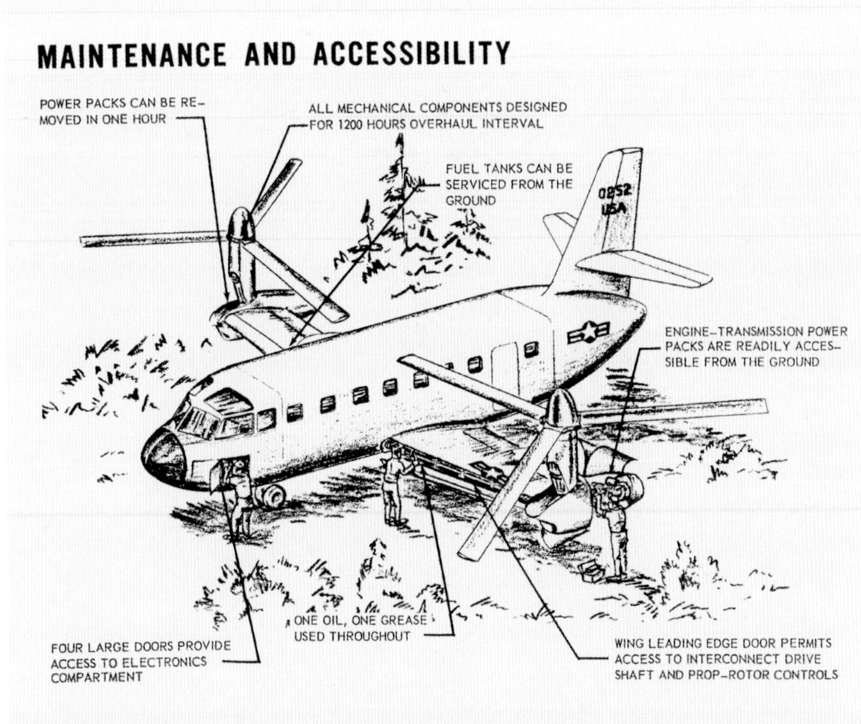

Left | In this picture from an old brochure, Bell praised the easy access to all-important systems and the simple maintenance of the D-252. *(Tommy H. Thomason Collection)*

Below | From the same brochure comes this picture that shows the folding feature of the fuselage and rotor blades. *(Tommy H. Thomason Collection)*

FOLDING ARRANGEMENT

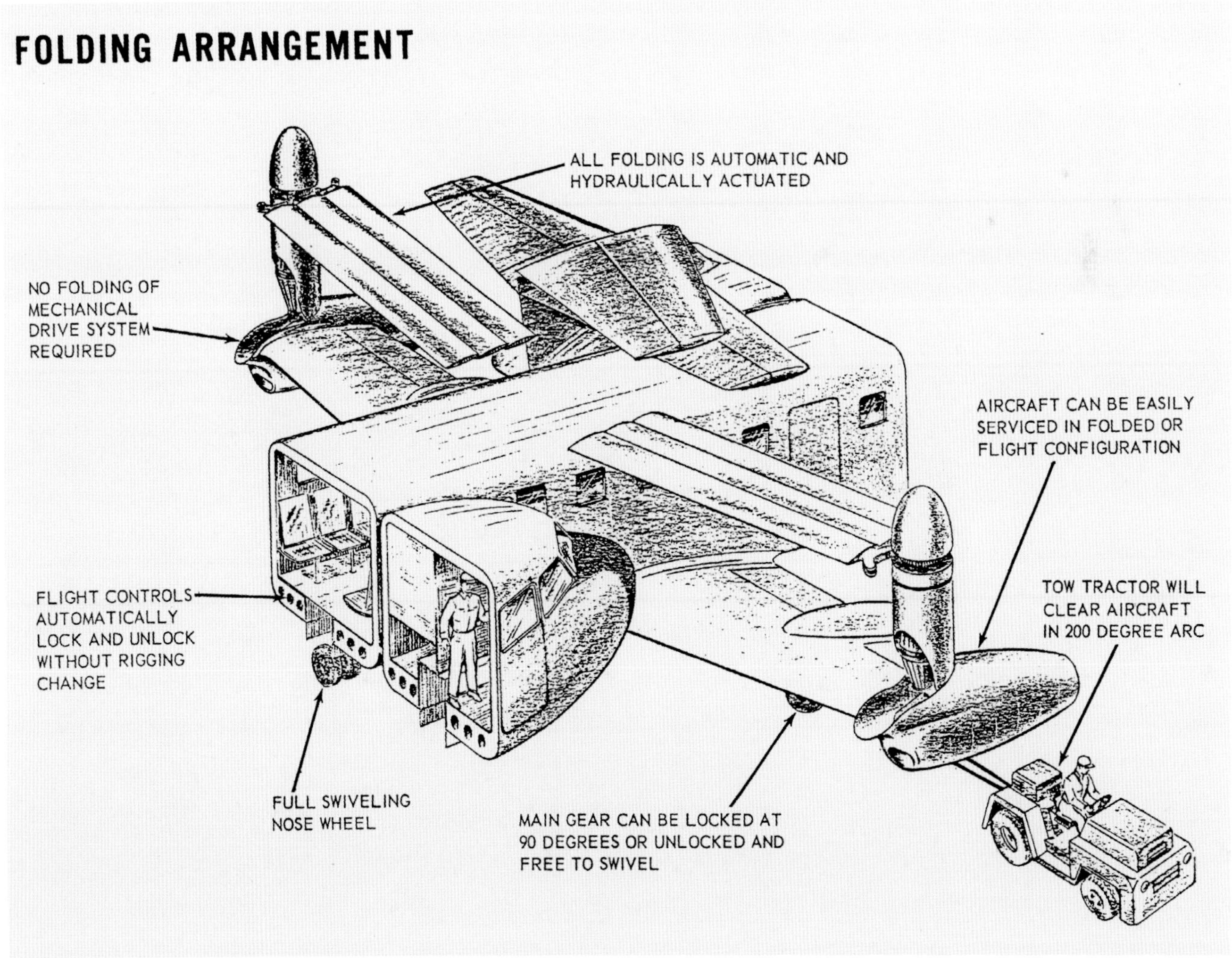

NAA Tilting-Wing Project	
Crew	2
Empty weight	unknown
Takeoff weight	4,994kg (VTOL),
	5,356kg (STOL)
Length	13,360mm
Height	4,521mm
Wingspan	15,240mm,
	18,640mm with propellers
Powerplant	4 propeller turbines,
	500 HP each
Top speed	445kph
Service ceiling	unknown
Range	370km (VTOL),
	960km (STOL)

In the rear part of this drawing is North American's proposal for the Tri-Service competition. The smaller airplane in front is the drawing of a concept designer.
(National Archives via Scott Lother)

NORTH AMERICAN AVIATION TILTWING PROJECTS OF THE 1960S

North American Aviation (NAA) took part unsuccessfully in the Tri-Service competition in 1961 with a four-engine tipping-wing design that was to have a mantled horizontal propeller at the tail to control nodding movements.

In the same year, North American Aviation suggested a similar craft (though of lesser size) to the Pentagon. It was to be used for numerous roles, from evacuating the wounded to close air support.

The payload in VTOL mode was to be 1,200kg and in STOL use 1,816kg. Four turbines, each producing 500 HP, drove propellers of 404cm diameter, and their slipstream touched almost the entire wingspan. NAA hoped to have a prototype assembled fifteen months after the design work began, and to deliver the first production planes nineteen months after its maiden flight. But since the U.S. forces showed no interest in this project, it was not pursued farther.

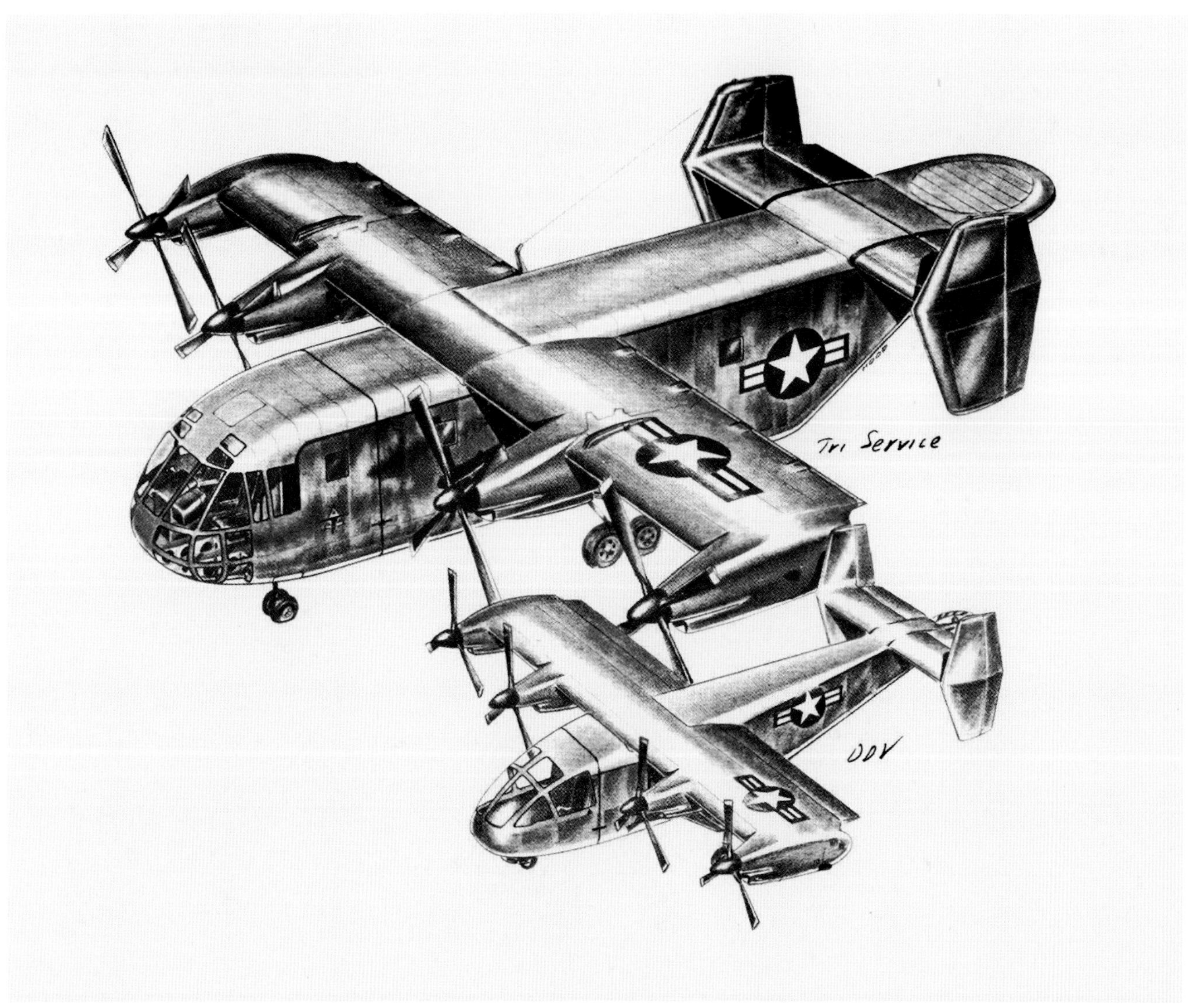

Above | Title picture of an NAA sales brochure for a small multipurpose airplane with tilting wings. (National Archives via Scott Lother)

Below | Note in this drawing too the horizontal mantled propeller on the tail, which was to control pitching movement. (National Archives via Scott Lother)

ARMY
V/STOL
MULTI - MISSION
AERIAL DELIVERY SYSTEM

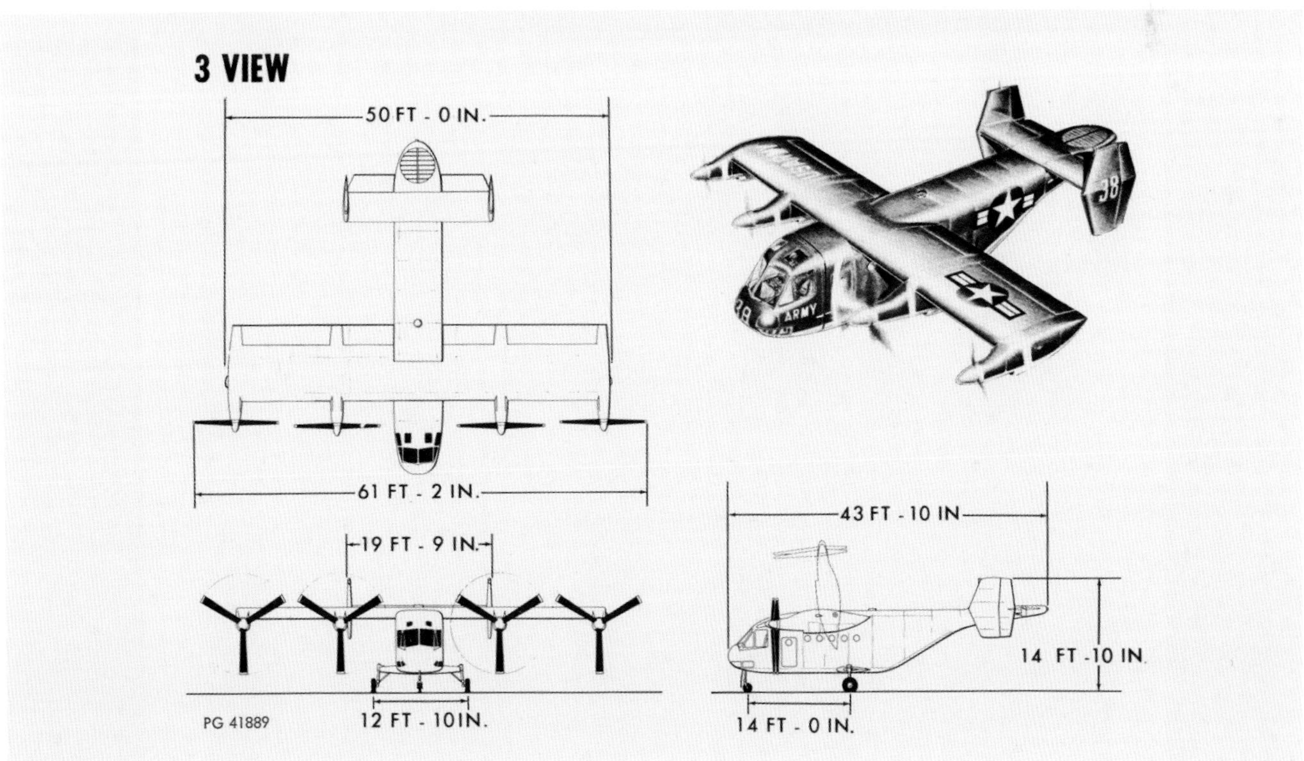

3 VIEW
50 FT - 0 IN.
61 FT - 2 IN.
19 FT - 9 IN.
PG 41889
12 FT - 10 IN.
ARMY
43 FT - 10 IN
14 FT - 10 IN.
14 FT - 0 IN.

GRUMMAN TILTWING PROJECTS OF THE 1960S

Grumman also developed several concepts for tiltwing airplanes in the 1960s, but did not realize any of them. The firm submitted the design of a tiltwing plane with butterfly control surfaces and two double engines, which operated two large propellers with wide blades, to the Tri-Service competition in 1961.

In 1965 Grumman took part in an AAFSS competition of the U.S. Army with Model 134E. This concept was based on the well-known Grumman OV-1 "Mohawk" but had tiltwings, four turbine engines, and a horizontal tail rotor to steer the transverse axis.

The "Gadfly," a much smaller plane than the 134E, was obviously meant to support the testing of the larger plane's tiltwing principle. No further data is known.

The Grumman model 134E was a tipping-wing variant of the well-known OV-1 "Mohawk." *(Northrop Grumman)*

A model of the "Gadfly." The small propellers on the side pods were supposed to control pitching movements in hover-hold. *(John Aldaz Collection)*

BOEING-VERTOL TILTROTOR AND TILTWING PROJECTS OF THE 1960S AND 1970S

After Vertol had been bought by Boeing in 1960, the firm became Boeing-Vertol. Referring back to the experience gained from the VZ-2A, numerous tiltwing projects began in the following years.

Boeing-Vertol's entry in the Tri-Service competition was the BV-137, a four-engine tiltwing plane that did not win out over the XC-142A. In 1965, the firm took part with the BV-147 in the U.S. Army's AAFSS competition.

The BV-147 was a two-seat, twin-engine shoulder-decker with tiltwings. The motors were further developed Lycoming T55 or General Electric T64 turbines producing ca.3,400 HP each; they were to drive four-blade propellers of 2.6-meter diameter. The maximum takeoff weight of the BV-147 was calculated at 8,160kg, its length was to be ten meters, its wingspan 7.60 meters. The main running gear retracted into side stump wings. In addition to the drop loads attached to the stump wings and/or rocket racks, the plane was to be equipped with two remote-control turrets for 7.62mm miniguns and/or 40mm grenade launchers under the nose and the fuselage. The turrets could be turned 220 degrees. As in a combat helicopter, the pilot was to use the rear seat and the gunner the front seat in the cockpit. But since the design was rejected, there was no further development of the BV-147.

In 1969, Boeing-Vertol published the study of a medium military transport plane in the framework of the "Light Intra-Theatre Transport" program (LIT) of the USAF. The craft had four motors and tipping wings, its payload in VTOL use was five tons and in STOL mode up to seventeen tons could be carried. Its uses as a search-and-rescue craft or a civilian passenger and freight plane were also suggested.

At the end of the sixties the firm came more and more to the conclusion that tiltrotors were superior to the tiltwing principle; thus Boeing-Vertol's developments were devoted more and more to that technology.

Below | In 1965 Boeing took part with the BV-147 in the U.S. Army's AAFSS competition. *(Boeing via HMB)*

Lower right | Artistic conception of the BV-147 from a Boeing sales brochure. *(Boeing via HMB)*

A Boeing study of a medium military transport plane (LIT) for a USAF competition. *(NASA)*

Boeing also suggested use of the IT design as a rescue plane. *(Boeing via HMB)*

BELL D-266

The Bell engineers knew that many of the problems that had plagued the XV-3 came from its helicopter-like rotors. To deal with these difficulties, they designed a new type of "Proprotor." This rotor had a strong twist from the hub through 40% of the blade length, to give good performance as a propeller. From this point to the tip, though, the blade had much less twist, to fulfill the function of a rotor.

By using this new proprotor, Bell completed a study, called D-266, of a tiltrotor test plane as part of the "Composite Aircraft Program" of the U.S. Army. It was to serve as the forerunner of three planned production versions, which were:

- A multipurpose airplane with ca.6,800kg takeoff weight and up to 1,816kg payload.
- A light transport plane with ca.13,600kg takeoff weight and up to 3,632kg payload.
- A medium transporter with 24,900kg takeoff weight and up to 7,620kg payload.

The D266 itself corresponded most closely in size and weight to the light transport plane. It had a takeoff weight of 12,700kg, an empty weight of 8,390kg, and was equipped with two T64-GE-16 turbines, each producing 3,435 HP, in tipping gondolas at its wing tips. The three-bladed proprotors had a diameter of 11.73 meters. Models of the D266 were subjected to intensive wind-tunnel tests, in which a possible cruising speed of 648kph was determined; the calculated top speed was over 710kph.

At the end of the 1960s and beginning of the 1970s, Boeing turned the focal point of its studies to the tiltrotor concept. *(Boeing via HMB)*

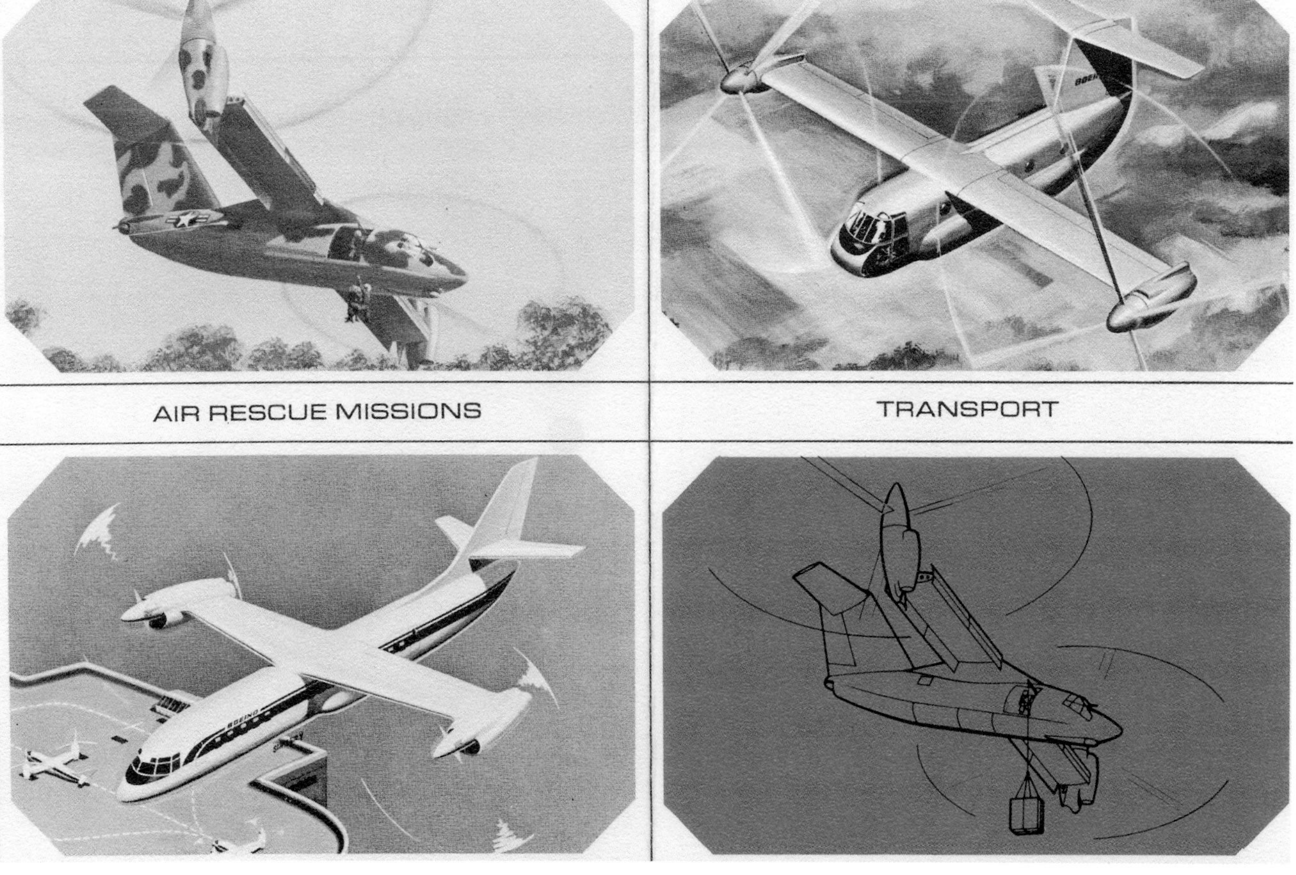

MILITARY PROJECTS IN THE USA AFTER 1945

But a prototype was never built, since the "Composite Aircraft" program was halted in 1969 for lack of financial means. An enlarged version, which Bell proposed as part of the "Light Intra-Theatre Transport" description, was also unsuccessful.

Right page | A model of the D-266 showing the tilting process of the proprotors. *(Bell via HMB)*

Below | The Bell D-266. *(Bell via HMB)*

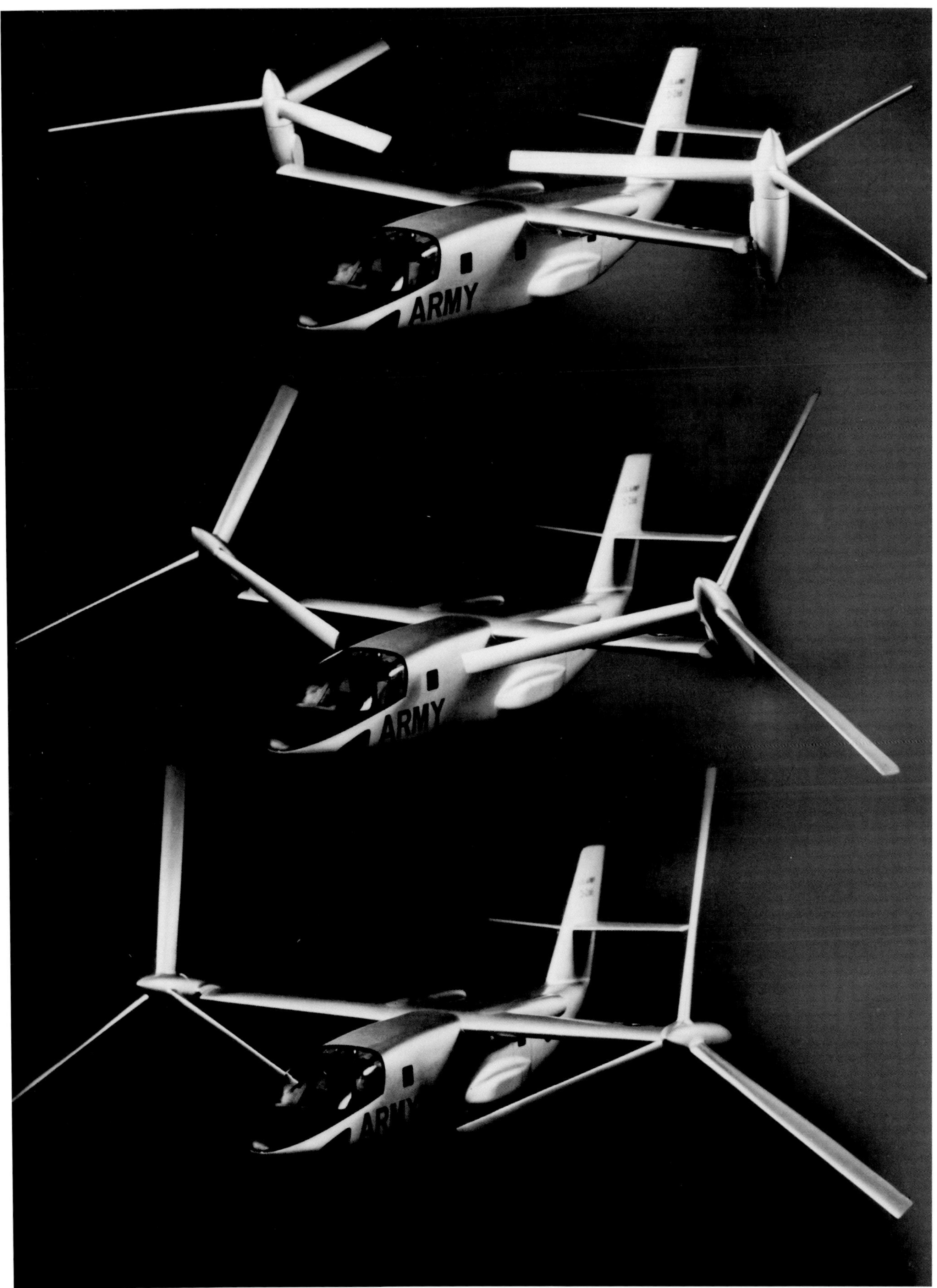

ARMY
ARMY
ARMY

BELL XV-15

Although the development of the D-266 had to be broken off because the "Composite Aircraft Program" had been halted, Bell decided to pursue this very promising path further and design a small test craft at their own cost. In their design the research gained with the XV-3 would be used, as would the proprotors developed for the D-266. Bell had calculated a takeoff weight of around 4,300kg for this type, called D-300, and planned to have the plane powered by two Pratt & Whitney PT-6 turbines, which would drive proprotors with a diameter of 7.62 meters. Models in 1/5 scale were subjected to intensive wind-tunnel tests from 1969 to 1973, while a full-size rotor was tested successfully at the NASA Ames wind tunnel in 1970. Because of the very promising test results at Ames, plus progress in the realm of automatic flight situation and powerplant regulating, NASA and the U.S. Army agreed in 1971 to finance jointly the development of a tiltrotor research airplane.

In the "Tilt Rotor Research Aircraft Program" (TRRA), Boeing-Vertol and Bell received contracts in 1972 to develop corresponding proposals until the start of 1973. Since it was to be a pure research program, not to be followed by contracts for series production, the plane should be designed as economically as possible.

Boeing-Vertol's proposal, the Model 222, was based on a modified Mitsubishi Mu 2J, which was to be fitted with new wings and two Lycoming T53L-13 propeller turbines at the wing tips. The powerplants themselves were fixed in place; only the jointless three-bladed rotors measuring 7.92 meters in diameter would tilt.

Bell's proposal (D-301) was based on D-300 and kept its rotors and gears, but was also fitted with the more powerful T53 turbines to meet the requirements for the ability to carry out hover-hold with one motor, and for heavier payloads. The T53 powerplant had also proved already in the CL-84 that its lubrication system could handle use in a vertical position.

Boeing-Vertol's Model 222 was based on the Mitsubishi Mu-2J, but could not prevail against the Bell D-301. *(Boeing)*

The jointless rotor developed by Boeing for the TRRA program was tested in NASA's Ames wind tunnel from August to December 1972. *(NASA)*

Artistic conception of a possible military version of the Bell D-301. Note the simple side engines, unlike those of the later XV-15.

In April 1973, Bell's concept was declared the winner, and on July 31, 1973, the firm received a contract to build two test models based on the D-301 and designated XV-15. As opposed to the original design, the XV-15 had double side engines to improve directional stability. The calculated empty weight was some 4,345kg; the takeoff weight 5,902kg. The fuselage of the XV-15, 12.83 meters long, was built conventionally and consisted mainly of light alloys and aluminum. In front was the acclimatized cockpit with double controls and zero-zero ejection seats for two pilots sitting side by side.

The wings were mounted high on the fuselage and angled 6.5 degrees negatively to give the rotors a sufficient distance from the leading edges of the wings. The whole trailing edge of the wings was taken up by two-part landing flaps, their outer two thirds also functioning as lateral rudders. In hover-hold the flaps were turned down seventy-five degrees to minimize the disturbing influence of the wings. To deal with the vibration problems of the XV-3, the wings were designed to be very robust, and the rotor hubs were placed as close to the wings as possible. On the wings there were also two fuel tanks with a total capacity of 829 liters. At the wing tips were two Lycoming LTC1K-4K turbines (modified T53-l-13B), which produced

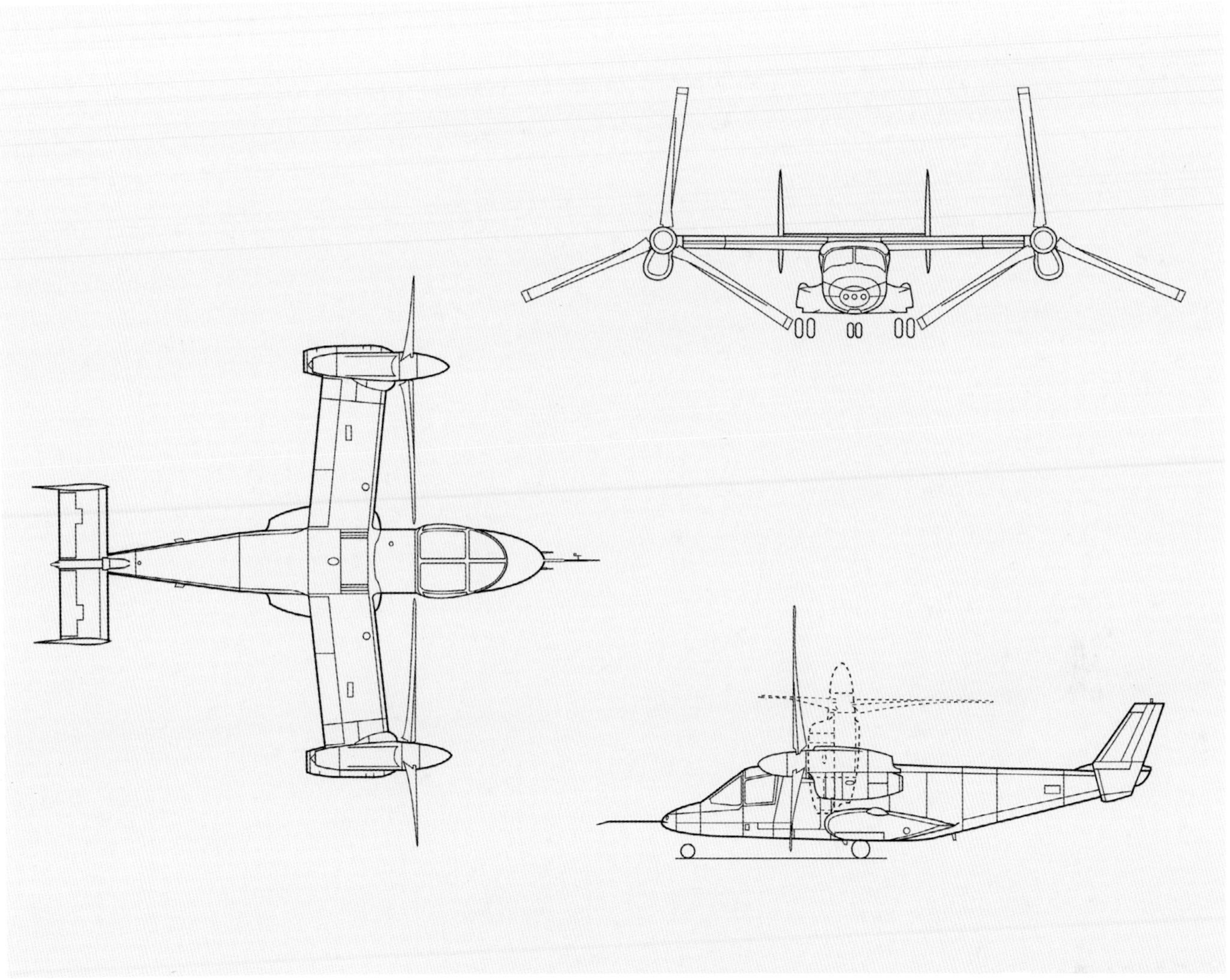

Three-side drawing of the Bell XV-15.
(NASA)

1,550 sustained HP and 1,800 if needed, and were linked by a transverse shaft.

The semi-rigid three-bladed rotors of the XV-15 measured 7.62 meters and consisted of stainless steel. The motor gondolas were tilted hydraulically ninety-five degrees: a complete transition took some twelve seconds. The nacelles could either be tipped freely, fixed at any chosen point, or set automatically to 0, 60, 75 or 90 degrees.

Steering in hover-hold was done via the cyclical and collective adjustment of the rotor blades; thus the cockpit layout was similar to that of a helicopter. A mechanical device coordinated the sending of steering commands from hovering to horizontal flight, in which conventional rudders took over the control. The XV-15 also had an automatic flight regulating system from the Calspan Corporation, but was not steered by a "fly-by-wire" system.

For reasons of cost, the main landing gear of the CL-84 was used for the XV-15 and enclosed in two side housings. The bow wheel had its place in the fuselage.

The rollout of the first XV-15 (N702NA) took place at the Bell Research Center in Arlington, Texas on October 22, 1976. After intensive ground tests, N702 finally lifted off for its first hover-hold on May 3, 1977, and was tested in the ensuing

Right page | The XV-15 in the wind tunnel at Ames, June 2, 1978. *(NASA)*

Below | The proprotors of the XV-15 were made of stainless steel; later tests with GFK rotors proved to be problematic. *(NASA)*

weeks for its hovering and slow flight characteristics. After these tests had gone off successfully, the gears and rotors were removed, taken apart, checked thoroughly and reinstalled.

Since NASA was facing further, promising flight-testing based on thorough wind-tunnel tests, Bell turned N702 over to the Ames research center in March 1978. After these tests had been completed successfully in June 1978, NASA technicians examined the plane thoroughly at Ames and overhauled it.

The XV-15 No.1 (N702) in flight at the Bell test center in Arlington, Texas.
(Bell via NASA)

Meanwhile, the second XB-15 (N703NA) neared completion and began its first ground tests at Arlington in August 1978. On April 23, 1979, N703 took off on its first flight, and made its first full transition on July 24 of that year. On December 5, 1979, N702 had an engine failure in flight, but thanks to the cross shaft that linked the two motors there was no threat to flight safety. Both rotors continued to turn as planned.

Bell first concluded its test flights in August 1980. The N703 had reached a height of 4,877 meters and a speed of 557kph during its testing, carried out a good hundred

At the end of April 1981, N702 was flown to Europe on a C-5A "Galaxy" and demonstrated its ability at air bases in Farnborough and Le Bourget before returning to Dryden.

N702NA

transitions, and proved to be quite problem-free. In mid-August 1980 Bell turned the second XV-15 over to the NASA research center at Dryden, where the two planes were tested together.

For test flights under military conditions, the plane was fitted with an APR-39 radar warning system and a chaff launcher. The U.S. Navy had already been interested in XV-15 and shared in its financing since 1979-80; thus N702 was tested in June and July 1982 first at the Navy base at China Lake, California, and then at Fort Huachuca, Arizona.

In August 1982, N702 finally made fifty-four takeoffs and landings on board the helicopter carrier USS Tripoli (LPH 10) off San Diego.

The VX-15 N702 in simulated rescue drills. For this purpose the plane was fitted with a winch. *(NASA)*

Further tests simulated rescue missions under combat conditions over the ocean in May 1983 and midair fueling in September 1984.

By 1986 the two VX-15s had spent 530 flight hours in all and carried out 1,500 transitions. During the testing by NASA, they proved that they were capable of autorotation (though they made no such landings), stayed in the air nonstop for an hour and forty-two minutes, reached an altitude of 6,888 meters with a 1,000kg payload on March 1990, and showed in short takeoffs with rotors tilted 60 to 70 degrees that they could lift off with a weight of 6,810kg. Although the XV-15 never attained the values calculated by Bell of a 611kph top speed or an 8,840-meter service ceiling, all those involved in the TRRA program evaluated the program as a success. The only negative note was a certain vibration level.

N702 returned to Bell in Arlington in June 1990, while N703 remained at Ames. N702 was used by Bell primarily as a concept demonstrator and advertising plane for the V-22 program, in which numerous "guest pilots" flew the plane and were convinced of its good flight performance. In such a flight on August 20, 1992, there was an accident caused by mechanical failure of the rotor-steering system in hover-hold. The plane turned over and was badly damaged, but no personnel

After the accident to N702, N703 was the only remaining XV-15. *(NASA)*

XV-15 N703 is now on display in the Steven F. Udvar-Hazy Center at Washington Airport.

Bell XV-15

Bell XV-15	
Crew	2
Empty weight	4,578kg
Takeoff weight	6,015kg
Powerplant	2 Lycoming LTC1K-41K turbines, 1,550 HP each
Top speed	557kph
Length	12,830mm
Height	3,860mm
Wingspan	9,800mm, 17,420mm with rotors
Service ceiling	8,840 meters
Range	825km

were injured. After over 840 hours of total flight time, N702 had to be written off, but the front of its fuselage was used by Bell to build a flight simulator.

N703 had been fitted in 1986 with new rotor blades of composite material, and was flown again by NASA pilots, though to a lesser extent. On September 6, 1991, though, a serious problem with a rotor sleeve occurred, which led to a forced landing. Since a large-scale inspection of the plane would have been made shortly thereafter, NASA decided to move this up and had N703 partly dismantled. A shortage of financial means led to the plane being left in that condition, until Bell had the plane reassembled at their own cost, so they could do further research in the V-22 program, pilot training and demonstration flights. N703 flew in this role until September 16, 2003, and accrued a total flight time of almost 680 hours in the hands of 410 pilots, until Bell donated it to the Smithsonian National Air and Space Museum in Washington D.C., where it is now on display in the Steven F. Udvar-Hazy Center at Dulles Airport in Washington.

On the basis of the XV-15, Bell conceived a whole series of further tipping-rotor airplanes. In the "Spectrum" program of the U.S. Army, there sprang from the Bell drawing boards in 1975 a family of airplanes (D-314A to D-314G) for various military tasks, extending from communications and observation planes to radar surveillance and transport machines and combat aircraft. Most of these designs resembled the XV-15 in appearance and dimensions; only the D-314E was a much larger variant that was to serve as a medium transport.

Under the D-314 designation, Bell made various studies for military variants of the XV-15. *(Bell, via NASA)*

V333 "SKYCAT"

The former Lockheed colleague and aeronautical engineer Hal Fogle built the V333 "Skycat" with private means in 1982. This tipping-rotor plane was to be a test craft for a possible warplane for near support, but never got off the ground. The "Skycat" was 7.01 meters long, had a wingspan of 6.1 meters, and was fitted with a 500 HP V-8 piston engine that drove two tiltrotors of 4.88-meter diameter. The plane is now at the Carolinas Aviation Museum in Charlotte, North Carolina.

The "Skycat" at the Carolinas Aviation Museum. *(Matt Muse)*

BELL "BAT"

In 1983-84 Bell designed this tiltrotor plane as an answer to the U.S. Army's "Light Helicopter Experimental Program" (LHX), in which a modern successor to the OH-58A and AH-1 reconnaissance and combat helicopters was sought. "BAT" stood for "Belt Advanced Tiltrotor." Bell presented an initial mockup of the craft in mid-1984, but the design was rejected by the Army shortly thereafter, since it did not satisfy the modified weight requirements (gross weight under 3,150kg). The "BAT" was to have an empty weight of 3,620kg and a top speed of 563kph. For its armament, four "Hellfire" antitank and four "Stinger" air-to-air rockets were foreseen. The plane was to be built mainly of composite materials and have "fly-by-wire" steering. With a short rolling start and a weight of 6,800kg, a range of almost 3,900km was supposed to be possible.

Bell "BAT."
(NASA)

BELL BOEING V-22 "OSPREY"

Chapter 4

The V-22 is the first series-produced tiltrotor aircraft in the world. A technological triumph of the USA. Yet the development of the "Osprey" was laborious, costly and full of problems. Critics of the craft frequently called for the end of the program. Even today there is heated debate in progress as to whether the V-22 can and will fulfill the hopes placed on it.

THE WAY TO THE V-22

In 1969, the U.S. Navy (USN) and U.S. Marine Corps (USMC) began to look for a new medium transport helicopter to replace the CH-46, which had been in service since the early-1960s. The task of the new type was to be, above all, the transport of soldiers and materials from landing ships to the coast. Under changing designations, a bewildering series of programs was initiated in the ensuing years, but all of them came to grief for lack of financial means.

In the course of this program, Bell submitted proposals again and again, such as the D-310 or D-311 study in 1974, a tiltrotor craft with two engines and butterfly control surfaces, or the D-321 study in 1978.

In 1980, the USMC began a new search to replace its obsolete CH-46 helicopter. The program called V/HXM (Vertical/Helicopter Experimental Marine) was very ambitious and set up requirements that could not be fulfilled by a conventional helicopter. The successor to the CH-46 had to be able to transport its twenty-four soldiers over a distance of 370km at a speed of 463kph; the CH-46 transported eleven soldiers over a distance of 176km at 195kph. Bell's proposal for this competition was the D-315, a tiltrotor craft with a takeoff weight of some 15,890kg and a cruising speed of 493kph. With a 2,270kg payload its range was to be 2,778km in VTOL or 4,445km in STOL mode. Four General Electric T700-GE-401 turbines, mounted in pairs in nacelles on its wings, were foreseen as its powerplants. In 1981, Bell modified the D-315 into the D-327 with T-controls and just two turbines.

On December 21, 1981, Secretary of Defense Caspar Weinberger nevertheless made known that the U.S. Department of Defense (DoD) intended to have such an aircraft developed for all service arms (Air Force, Army, Navy and Marine Corps), for which reason the V/HXM description was dropped for a time. The reason for this decision was, not least, the failed rescue of the hostages in Iran in April 1980 ("Operation Eagle Claw"), which clearly showed the inadequacy of the available helicopters. After a requirement catalog for the craft to be designed had been published in 1982, the V/HXM program finally became the JVX (Joint Services Advanced Vertical Lift Aircraft Experimental) Program.

The leadership of the entire program belonged to the U.S. Navy and the Marine Corps, since they needed the largest number of the new aircraft (552 of them). The USAF wanted eighty of them to replace their obsolescent HH-3E and MH-53 for special operations, while the Army wanted to buy 231, to be used mainly as

The CH-46 had already been in service with the U.S. Marines since the 1960s. *(DoD)*

Above | The D-310 (or D-311 USMC version) was Bell's contribution to the "HX" program of the U.S. Navy in 1974. Like many other Bell designs in those days, the D-310 also showed numerous points in common with the XV-15. *(Bell via NASA)*

Right | The folding rudders and wings were one of the requirements of the USMC. The butterfly control surfaces of the D-321 were replaced in a later design by those in T-form. *(Bell via HMB)*

Above | Drawing of a transition study between the D-315 and D-327. *(Bell via HMB)*

Below | One of the earliest Bell-Boeing JVX designs. Note the side drop tanks. *(Bell via NASA)*

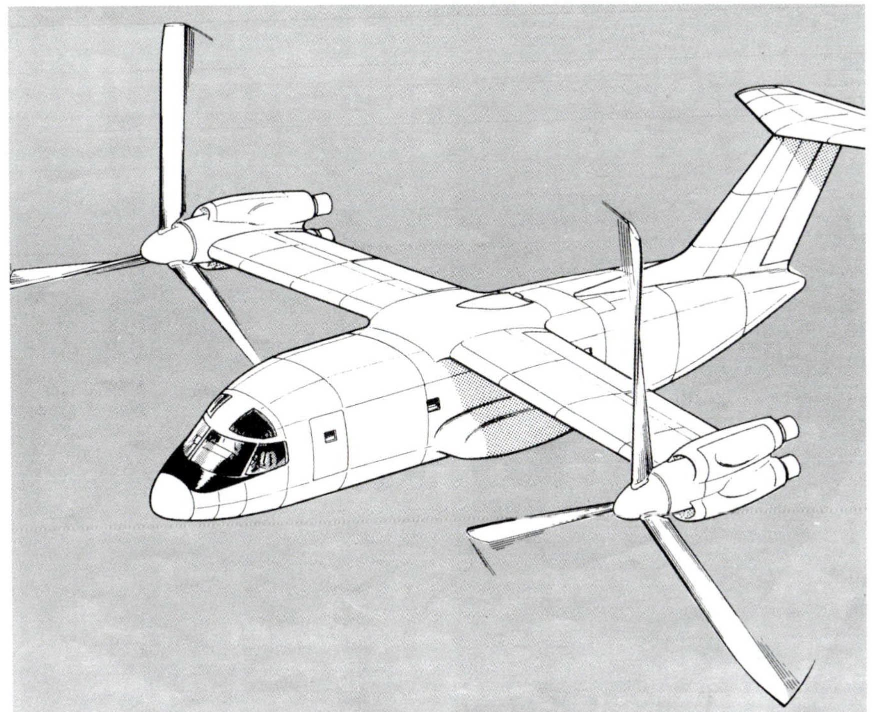

transports and MEDEVAC craft. The Navy intended to use fifty for fleet supplying, SAR and special tasks, plus an unknown number of craft for submarine hunting. In the JVX description, among others, the following performances and characteristics were expected:

- Cruising speed: 463kph
- Top speed: 509-556kph
- Range: to 3,890km nonstop on crossing flights
- Service ceiling: 7,925-12,192 meters
- Payload: twenty-four fully equipped soldiers or 6,804kg externally in short-haul action
- Empty weight: Maximum 14,405kg
- Takeoff weight: Maximum 21,546 (VTOL), 24,948kg (STOL)
- Wing folding for use on carriers
- No more than 5.52 servicing hours per flight hour (goal 2.26 hours)
- Ability to operate on an atomically, biologically or chemically contaminated battlefield.

Bell, Boeing-Vertol, Grumman, Lockheed, Aerospatiale and Westland showed interest in this competition. The Pentagon urged the interested firms to find partners for the development, so that Bell and Boeing Vertol cooperated. This team turned in its first proposal on February 17, 1983; it was based on the Bell D-327 and designated 901-X.

Although the Department of Defense had intended to finance two competing designs in a first phase of development, from which the more suitable would finally be chosen, this plan had to be given up, for all the other parties had withdrawn because of the demanding goals of the program. Only a tiltrotor aircraft appeared to be capable of fulfilling the requirements – a kind of technology in which Bell was years ahead of other firms.

Although the Pentagon had briefly considered calling off the competition because of the changed circumstances, it decided on April 26, 1983 to issue a contract to Bell Boeing for a first stage of development.

On January 15, 1985, the type formerly called JVX was officially named V-22 "Osprey" (sea eagle).

JVX design of 1983-84. (Bell via NASA)

welcome to the
BELL BOEING V-22 OSPREY ROLLOUT

DEVELOPMENTAL HISTORY

In May 1986, Bell and Boeing were given the green light to begin the "Full Scale Development" (FSD) of the V-22 and the design of six FSD prototypes. The U.S. Army, to be sure, left the program for financial reasons in 1987, but the work was continued. The first V-22 was displayed to the public at the Bell works in Arlington, Texas on May 28, 1988.

The first flight, planned initially for June, then for mid-August and finally for December of that year, had to be postponed until March 19, 1989, because of delays in turbine and gear tests and problems that had been discovered in ground testing. "Osprey" No.2 and 3 made their first flights in Arlington on August 9, 1989, and May 9, 1990. Prototype No.4 was finished at the Boeing works in Wilmington, Delaware and first took to the skies on December 21, 1990.

On September 14, 1989, Plane No.1 carried out its first full transition, and in October of that year it reached a speed of 463kph on a horizontal flight. This achievement was exceeded in August 1990 with 646kph (though in a diving flight).

While Bell took over the general testing of the flying characteristics at Arlington, testing the special systems was to be done by Boeing in Wilmington. Planes No.3 and 4 made a total of fifteen takeoffs and landings on board the USS Wasp (LHD-1) from December 4 to 7, 1990.

At the end of February 1991 the four prototypes had already made 340 flights over 400 flight hours, without any serious difficulties.

This changed, though, with the first flight of the fifth prototype on June 11, 1991. From the start of the flight on, the plane reacted contrarily to the steering orders of the test pilots. When the pilots made a first attempt to land after about three minutes, the left engine nacelle touched the ground; in a second try, so did the proprotor. The craft turned over and burned out. The crew escaped with slight injuries. The cause of the accident, as it turned out, was a wrongly cabled flight situation control system. It is especially piquant, though, that the system's self-testing program had not been carried out before the takeoff.

The other four aircraft continued their testing as of September 10, 1991.

Prototype No.4 was tested from February to July 1992 in a climate chamber at Eglin AFB, Florida, at temperatures from -54 to +52 degrees Celsius, in icy rain, snow, and wind velocities up to 83kph. When No.4 flew from Eglin to the U.S. Marine air base in Quantico, Virginia on July 20, after the end of the tests, where a series of demonstration flights was to take place, the next accident happened. Approaching a landing, the right engine nacelle caught fire and the craft plunged into the Potomac River. All seven men on board lost their lives.

The cause was obviously an unsealed gearbox, from which oil had leaked and had gathered in the area of the air intake. When the pilot tipped the engine nacelles to the vertical, the oil flowed into the turbine and caught fire. This alone would not have been a problem that would lead to a crash. After all, the second turbine should have supplied both proprotors with power via a cross shaft in an engine failure, but for reasons of weight, this shaft had been made of composition material and not of metal. When the fire reached the shaft, it burned out within a few seconds. With just one rotor, the V-22 could no longer be controlled and thus crashed.

Prototype No.4 on board the USS Wasp early in December 1990. *(USN)*

To take up as little hangar or deck space as
possible, the rotor blades of the V-22 are
automatically folded at first ...

... before the wings are automatically
turned ninety degrees and stopped.

Prototype No.1 during a transition.
(Bell via NASA)

Left page | An early V-22 in hover-hold at the Bell testing grounds in Arlington, Texas. *(Bell via NASA)*

This accident at first brought on a ban on flying all V-22s, and almost ended the whole program. Prototype No.6, which was nearing completion in Arlington, was not finished. The reason for this was not just the crash, but also the fact that the financing of the project was now very slow. Secretary of Defense Richard Cheney had already tried several times since April 1989 to end the development of the "Osprey." The V-22, he said, was too costly (the estimated price per plane at the time was some 34.5 million dollars), too complex, too heavy, and its technology was not yet mature. The end of the Cold War in 1989-90 did the test; from everywhere came calls to decrease the defense budget. To be sure, Cheney encountered stubborn opposition from Congress. The program was continued until the Clinton administration came into power early in 1993 and every dollar had to be fought for. The flights with the original test aircraft were resumed on July 18, 1993, after the craft had been modified, resulting from the information on the accident of July 20, 1992.

After Bell and Boeing had presented their proposals for a new phase of development (EMD – Engineering and Manufacturing Development, more or less a design for series production) in April 1993, the Pentagon issued a contract in April of the next year for $2.65 billion dollars which included the building of four new, improved prototypes and six pre-series craft, for flight testing (OPEVAL – Operational Evaluation).

The new EMD prototypes had almost no external changes from the planes of the FDS phase, but their structure and equipment were designed anew in almost every feature. Besides heightened safety and reliability, weight and cost savings were also emphasized. "Osprey" No.1 was already some 454kg over its intended empty weight on its first flight. What with added equipment and various modifications, this excess had already risen to 1270kg by the end of 1990. The price per V-22 had risen by the start of 1993, through limiting the total number of planes to be built and delays in development, from the originally planned $16 million to an estimated $41.8 million dollars.

Prototype No.3, built by Boeing in Wilmington, is seen here landing at Patuxent River. *(USN)*

In April 1995, the building of the first of four new EMD prototypes, which made its maiden flight at Arlington on February 5, 1997, began. By August 23, 1998, the four EMD aircraft had spent a total of 627.7 hours in the air on 316 flights. But again, development fell behind schedule. The reasons were a greater amount of servicing than expected, plus a much too narrow time limit, which left no room for unexpected events (which practically had to occur on test flights). In January 1999 carrier landings and takeoffs from the deck of USS Saipan (LHA-2) were carried out, in which there were almost collisions with deck structures because of errors in steering software.

The first pre-series craft was delivered on May 25, 1999, and as of that summer two prototypes were revised to the condition of the planned CV-22 Air Force version, receiving terrain radar and the possibility of attaching drop tanks. In this configuration they carried out low flights and simulated combat actions. In August 1999 the improved steering software was tested again on board the USS Saipan, without any problems being found. The official action testing of the "Osprey" began on October 1, 1999. By that time the V-22s had attained a total of 3,600 flight hours.

One of the four EMD prototypes in October 1998. *(USN)*

When an MV-22 stationed at the Yuma Marine Corps base in Arizona tried to land at the Marana Airport near Tucson after a simulated rescue mission on April 8, 2000, there was another serious accident. Because of a pilot error, the aircraft went into a much steeper dive than was allowed (over 610 m/min, instead of the maximum 240m/min), going under the minimum speed of 74kph. There was a "vortex ring state" or "settling with power" situation, which can happen to any helicopter, and in which the rotor is in its own slipstream. In this condition too little lift, or none at all, is produced any more. This problem was probably worsened by further MV-22s flying in a close formation. The pilot of the afflicted "Osprey" lost control of his craft, it crashed to the ground from some seventy-five meters up, and exploded. All nineteen Marines aboard lost their lives. One of the other MV-22s was forced by the explosion to make such a hard landing that it had to be written off later.

Despite this tragic event, the EMD phase was declared ended on April 30, as was the action testing in August 2000. On October 13, 2000, the Navy made known that the "Osprey" was regarded as suitable for action from land bases. Problems with the automatic flap and folding actions of the wings and rotors still prevented action from ships. Only after another improvement on the part of industry and successful testing on board the USS Bataan (LHD-5) in mid-November 2000 was the model also found usable for sea action. This report would have cleared the way for series production, about which a decision was to be made in December of that year.

On December 11, 2000, though, an MV-22 crashed during a night flight near Jacksonville, North Carolina, and four Marines were killed. The pilot and co-pilot of the craft were the most experienced pilots in the entire V-22 program. All "Ospreys" were banned from flying until the accident could be explained, and the decision about series production was postponed to an undetermined time. On April 5, 2001, the USMC made known that the accident had been caused by an unsealed hydraulic line and faulty steering software. This error led to the craft unexpectedly and abruptly gaining or losing speed, while the pilots tried to deal with the occurring difficulties. The Marine Corps thus required a reworking of the hydraulic system and the faulty software.

A "Blue Ribbon Panel" established by Secretary of Defense William Cohen found in a hearing on May 1, 2001, that the "Osprey" was not yet ready for action. As before, the areas of safety, reliability and training of crews were still problematic. The tiltrotor technology in itself was evaluated as thoroughly practicable. The panel thus recommended that the program be continued, but the rate of the produced aircraft was to be limited to the absolute minimum needed to keep the production lines open (seven to twelve per year). This was only to change when all identified faults were corrected. Another burden for the V-22 program was that at the beginning of 2001 the commandant of the Marine Corps Air Station at New River had to admit that he had advised his men to manipulate the servicing of the "Ospreys" so that the craft appeared to be more reliable.

Left | Comfort is not provided for the twenty-four Marines on board an "Osprey." December 1, 1999, New River Marine Corps Air Station, North Carolina. (USMC)

Below | The fourth EMD prototype in flight. (USN)

Bell and Boeing literally suggested hundreds of changes to the V-22, but not all of them had to be carried out to be able to resume the test flights. But the necessary modifications took longer than expected, so the MV-22 could resume its flights only on May 29, 2002. The main differences between the craft that had been grounded at the end of 2000 and those that resumed the flight program some seventeen months later consisted above all of new, more resistant hydraulic lines, improved software, and a new warning system for dangerous flight conditions and failing functions. Craft with these modifications were designated "Block A." Although a number of new action problems occurred after the test flights were resumed, caused by problems with the hydraulics, engine damage and pilot errors, there were no more crashes. The Pentagon also backed off from some of its requirements. Thus it was no longer necessary to have the V-22 carry out aerial combat maneuvers; defensive maneuvers should suffice. Capability on an ABC-polluted field and the possibility of autorotation were also eliminated. To avoid crashes because of the "vortex ring state," certain flight maneuvers were also banned. Finally the Department of Defense approved series production of the "Osprey" on September 28, 2005.

This craft (Serial No.165838) was the 24th V-22. It lost parts of its proprotors in a test flight to determine its behavior in ice and snow over Nova Scotia, Canada on November 26, 2004, but was able to land safely. *(USN)*

An MV-22B of the VMX-22 is prepared for
fueling on the deck of USS Wasp (LHD-1).
The craft is coated experimentally with new
lightweight paint which also reduces the
IR signature. Atlantic Ocean, November 15,
2005. *(USN)*

VARIANTS

From the beginning of V-22 development it was clear that various versions of the "Osprey" had to be designed for the various needs of the forces. Among them were or are:

MV-22: Version for Marine infantry. Used chiefly to transport soldiers and equipment, such as from landing ships to land.

Since the new design of 1993, production models have been designated MV-22B; the two EMD prototypes of the MV-22B unofficially also being named MV-22A or V-22A. Among the MV-22B there are still different "blocks" established. Bell and Boeing, after the crash on December 11, 2001, had reworked the design again and identified hundreds of possible improvements, not all of which could be carried out at once.

Block A: Craft with the minimum of necessary changes after the flight ban of December 2000. Were and are used only for testing and training.

Block B: Improved access to engines, generally improved ease of servicing and reliability. First MV-22B "Block B" was delivered to the Marine Corps on December 8, 2005. Present action craft.

Block C: Planned improvements for heightened action abilities, such as weather radar, additional ALE-47 decoy launchers aimed to the front and improved air conditioning.

MV-22B of VMM-263 of the USMC on the landing strip at Al Asad Base, Iraq, October 4, 2007. *(USMC)*

An MV-22B of VMM-261 of the USMC
with a 155mm howitzer as an external load.
(USMC)

CV-22: U.S. Air Force version for long-haul special actions in U.S. Special Operations Command (USSOCOM). Has additional tanks for increased range, terrain radar and much avionic equipment. The CV-22 is 85% identical to the MV-22. Easy to identify from outside by the radome of the terrain radar.

Production models have been designated CV-22B since new design of 1993; the two EMD prototypes of the CV-22B are also known unofficially as CV-22A or V-22A. Within the CV-22B there are also different "blocks" defined.

Block O: Corresponds to Block A.

Block 10: Corresponds to Block B but also has forward-aimed ALE-47 launcher. First craft delivered on March 1, 2006.

Block 20/25: Is to have better action capability through heightened maneuverability and improved navigation systems. Block 20 for USSOCOM, Block 25 for USAF. Not yet produced.

Block 30: Is to have increased protection from possible threats through improved countermeasures and reduced radiation in electromagnetic realm. Not yet produced.

CV-22B of the USAF. *(USAF)*

The CV-22B is used by the USAF mainly
for special operations behind enemy lines.
(CSAF)

HV-22: U.S. Navy version. Should be used for special actions, CSAR (Combat Search and Rescue) and fleet supplying. But in 1992 the Navy decided to obtain the MH-60S for these tasks. No HV-22 built as yet. If it is, the Navy will probably get modified MV-22s.

AV-22: Study for a combat version of the "Osprey" with tandem cockpit, Gatling gun under the nose and armament with linked air-to-ground and air-to-air rockets. Although Bell halted the work on this concept at the end of the 1980s, such a version would make sense. The combat helicopters of the Marines, which are supposed to escort the "Osprey" and give it fire support (AH-1, "Super-Cobra") are actually some 200kph slower and also have a lower maximum altitude and range than the MV-22B. In action the "Osprey" must thus wait for their escorts in doubtful cases and give up their speed advantage.

EV-22: Study for an early-warning version (AEW) of the V-22 with triangular radome on the fuselage, or planned "Phased Array" antennas.

Bell advertisement for a possible EV-22. Note the British roundels and the accompanying F-32 fighters. Bell and Boeing advertise the EV-22 as a radar early-warning craft for the new Royal Navy carriers. *(Bell)*

KV-22: Study in 2001 of the utility of revised MV-22s as tankers for the Marines.

SV-22: Version planned at the beginning of development for fighting submarines. Should have been stationed on US Navy ships. Halted at the end of the 1980s.

VV-22: Study of the usefulness of the V-22 as a helicopter for the U.S. President ("Marine One"), already set up by the end of the 1980s. The VV-22 took part in the VXX competition in 2003, in which a replacement for the obsolete VH-3D helicopter of the President was sought. The VV-22 lost, because of its delayed development, to the VH-71 "Kestrel," a variant of the AgustaWestland EH101. The obtaining of the "Kestrel," though, was ruled out in April 2009.

Bell advertisement from the 1980s for the planned SV-22 submarine-fighter version. *(Bell)*

A CV-22B of the USAF on a training flight over Colorado. *(USAF)*

The V-22 was developed equally by Bell Helicopters Textron of Fort Worth, Texas and Boeing helicopters of Philadelphia, Pennsylvania, which now share its production at the same ratio. The fuselage is made in Philadelphia, the power system, wings and other parts in Fort Worth. The engines come from Allison in Indianapolis, Indiana, today a branch of Rolls-Royce. The final assembly of the V-22 takes place in Amarillo, Texas. Besides these three main contractors there are literally hundreds of others scattered all over the USA, plus a few outside the USA.

The number of V-22s needed has been reduced more and more by the Pentagon during development. In 2009, as since 1997, the building of 458 of them is envisioned, which should take until 2017.

Planned Numbers

Year	USMC	USN	USAF	U.S. Army	TOTAL
1982	552	50	80	231	913
1989	552	50	55	0	657
1994	425	48	50	0	523
1997	360	48	50	0	458

From 1988 to 1991 components for a total of six FSD prototypes were made. Five of the craft were finished; the sixth one was not completed. Its fuselage ended up as a shooting target.

In 1997-98 Bell and Boeing built four EMD prototypes, designated MV-22 and CV-22.

The first pre-series craft (MV-22B and CV-22B) were delivered as of 1999, but because of financial modalities they were planned for the fiscal year (FY, runs from October 1 to September 30).

There were also thirteen "Ospreys" (seven MV-22B and six CV-22B) obtained in the last few years not via the regular budget means of the Department of Defense, but via special means for wartime ("wartime supplemental funding," WSF) as replacements for older helicopters lost in combat.

FY	MV-22B	CV-22B	Total
1997	5	0	5
1998	7	0	7
1999	7	0	7
2000	11	0	11
2001	0	0	9
2002	9	0	9
2003	11	0	11
2004	9	2	11
2005	8	3	11
2006	9	2	11
2007	14	2	16
2008	19	5	24
2009	30	6	36
WSF	7	6	13
Total	146	26	181

An MV-22B of VMM-263 taking off from the deck of USS Bataan (LHD-5) in the Atlantic, July 8, 2008. *(USN)*

Thus by the end of the 2009 fiscal year a total of 181 pre-series and production craft of the MV-22B and CV-22B variants plus ten prototypes had been built. For the 2010 fiscal year the regular purchase of thirty MV-22B and five CV-22B is planned. HV-22 craft for the Navy have not yet been produced.

In 2009, the Pentagon stated the price for obtaining a single V-22 as $119.5 million (system price), which is approximately $84 million dollars. The "fly away" price of an "Osprey" is $92.1 million, or around $64 million dollars.

Orders from other countries did not exist as of August 2009. Although it was heard repeatedly that Israel was interested in buying "Ospreys," no concrete plans are known to date. At the end of the 1990s the British Royal Navy briefly considered obtaining the V-22, but dropped this idea for lack of financial means. In the mid-1980s Bell offered the V-22 to Australia in vain. Just as unsuccessful was an attempt undertaken along with Dornier at the end of the 1980s to offer the "Osprey" to the German Defense Ministry. At this time the V-22 is one of the applicants for a Norwegian competition for a new all-weather SAR helicopter (Norwegian All Weather Search and Rescue Helicopter = NAWSARH).

Export contracts for the V-22 might come in only when the type has shown, in some years of action with the Navy and Air Force, that it is dependable and safe.

GENERAL STRUCTURE

The V-22 consists to a great extent of carbon-fiber (CFK) and GFK (percentages of weight of a cell of the prototype: CFK 59%, GFK 10%, metal 20%, other materials 11%). The high degree of composition materials helps to keep the weight of the cell within acceptable limits for VTOL use and indicates a better rigidity/weight ratio and higher corrosion resistance than the conventional metal structure.

The cockpit offers seats for two pilots side by side who can control the craft from either position. The seats are armored and made of boron carbide. By the cockpit door is a wide folding seat for a loadmaster or on-board engineer. The V-22 has a so-called glass cockpit with four large color monitor screens (MFD) and a fifth MFD in the central console, which display the most important flight, navigation and sensor data in color.

Under the nose an AN/AAQ-27 infrared sensor (FLIR) is mounted. It can swing thirty degrees to either side and from +14 to -23 degrees vertically. The FLIR's pictures can be shown on an MFD on night and bad-weather flights. The CV-22 also has an AN/APQ-186 terrain radar set.

Behind the cockpit is the 6.35- by 1.68- by 1.8-meter cargo space, in which twenty-four fully equipped soldiers and a loadmaster can sit on folding seats or up to 9,072kg of freight can be stored. Alternatively, nine to twelve stretchers for wounded men can be carried. If need be, up to thirty-two men can find room on the floor of the cargo space. As external freight the V-22 can transport up to 6,804kg on two hooks. The cargo space had a lowering loading ramp, plus a door on the right side. There a winch capable of lifting 272 kg can be installed. The cockpit and cargo space of the V-22 are not pressurized.

Right | Overview of the materials used in the V-22 and their shares of the structural weight. *(DoD)*

Below | The cockpit of the V-22 is dominated by modern monitor screens. *(USMC)*

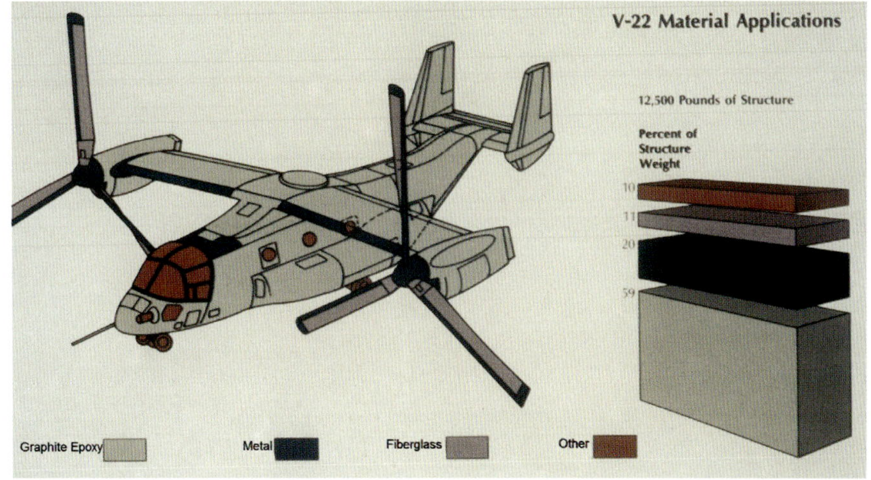

The cargo space of the V-22 offers room for twenty-four fully equipped soldiers. *(DoD)*

CV-22B of the 8th Special Operations Squadron in landing flight, May 11, 2008. *(USAF)*

The bow wheel is retracted into the fuselage, the two main landing gear units into side pods, which also contain fuel and avionics.

To allow space saving stowing on ships, the wings can automatically be turned ninety degrees and the rotor blades can be folded. The required hangar space is thus only 19x5.6 meters.

The engine nacelles can be tilted ninety degrees in twelve seconds. Each contains a Rolls-Royce AE 1107/C Liberty turbine producing 6,150 HP and driving the 11.61-meter proprotors. In all, the engine nacelles can tip ninety-six degrees. The proprotors drive the three strongly twisted blades in opposite directions. The two turbines are linked by a transverse shaft in case one turbine fails. Powerplant control is completely digital through a FADEC system.

Besides pure vertical takeoffs, the V-22 is also capable of short takeoffs, which increase its payload considerably. The "Osprey" then tips its engine gondolas some forty-five degrees and requires a run of forty-six meters to lift off and eighty-five meters to be able to rise above a barrier fifteen meters high.

The MV-22 has fuel tanks wit a total capacity of 5,480 liters in its side pods. The CV-22, through auxiliary tanks in its wings, has the possibility of carrying 7,730 liters of fuel. For long flights, one or two auxiliary tanks, each holding 3,032 liters, or three holding 1,630 liters, can be installed in the cargo space. The MV-22 also has a rigid air-refueling sonde; that of the CV-22 is retractable. The "Osprey" is thus theoretically capable of flying to anywhere in the world.

The V-22 has a threefold redundant digital fly-by-wire flight situation control and steering system. In horizontal flight the craft is steered by conventional rudders and flaps; in hovering flight by the cyclical and collective adjustment of the propro-tors and thrust changes in the engines. The transition between the two steering modes can be done gradually under computer control; the closer the proprotors come to the horizontal, the more the flaps and rudders take control. It is, though, a problem that the pilot has no control over collective blade adjustment, for this takes place automatically via the lever for thrust steering. Pilots who were trained on helicopters have had problems with this system, which have led to pilot errors.

Flaps, rudders and engine nacelles are moved hydraulically, and the threefold redundant system works with an extremely high pressure of 345 bar. This pressure allows the use of smaller pumps and activation cylinders, but also allows the use of lines made of titanium and highly firm steel.

Unlike a helicopter, the V-22 cannot use autorotation in time of need, which has brought it some criticism. According to statements from Marine Corps pilots, the craft can still be landed in gliding flight just as well as a C-130. The big proprotors are designed so that they go to pieces in a crash landing, so as not to endanger the fuselage. Then too, the turning direction can assure that a large part of the pieces are thrown away from the fuselage.

The CFK and GFK elements of which the greater part of the cell consists show a high shot-resistance. The fuel tanks are self-sealing up to a direct hit of 12.7mm caliber. Load-bearing parts of the craft are designed so that they can also with-stand shots of 23mm caliber.

The V-22 has an AN/APR-39A(V) radar warning receiver, a device that warns it of contact by laser (AN/AVR-2A LDS), and a flying-body warning system (AN/AAR-47 MWS). The received signals are automatically processed, portrayed on a cockpit monitor screen, and the crewmen are informed by light and sound signals. In the rear part of each side pod is an ALE-47 launcher, which can throw out IR flares or chaff in times of danger.

The armament of the MV22B consists of one 7.62mm MG M240 mounted on the rear loading ramp. Machine guns in the side doors or windows, such as other Navy helicopters carry, are impossible because of the big proprotors and engine nacelles. In 1999-2000 the armament of the V-22 was planned to include a three-barrel 12.7mm MG GAU-19 Gatling MG in a turning turret under the nose, but this was not installed. Since 2007 BAe Systems has worked on the development of a retractable, remote-controlled weapon station under the fuselage, which is to carry a 7.62mm GAU-17 minigun.

Above | EMD prototype No.3 deploys flares in a test flight over Edwards AFB in October 2004. (USAF)

Right | For use in Iraq a 7.62mm MG M240 was installed on the rear-loading ramp of the MV-22B of the USMC. It was operated by the loadmaster. For service in Afghanistan a 12.7mm MG is also planned for installation. (USMC)

TRAINING AND OPERATIONS

The first unit of the USMC to receive the MV-22 was the VMMT-204 training unit, which began training crews for the "Osprey" in March 2000. The VMX-22 examination and testing unit was formed on August 28, 2003. By mid-2009 the USMC had five MV-22B units plus one being reequipped. The first of these units was VMM-162, which was declared ready for action on March 3, 2006. It was followed by VMM-162 (August 31, 2006), VMM-266 (March 23, 2007), VMM-261 (April 10, 2008), and VMM-365 (January 15, 2009). The VM-264 began its conversion to the MV-22B in April 2009; the process was to be finished in October of that year. All the action units are stationed at the New River base in North Carolina and previously flew the CH-46 for years.

On September 17, 2007, the USS Wasp (LHD-1) left the USA for Iraq carrying ten MV-22Bs. This way was chosen because of the lack of tankers and a de-icing system that still did not work without problems, which ruled out a flight over the North Atlantic.

MV-22B of the VMM-263 on the deck of USS Wasp (LHD-1) prepare for a flight to the Al Asad base in Iraq. Gulf of Aqaba, October 4, 2007. *(USN)*

The VMM-263 left its ten aircraft in Iraq and was replaced by VMM-162, which brought two more MV-22Bs. The VMM-266 was stationed in Iraq from October 2008 to April 2009, and what with the decrease in U.S. troop presence there, may be the last MV-22B unit operating out of the Al Asad base in Anbar Province. The "Osprey" flew mainly routine missions during this time, transporting men and materials. In only a few cases did MV-22Bs bring combat troops to their areas of service. In all, the aircraft flew over 4,600 missions and spent some 9,700 hours in the air. Since the end of May 2009 the VMM-263 has been stationed with ten MV-22Bs on board the USS Bataan (LHD-5). An amphibian attack ship, and forms the transport element of the 22nd Marine Expeditionary Unit (MEU). In the future every MEU is to receive its own "Osprey" unit.

During their service in Iraq (October 2007 to April 2009) the MV-22B mainly flew routine missions to transport men and materials. *(USMC)*

The reports on the service of the "Osprey" in Iraq are contradictory. The Marines themselves say they are very satisfied with the performance of the craft and praise its speed and range was well as its high altitude, which allows it to fly beyond the range of light weapons. A report of the Government Accountability Office (similar to the German Bundesrechnungshof) of May 2009, though, comes to different conclusions. Although it also praises the speed and range of the type, the report criticizes the still-lacking reliability and ease of maintenance. On an average, only 57% to 68% of all MV-22Bs stationed in Iraq were ready for action. Compared to this, in units that flew the CH-46 or MH-53 and were also stationed in Iraq, an average of over 85% of the helicopters were ready for action. The relatively meager readiness of the "Osprey" did not apply only to those stationed in Iraq and exposed to bad conditions, but also to units in the USA.

Only rarely does the MV-22B transport combat troops into action. *(USMC)*

A number of "Osprey" components did not reach the expected life span. The turbines of the craft stationed in Iraq had to be replaced after 380 hours of running. Other parts reached only 10% of their guaranteed life cycle. The sharply increased need burdened supplying with spare parts so much that parts in the craft stationed in the USA finally had to be removed. The unexpectedly high spare-parts need made stationing on ships difficult, as they were scarcely able to carry such a large quantity of parts. Since 2006 there have also been a series of problems with the foreign-body removers in the engine air intakes (EAPS). Engine fires, faulty microchips and loose bolts in the rotor steering, which led several times to grounding of all "Ospreys."

According to this report, loadmasters and group leaders complain about the poor overview ("situational awareness") that the cabin of the MV-22B affords them. Two tiny windows, unlike the CH-46 with its numerous large windows, allow hardly any observation of the landing zone.

The unreliability of the de-icing system is seen as highly problematic, as it has already led to the VMM-263 being moved to Iraq by ship. Actions at great heights and in cold weather thus involve great risks. Yet the Marines plan to transfer a unit of "Ospreys" to Afghanistan in the autumn of 2009.

The first completely action-ready CV-22B Block 10 aircraft was delivered on March 20, 2006 to the 71st Special Operations Squadron (SOS) of the U.S. Air Force at Kirtland AFB, New Mexico. By mid-2009 two other units of the USAF were equipped with CV-22Bs, the 20th SOS at Cannon AFB, New Mexico, and the 8th SOS at Hulburt Field, Florida.

Unlike the USMC, the Air Force "Ospreys" have not yet flown any missions in Iraq, but have mainly tested rescues and special operations. Four CV-22Bs of the 8th SOS, though, took part in joint maneuvers with the USAF and the forces of Mali and Senegal in November 2008. With tanker support, they flew nonstop from Florida to West Africa.

On March 16, 2009, the 8th SOS became the first USAF unit supplied with "Ospreys" to be declared ready for action. In June 2009 two CV-22Bs of this unit transported almost twenty tons of humanitarian goods to distant villages in Honduras that were not reachable by road.

Despite over twenty years of development and almost thirty billion dollars spent on development costs, the V-22 still does not seem to be totally developed. Their achievements could not convince their critics to this day, and so after the end of the Iraq conflict voices were again heard demanding new testing, and even a definite end to the "Osprey" program. Whether the craft will ever really fulfill the expectations placed on it remains to be seen.

Bell Boeing MV-22B "Osprey"

Crew	2+1
Empty weight	15,030kg
Takeoff weight	23,860kg (VTOL), 28,855kg (STOL)
Powerplant	2 Rolls-Royce AE 1107C Liberty turbines, 6,150 HP each
Top speed	564kph at 4,572-meter altitude
Length	15,470mm
Height	6,730mm (powerplants vertical)
Wingspan	15,120mm (including engine nacelles), 25,740mm with rotors
Service ceiling	7,620 meters
Range	520km with 5,448kg payload (VTOL) or 1,140km (STOL)
One-way range	3,590km with auxiliary tanks

CV-22B of the 8th SOS about to land near Bamako, Mali, November 2008. *(USAF)*

A CV-22B "Osprey" and an MH-53 "Pave Low" over the coast of Florida on August 20, 2008. *(USAF)*

Special-action aircraft of the Air Force are winched down from a hovering CV-22B of the 8th SOS at Hurlburt Field, Florida, May 22, 2007. *(USAF)*

MILITARY PROJECTS AND PROTOTYPES OUTSIDE THE USA AFTER 1945

Chapter 5

Only a few countries outside the USA had or have the technological foundation for building tiltrotor or tipping-wing aircraft. They naturally include the countries of Western Europe, Canada and Russia. Surprisingly, Brazil also joined this group in the 1950s, though, with German assistance, so to speak.

Despite the wealth of projects, only a few prototypes were built, of which one in particular, the Canadair CL-84, ranked among the most successful airplanes of its kind and just barely missed series production.

BRAZIL

HC-1 "Convertiplano"

Prof. Heinrich Focke, father of the Fw 61, and some of his former colleagues went to Brazil in 1951 to work for the CTA (Centro Tecnico Aeroespacial). There Focke and his team designed a tiltrotor plane designated HC-1 "Convertiplano" in 1952. The plane had four large tilting propellers, each with three blades, which were attached to two shafts in the front and the fuselage at the rear.

Since Great Britain was not ready to deliver the originally planned propeller turbines of the Armstrong Siddeley Double Mambo, Focke and his colleagues designed the HC-1 so that a Wright R-3350 eighteen-cylinder radial engine producing 2,200 HP could serve as a power source. Focke did particularly keep in mind that the higher weight and heavy vibration level of the powerplant could be problematic. The motor was housed in the central fuselage, behind the cockpit, and drove all four propellers via gears and shafts. The powerplant was

In order to reduce costs Professor Focke used the wing and the undercarriage of a Supermarine Spitfire for the "Convertiplano." *(Jens Baganz)*

supplied with cooling air through a slit in the fuselage behind the cockpit. After a few test runs on the ground, the project was halted in 1953. The design and building of the HC-1 had consumed some eight million dollars by that time, and testing the plane threatened to last longer than the Brazilian officials were willing to wait, so they halted their financial support.

Then Prof. Focke designed a small helicopter, the BF-1 Beija Flor, for the CTA, but it too failed to go beyond the prototype stage.

GERMANY

Although the German aircraft industry was as good as dead after 1945 and the building of airplanes was banned until 1955, German firms were able to move quickly to the top in the world. The technically noteworthy and futuristic STOL and VTOL projects of that time bear a clear witness to this.

Although the Ministry of Defense (BMVg), in cooperation with the Economic and Commercial Ministry and Lufthansa (DLH), announced a competition in May 1969 for a civilian and militarily useful VTOL transport plane, the interest of officialdom grew steadily less. In 1971 all the public funds for this area were finally canceled, which meant the end for VTOL research in Germany. If one can believe contemporary sources, political indecision and short sight in particular led to this decision.

Dornier Do 29

With the successful Do 27 single-engine multi-purpose plane, which offered outstanding short-takeoff and landing qualities, Dornier had successfully returned to aircraft building in the mid-fifties. On the basis of that type, Dornier already was considering the building of a version with considerably improved STOL qualities in mid-1955, but the possibility of vertical takeoffs and landings or hover-hold was not aimed at. To be sure, in 1957 Dornier received an official contract from the Ministry of Defense to build three test planes, and the designing work, in collaboration with the Deutsche Versuchsanstalt für Luftfahrt (today DVLR) had already begun a year before. The structure of the Do 29 was about 70% the same as that of the Do 27.

The most noticeable sign of change was the new fuselage front with a very glassed cockpit for a pilot who had a Martin-Baker ejection seat, plus two Lycoming GO-480-BI-A6 piston engines, each producing 270 HP. Through a gearbox they operated two contra-rotating pusher airscrews that could tip ninety degrees downward. To avoid a power loss on one side if one motor failed, the two motors were linked with each other at the gearbox by a cross shaft. The Do 29 also received larger control panels, a new, more rugged chassis, a wingspan lengthened by 1.2 meters, bigger double-section flaps and modified wing tanks.

The maiden flight of the first prototype V1 took place in Oberpfaffenhofen on December 21, 1958, but the actual flight testing was begun only in March of the following year.

An interim report of early December 1959 granted the Do 29 good steering and flight stability, but also determined that the achieved performance in all areas was below expectations. Instead of the calculated 330kph, the top speed was only 230kph, and instead of an expected landing speed of 25kph, this was 70kph. The predicted takeoff and landing distances (25 meters each) did not agree with the test results (80 and 45 meters).

On December 4, 1959, the second prototype, called V2, took off on its first flight, and was subjected to further tests until June 1960. Then pilots of the Luftwaffe's Test Center 64 in Oberpfaffenhofen first flew V2. After a long pause, flight testing was restarted on June 2, 1962. On July 5, 1962, there was a landing accident in which the plane turned over. The pilot was unharmed and the damage to V2 was minor, but the plane was written off. The test program was then resumed with V1 until the summer of 1963. Planned further development for military and civilian uses and fitting with propeller turbines did not take place, and the planned third prototype was never built. Yet the Do 29 provided valuable research results and remains to this day unique in its conception. The Do 29V1 was on display in the Federal Luftwaffe Museum in Berlin-Gatow until March 2009 and has been on view in the Dornier Museum in Friedrichshafen since July 2009.

Dornier Do 29	
Crew	1
Empty weight	2,180kg
Takeoff weight	2,490kg
Powerplant	2 Lycoming O-480-BI-A6 6-cylinder piston engines, 270 HP each
Top speed	230kph (calculated 330kph)
Length	9,500mm
Height	2,700mm
Wingspan	13,200mm
Service ceiling	6,500 meters
Range	400km

Right | The motors of the Do 29 could be tilted downward up to ninety degrees. *(EADS)*

Below | Although the STOL qualities of the Do 29 were worse than expected, the plane got by with a takeoff length of eighty meters. *(EADS)*

With tilted motors, the Do 29 had astonishing slow-flight capability. *(EADS)*

Weser-Flugzeugbau Tipping Rotor Projects

At the beginning of the 1960s the designers at the Weser-Flugzeugbau GmbH designed various types of tiltrotor airplanes. At the 1963 air show in Le Bourget the model of a type called P-16 was displayed, which had two mantled propellers integrated in the control surfaces. In hover-hold and slow flight they took over the control of the pitching and yawing movements, and were to be covered in cruising flight. This feature was also seen in the P-23 and P-27 projects. Unfortunately, little is known of all these projects. Prototypes were never built.

The P-16 was intended for military tasks, including fighting against enemy helicopters. Their payload was to be 900kg, and the two propellers were to have a diameter of four meters.

Weserflug WFG P-16	
Crew	2
Empty weight	3,900kg
Takeoff weight	unknown
Powerplant	2 Bristol Siddeley Gnome propeller turbines, 1,350 HP each
Top speed	670kph
Length	11,200mm
Height	3,300mm
Wingspan	8,600mm
Service ceiling	unknown
Range	400km

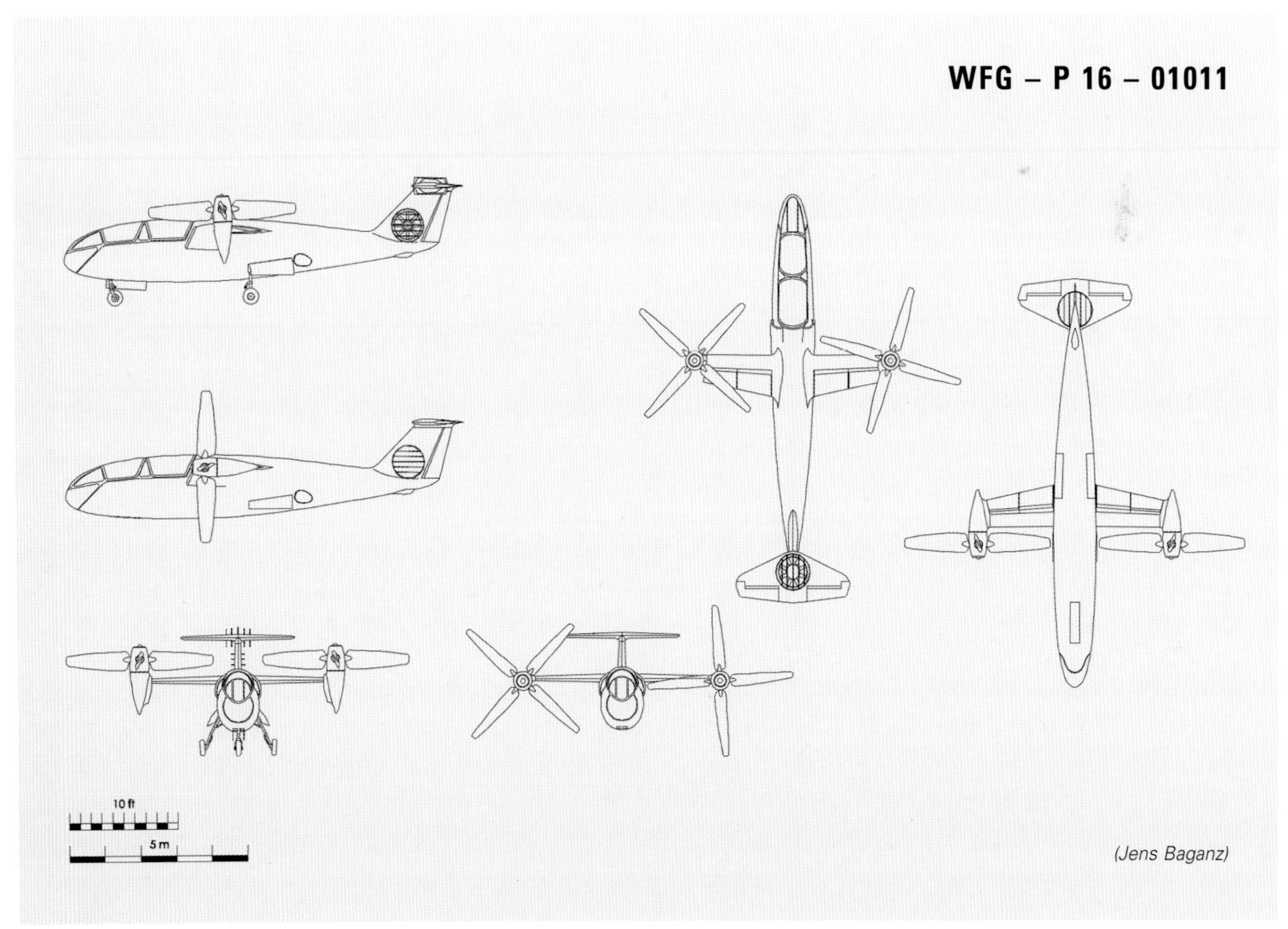

(Jens Baganz)

Weserflug WFG P-23

Crew	2
Empty weight	7,400kg
Takeoff weight	unknown
Powerplants	2 Lycoming T55-LTC4K1
	propeller turbines,
	2,940 HP each
Top speed	650kph
Length	13,600mm
Height	4,900mm
Wingspan	11,600mm
Service ceiling	unknown
Range	400km

The P-23 was intended as a light transporter for civilian and military uses. It was to be able to carry 1,850kg of freight or twelve passengers, or thirteen fully equipped soldiers, and to have a propeller diameter of five meters.

Scarcely anything is known of the WFG P-24 and P-27 projects. The P-24 was planned as a transporter and was to be able to take in a 1.5-ton truck over its rear-loading ramp. The P-27 was conceived as a military multi-purpose plane that could carry twelve fully equipped soldiers or be used as a fighter. For this purpose the P-27 was to be fitted with an internal weapon shaft.

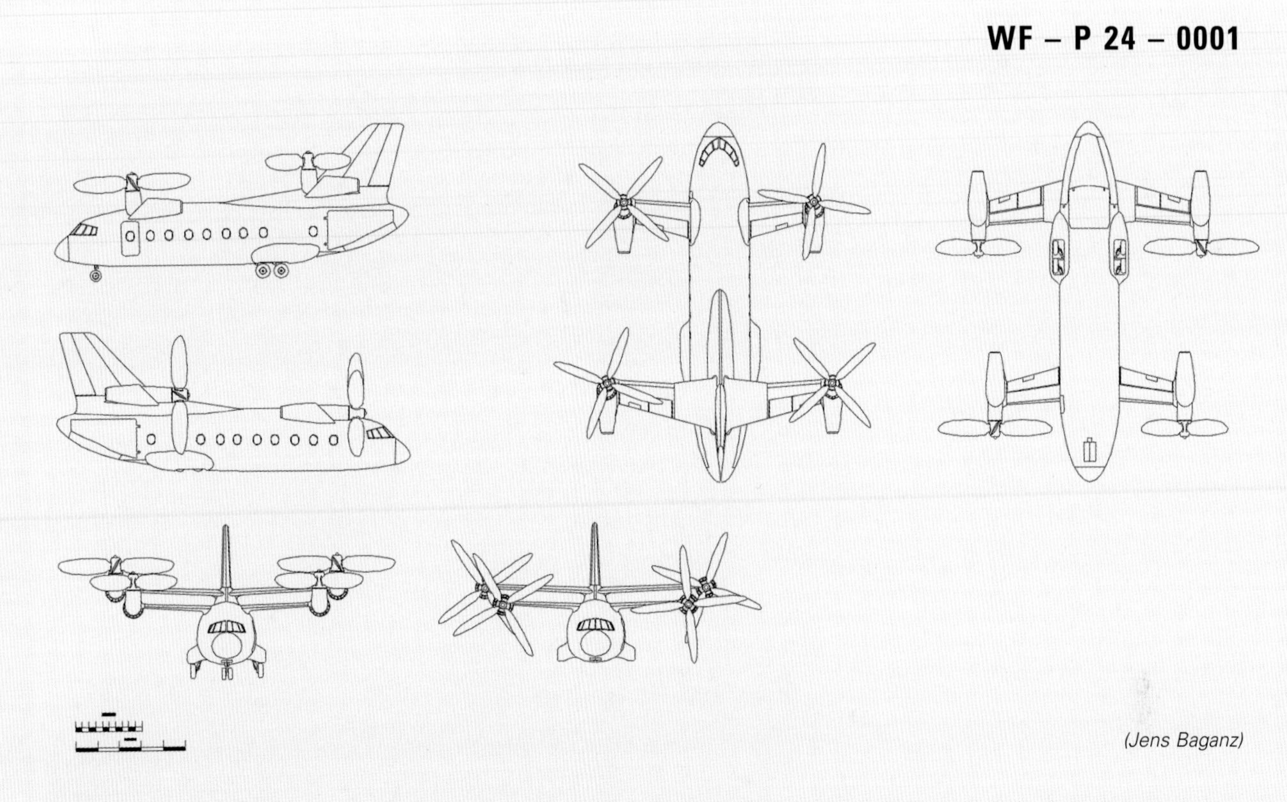

WF – P 24 – 0001

(Jens Baganz)

WFG – P 27

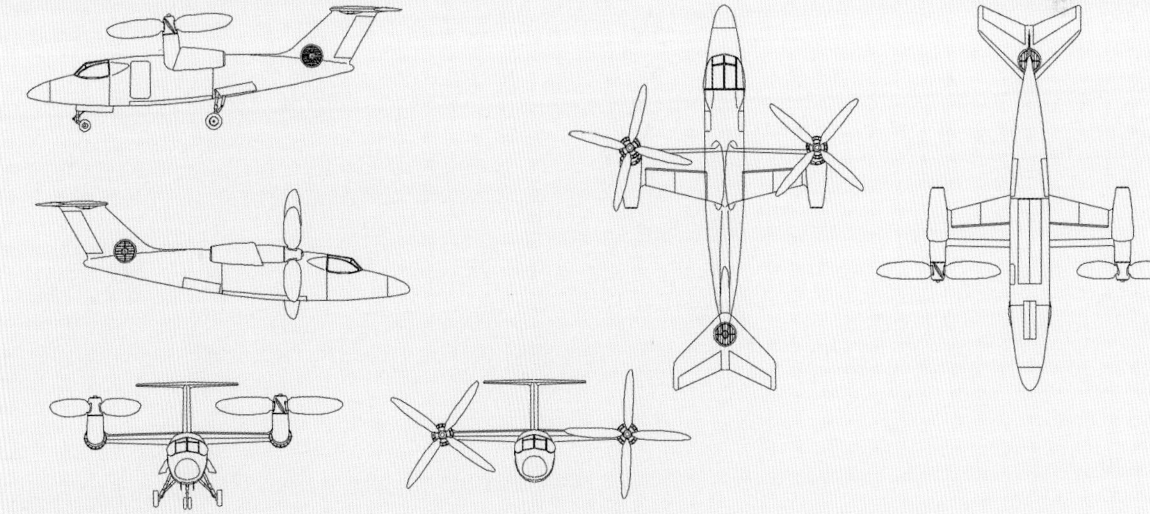

(Jens Baganz)

Vereinigte Flugtechnische Werke VC 400

The Vereinigten Flugtechnischen Werke (VFW) was formed at the end of 1963 by the merger of the Focke-Wulf and Weser-Flugzeugbau firms. In 1964, Heinkel Flugzeugbau joined the new firm.

At Heinkel in Munich, the first studies of building a VTOL transport plane, the He 212, with tipping wings, had already been made in 1963. After the merger with VFW these studies formed the basis for the design of a four-engine transport plane with tipping tandem wings (VC 400), from which the designers wanted to develop a whole family of tilting-wing aircraft.

One of these studies (VC 200) was for a fighter with tilting tandem wings and four propellers, driven by two turbines mounted in the rear fuselage and producing 1,800 HP each. The maximum weight for a vertical takeoff was calculated as 6,000kg. Between the tandem wings was a large fuselage shaft, which could take a load up to 1,800kg in VTOL mode or up to 2,400kg for STOL operation. There were also, on the one hand, to be cannon or weapon mounts, or, the designers also suggested a removable rack under the fuselage in which two wounded men could be transported.

VFW planned a whole family of VTOL airplanes in the 1960s, from a small fighter to a big transporter. *(EADS)*

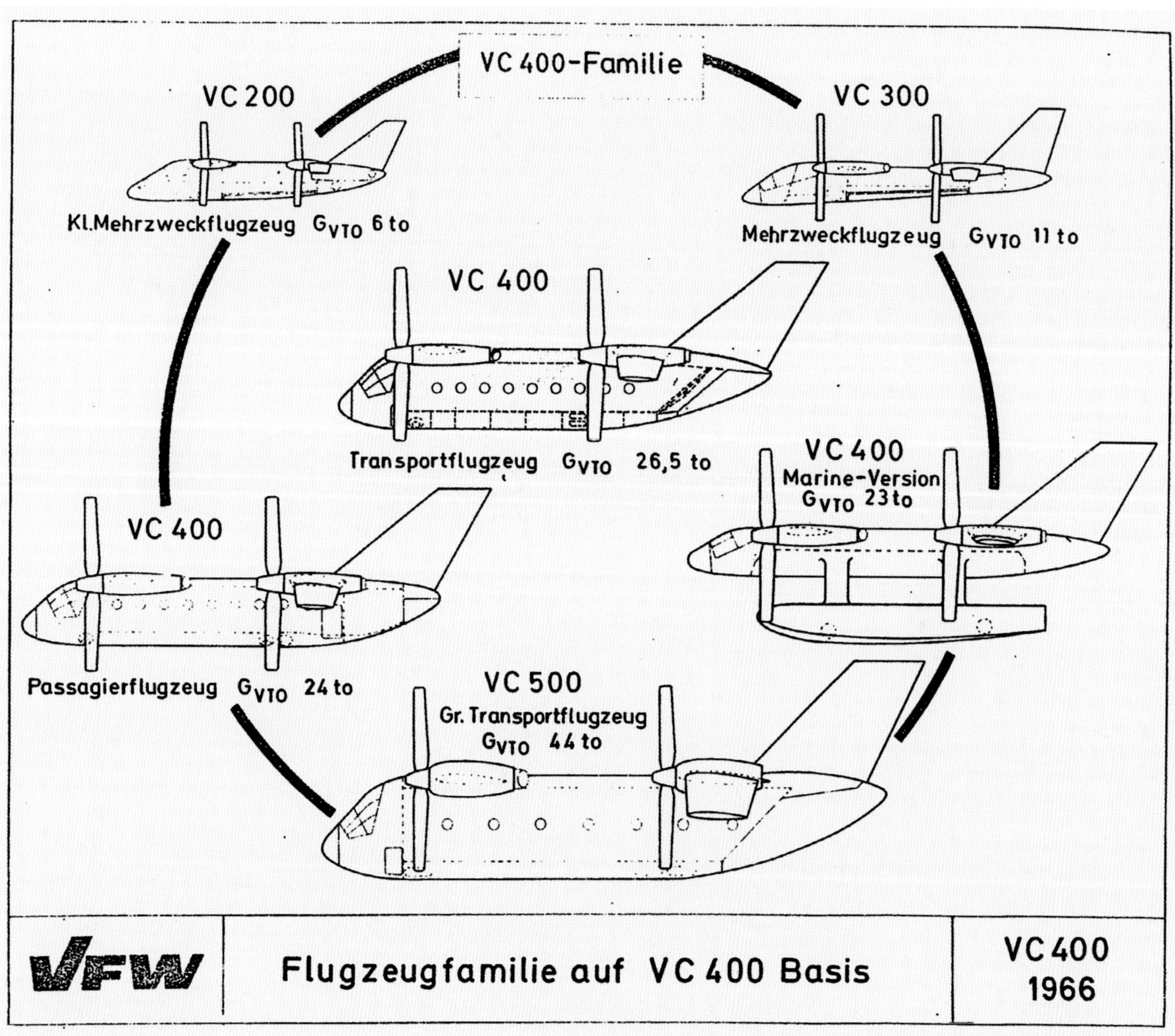

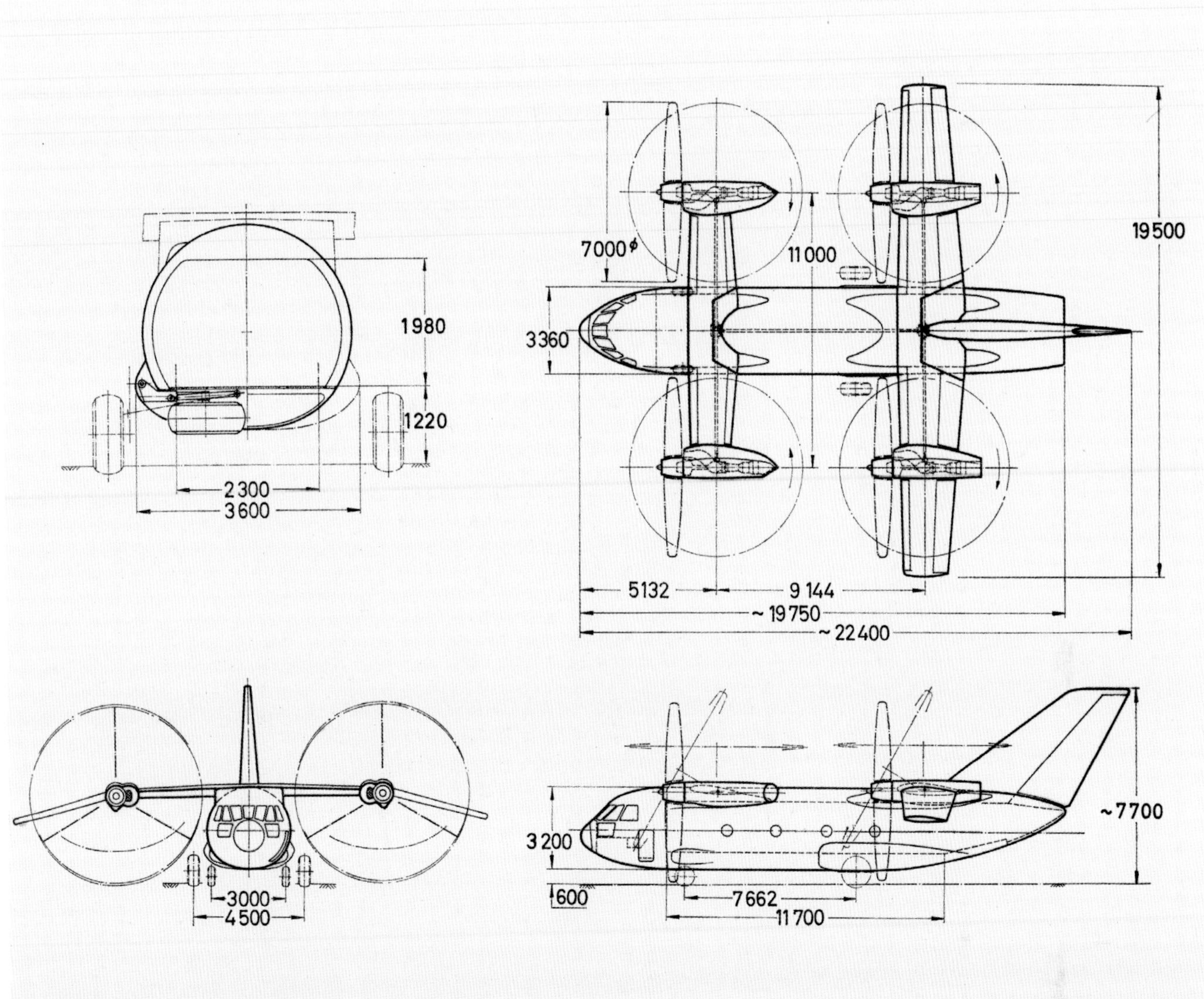

Four-side view of the VC 400. *(EADS)*

The VC 300 project looked like an enlarged VC 200, but the 1,800 HP power-plants were to be carried in nacelles on the tilting wings. For a vertical takeoff, the calculated takeoff weight was about 11,000kg and the payload 3,800kg. For a short takeoff, however, 4,800kg was to be possible. The VC 300 was also to have a long fuselage shaft for drop weapons and a removable rack underneath the fuselage that could, for example, carry up to twelve fully equipped soldiers. The two concepts never got beyond the initial stage.

In 1966, VFW explored the possibility of an armed version for the German Navy, which was to be used only secondarily as a transport. They envisioned not only a version with a boatlike lower fuselage, but also two variants with floats. These three concepts were never followed up.

The development of the VC 400, though, was carried out as of 1967 with means from the Ministry of Defense. The goal at first was the building of a test rig and two test planes by 1970-71. It is interesting that Siegfried Günther, who already had a decisive role in designing the Heinkel He 111 in the 1930s, was the project leader of the VC 400 design team in Munich.

The military version of the VC 400 with a rear-loading ramp. *(EADS)*

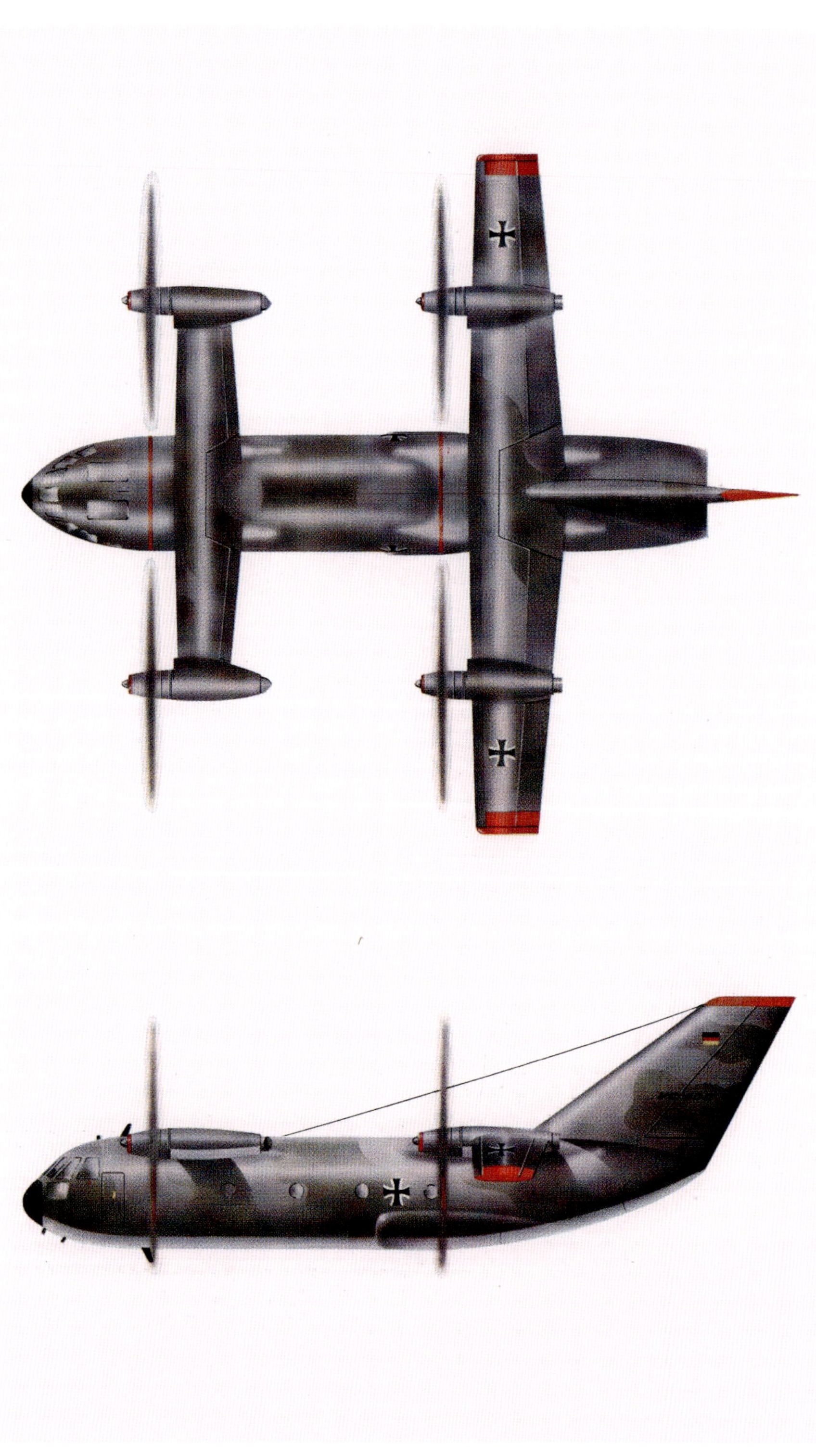

During the design work, measurements, weights, loads and motors changed several times. For the test flights in the first design phase, four Lycoming LTC-4-B11 turbines of 3,400 HP each were planned for; as of 1968 there were four General Electric GE64-GE-16 turbines of 3,980 HP each, which were to drive three-bladed propellers of seven-meter diameter. In case of an engine failure, the turbines were linked by cross shafts. In hovering flight the steering was done on the longitudinal and transverse axes with the help of modifications to the propeller thrust, and on the vertical axis by the elevators. The tandem wings could be tilted ninety degrees and had landing flaps on the trailing edges, which in their inner areas also served as ailerons and in their outer areas as transverse rudders. Besides pure vertical takeoffs, the plane was also to be capable of short rolling takeoffs, which would increase the load limit considerably. The two steerable bow wheels were retracted into the fuselage; the main landing gear into side pods. VFW planned to build two versions, which would differ in their fuselage shape: a military version with a rear loading ramp and strengthened fuselage floor for up to 4,840kg loads (VC 400), and a civilian passenger variant for fifty-eight passengers (VC 400P). Both were to be ventilated throughout.

Examples of loads for the VC 400. *(EADS)*

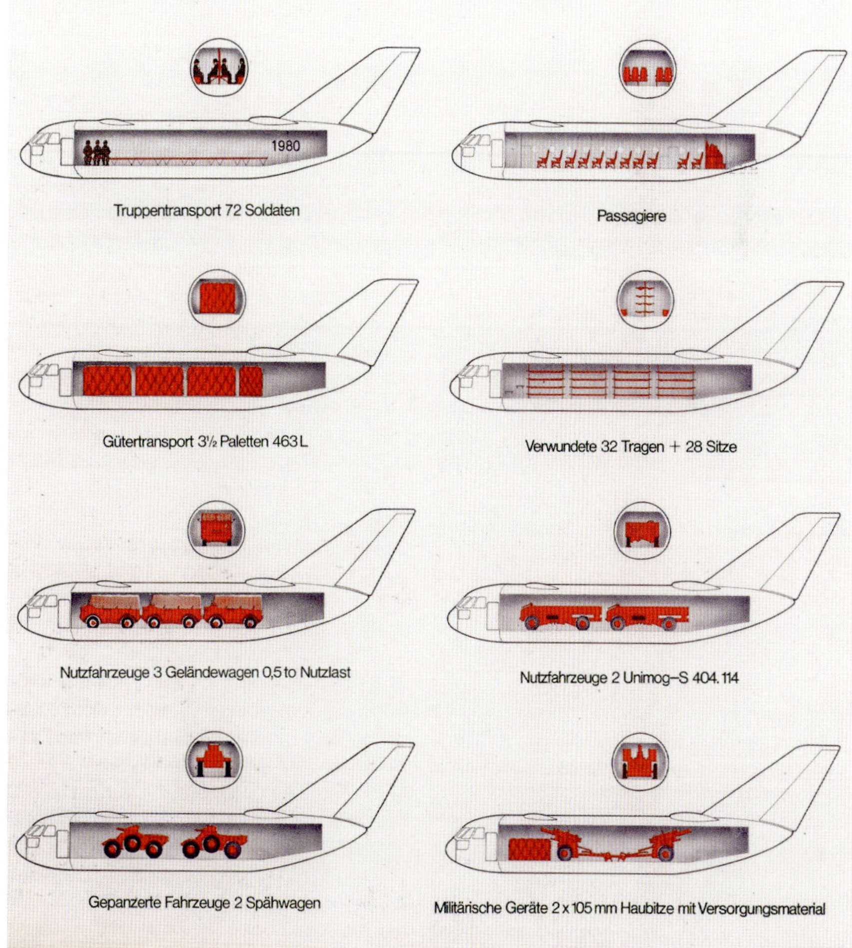

VFW VC 400

Crew	2
Empty weight	15,700kg
Takeoff weight	23,500kg (VTOL),
	29,000kg (STOL)
Powerplant	4 General Electric
	GE64-GE-16 propeller turbines,
	3,980 HP each
Top speed	790kph
Length	22,400mm
Height	7,700mm
Wingspan	19,500mm
Service ceiling	10,400 meters
Range	880km with maximum payload,
	STOL conversion range 6,200km

By 1970, various models had been tested a total of 7,000 hours in a wind tunnel, and in 1971 the design work for the VC 400 was practically finished. The test rig for propellers and motors was nearly finished, and VFW was confidently ready to begin building the first test planes when the project was halted for financial reasons.

Model of the VC 400 with tipped wings.
(EADS)

Model of the VC-400 in flight. *(EADS)*

Vereinigte Flugtechnische Werke VC 500

The VC 500 was developed by the Munich works of the VFW and was basically an enlarged version of the VC 400. In this model the data changed many times in the course of development. VFW took part with the VC 500 in October 1969 in the competition for a VTOL transport plane with civilian and military uses. The Ministry of Defense (BMVg), in cooperation with the Economic and Traffic Ministry and Lufthansa (DLH), had announced it that May. The winner of this competition, to be sure, was not the VC 500, but the Dornier Do 231, a further development of the Do 31. But in 1971 this program was broken off for financial reasons.

The main difference between the VC 500 and VC 400 was, besides the dimensions, the lack of a connection of the engines by transverse shafts for protection against thrust losses. Instead, each propeller was driven by two coupled T64-GE-S5C-1

Three-side view of the VC 500. *(EADS)*

VFW VC 500 (1969)

Crew	2
Empty weight	29,605kg
Takeoff weight	42,765kg (VTOL), 46,800kg (STOL)
Powerplant	8 General Electric T64-GE-S5C-1 turbines, 5,417 HP each
Top speed	800kph
Length	31,760mm
Height	9,600mm
Wingspan	21,800mm
Service ceiling	unknown
Range	800km with maximum payload, VTOL conversion range 3,380km

turbines (2x5417 HP), one of which could take on the tasks alone if need be. But
VFW also decided to use a version of the T64 still being developed, with some 6,000
HP, or a General Electric powerplant with some 10,000 HP (GE 1/S1A-2T) planned
for 1975. The latter, to be sure, had made a return to the connection by transverse
shafts necessary, since only four turbines were to be installed.

The military transport plane was to be equipped with a rear-loading ramp and be
capable of carrying up to 8,160kg of freight. The civilian passenger version was planned for a maximum of ninety-seven passengers. The VFW engineers also planned on
using conventional propellers of eight-meter diameter, but also considered airscrews
with a blade length that could be shortened in flight to 5.5 meters, plus the use of
propellers with variable shortening to improve their effectiveness at cruising speeds.
In 1971 this project was also brought to a final stop.

Model of the VC 500 in Lufthansa colors.
(EADS)

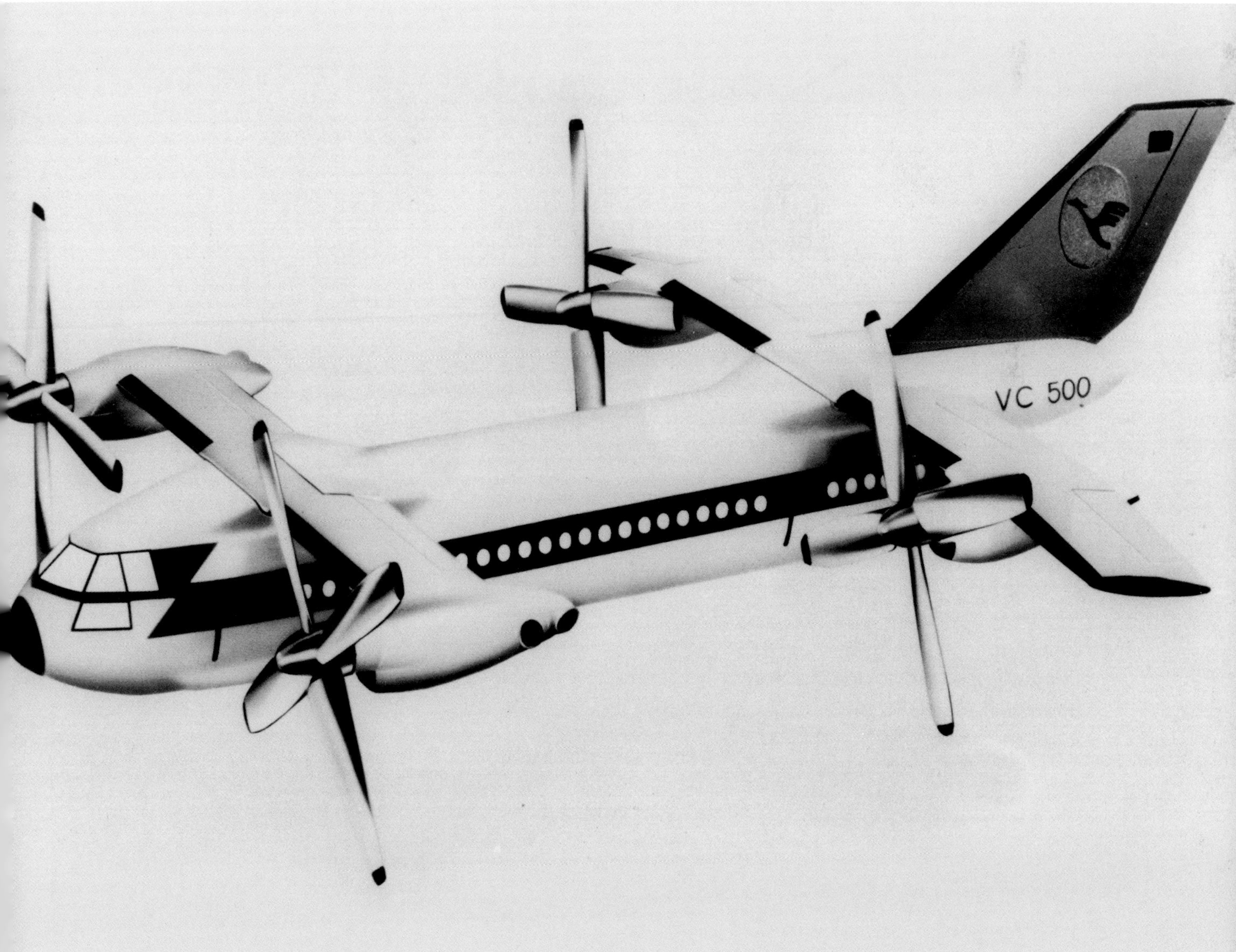

Messerschmitt-Bölkow-Blohm Bo 140

The Bo 140 by Messerschmitt-Bölkow-Blohm GmbH (MBB) was designed within three months in 1969 as an answer to the already mentioned competition for a VTOL, transport (see VC 500). Of course the Bo 140 was also a four-engine tipping-wing craft, but with only one main wing.

The designers regarded this configuration as aerodynamically more favorable and also wanted to keep the fuselage free in this way from drive elements like shafts and gears. MBB envisioned the installation of four General Electric GE1-S1A-1T turbines, each producing 11,400 HP, and linked together by a cross shaft), that drive four-bladed rotors of 8.24-meter diameter. Because of many years' experience with the jointless rotor of GFK designed for the Bo 105, MBB planned to use such rotors in the Bo 140. A great advantage of such a rotor/propeller is the possibility of cyclical and collective blade adjustment, whereby MBB hoped to simplify the steering and hovering at slow flight. The cyclical adjustment was to provide control of the pitching movements and the collective the steering of rolling movements, while yawing should be handled by means of the opposed activation of the wing flaps. According

Below | Artistic conception of the Bo 140 military version *(EADS)*

Right page | Three-side view. *(EADS)*

to the requirements, MBB conceived a military version, Bo 140-M, and a civilian type, Bo 140-X, which would differ only in their running gear and the bottom and rear of the fuselage.

The Bo 140-M had a rear loading ramp and a reinforced cabin floor, plus robust tandem running gear that could be lowered to make loading easier. The Bo 140-M was thus laid out to transport ninety fully equipped soldiers or an 11,000kg payload, with the payload doubled (21,400kg) for short takeoffs. The civilian version offered space for eighty passengers with luggage (8,750kg payload). The cabins of both versions were to be ventilated throughout. In building the Bo 140, large amounts of materials like titanium and various plastics were to be used, making up 20.3% of the empty weight.

Since the official agencies showed no interest in the Bo 140 and private development of the type had overburdened MBB, the program was dropped in 1971.

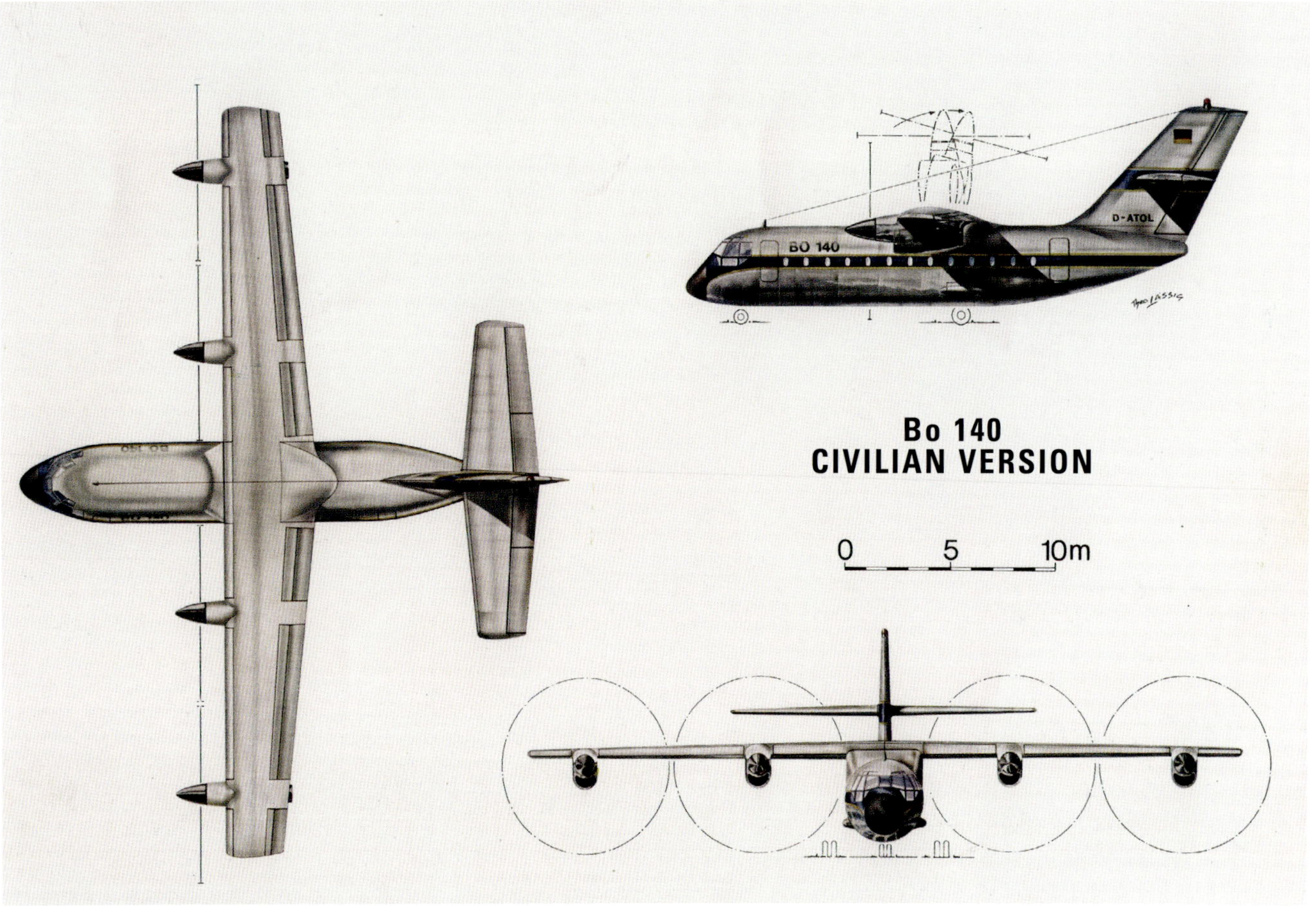

Above | Three-side view of the civilian
Bo 140. *(EADS)*

Left | Artistic conception of the civilian
Bo 140. *(EADS)*

FRANCE

Nord Aviation 500 "Cadet"

In 1962, the French state aeronautical organization Nord began to take an interest in the possibility of using mantled propellers for VTOL airplanes. To test the viability of this concept, the agency designed a small research airplane, the Nord 500, the look of which was to change several times in the course of development. A full-scale model of the type was already displayed at the air show at Le Bourget in 1965, but the building of two prototypes only began in 1966.

The first prototype of the Nord 500 under construction. *(EADS)*

The Nord 500 on hovering tests. Note the cables that prevent the plane from lifting off. *(EADS)*

Nord 500	
Crew	1
Empty weight	1,000kg
Takeoff weight	1,250kg
Powerplant	2 Allison 250-C18 turbines, 317 HP each
Top speed	350kph (planned)
Length	6,570mm
Height	2,170mm
Wingspan	6,140mm
Service ceiling	unknown
Range	maximum flight duration 15 minutes

The N 500 was a small airplane. It was only 6.58 meters long, had a wingspan of 6.14 meters, and had a payload of only 120 kilograms. Its two mantled, five-bladed tilting propellers of 1.58 meter diameter were driven by two Allison 250-C18 turbines 317 HP each, mounted on the fuselage. At the end of the mantles were four diamond-shaped guiding panels that the pitching steering moved collectively and the yawing steering moved differentially. Steering around the longitudinal axis (rolling) was done with the help of different thrust changes of the propellers.

The first prototype was used as of April 1967 for mechanical tests and ground testing. The second N 500 began its ground testing in February 1968 and made its first bound flight on July 23, 1968. The flight itself lasted fewer than twenty seconds and the Nord 500 reached a height of only about one meter. The plane was very unstable and hard to steer, so the designers decided to rework the flight regulation system thoroughly. Although the ground testing was continued, the plane seems to have never again risen into the air. A third, slightly larger prototype with four seats and stronger powerplants (Allison 250-C20) with 370 HP each was not built. After Nord and Sud Aviation had merged to become Aerospatiale in 1970, the program seems to have been halted at last.

An enlarged four-seat military version of the Nord was not built.

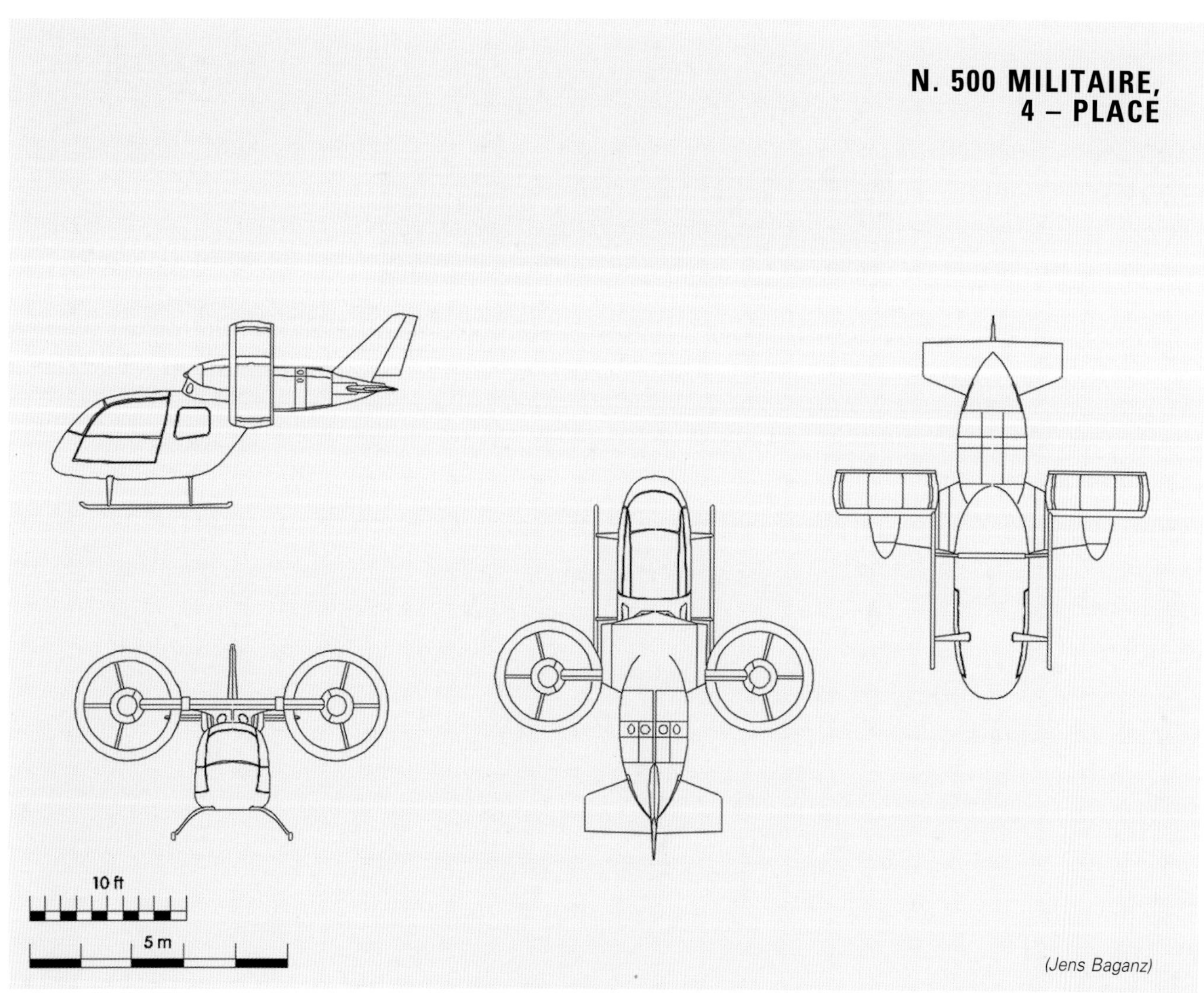

Nord 501 (fighter)

Crew	2
Empty weight	2,100kg
Takeoff weight	4,000kg
Powerplant	2 Lycoming T55-L-2B turbines, 2,100 HP each
Top speed	600kph
Length	8,000mm
Height	unknown
Wingspan	4,500mm
Service ceiling	unknown
Range	maximum flight time 1 hr 20 min.

Nord Aviation Projects

During the second half of the 1960s, the designers at Nord designed a whole row of VTOL planes with tilting-mantle propellers. The Nord 500 "Militaire" fighter or Nord 501 was built according to a contract from the French Defense Ministry in 1966-67. A model of this design was displayed at Le Bourget in 1969.

Nord made another study of a VTOL fighter plane with mantled propellers. It was named "Estocade" (Death Stab) and existed in two versions. An early variant had a turret with MG or MK and separate cockpits for the pilot and gunner. A later drawing showed a shared cockpit for both crewmen and no longer had a turret. Both designs were ca.10 meters long and 3.50 meters high, with a wingspan of ten meters as well. Further data on the "Estocade" study are not available.

The landing skids of the Nord 500 "Militaire"/Nord 501 were designed as retractable to minimize the model's air resistance.

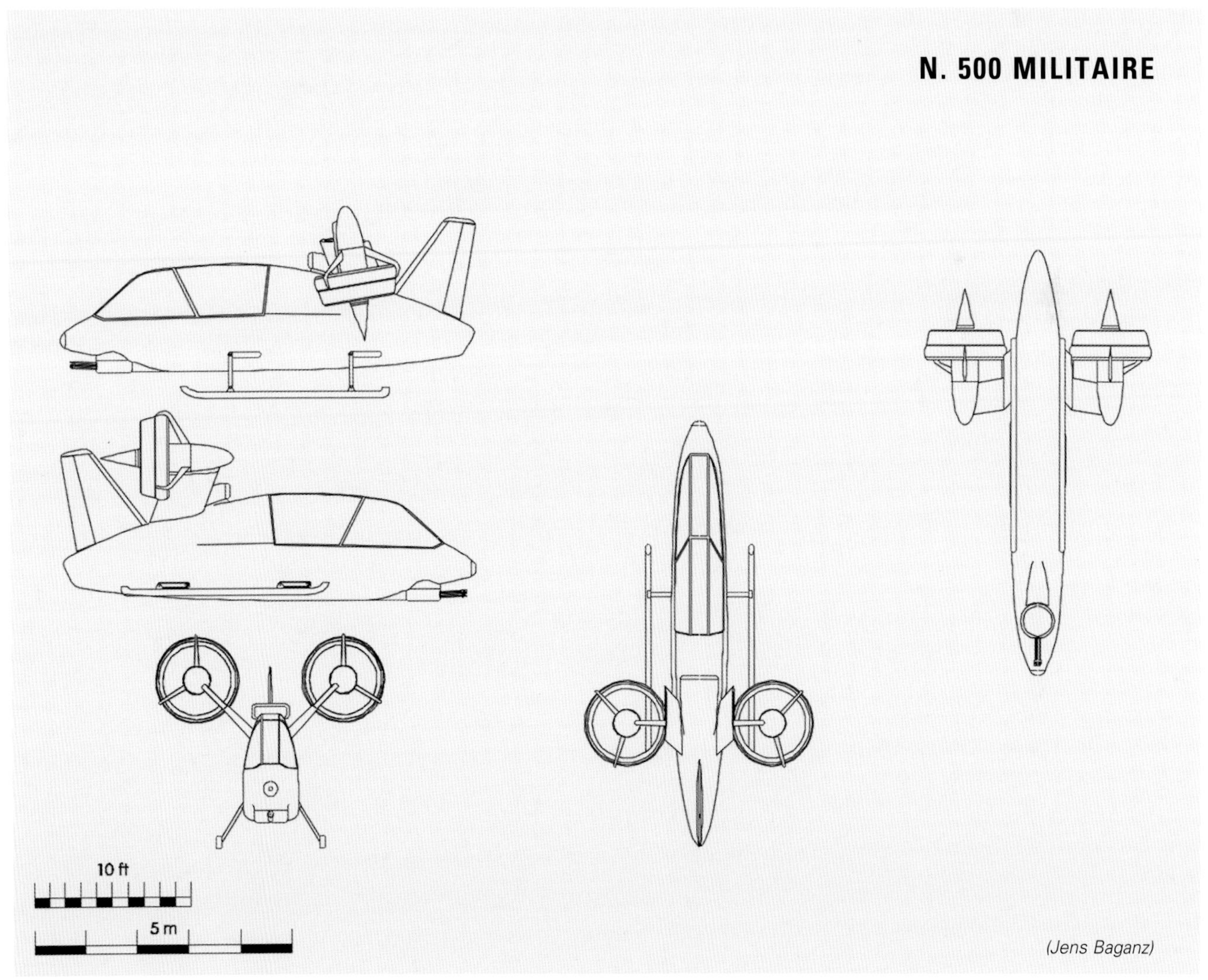

(Jens Baganz)

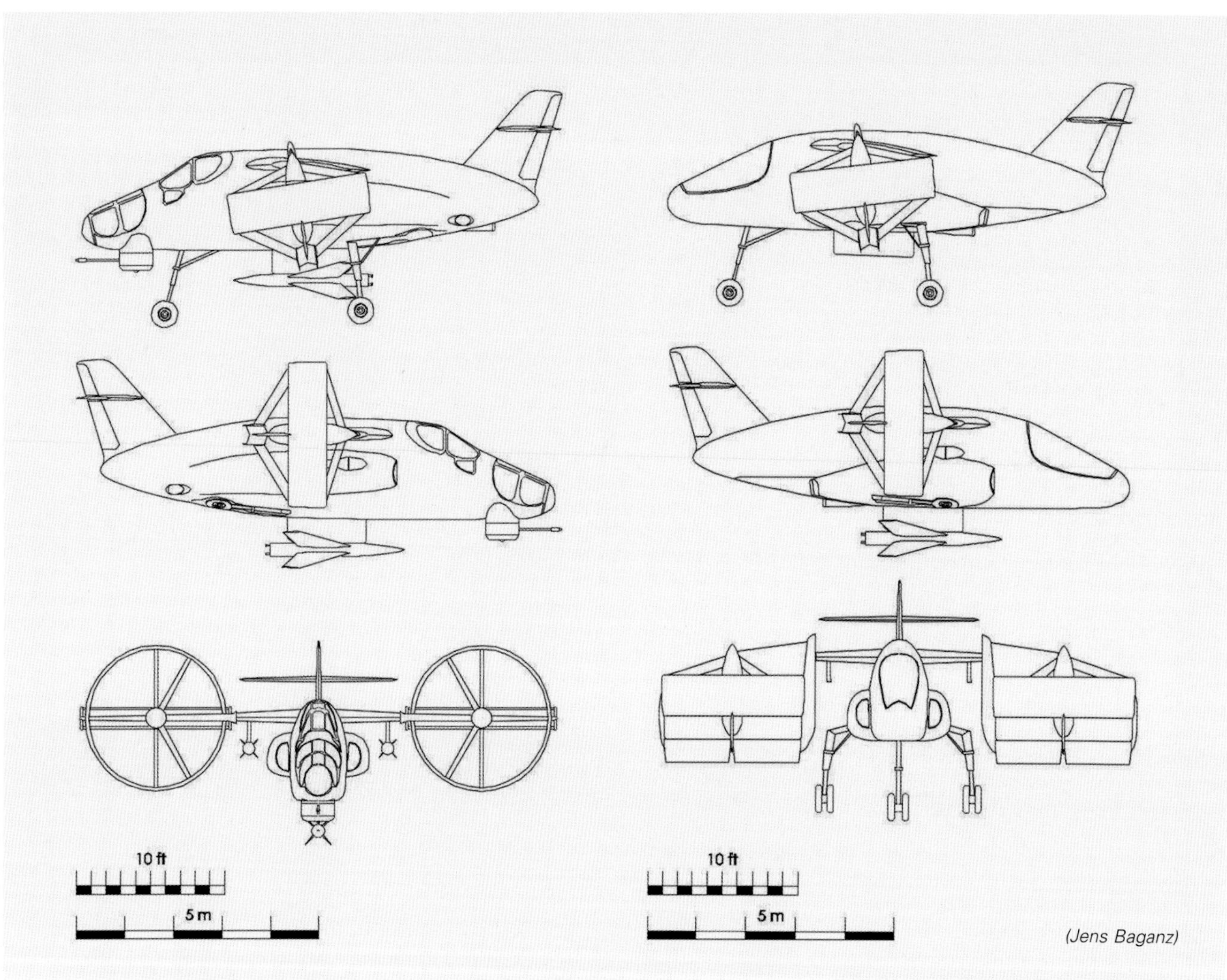

The "Estocade" study existed in two versions, the earlier one at left, the later type at right.

GREAT BRITAIN

Saunders-Roe Tipping-Wing Projects

The Saunders-Roe P.211/1 was a concept born in 1958, for a flying boat with tilting wings, which was to be used to fight submarines. The takeoff weight of the plane was calculated at around 45,400kg, the wingspan was to be some 36.6 meters. Four Rolls-Royce Tyne turbines, each producing 5,500 HP, were foreseen as its powerplant.

The P.539 concept for a test plane with partly tilting wings originated in 1967. The de Havilland Gnome turbines mounted in the fuselage over the cockpit drove two four-bladed propellers via shafts and gears. Their thrust was to be deflected by large flaps along the entire trailing edges of the wings ("deflected slipstream"), similarly to the Ryan VZ-3 and Fairchild VZ-5 STOL test machines. Along with a maximum wing tilting of about forty degrees, this was calculated by the designers to suffice to let the craft lift vertically, land and hover. But the two concepts were not followed up further.

SARO P.211/1

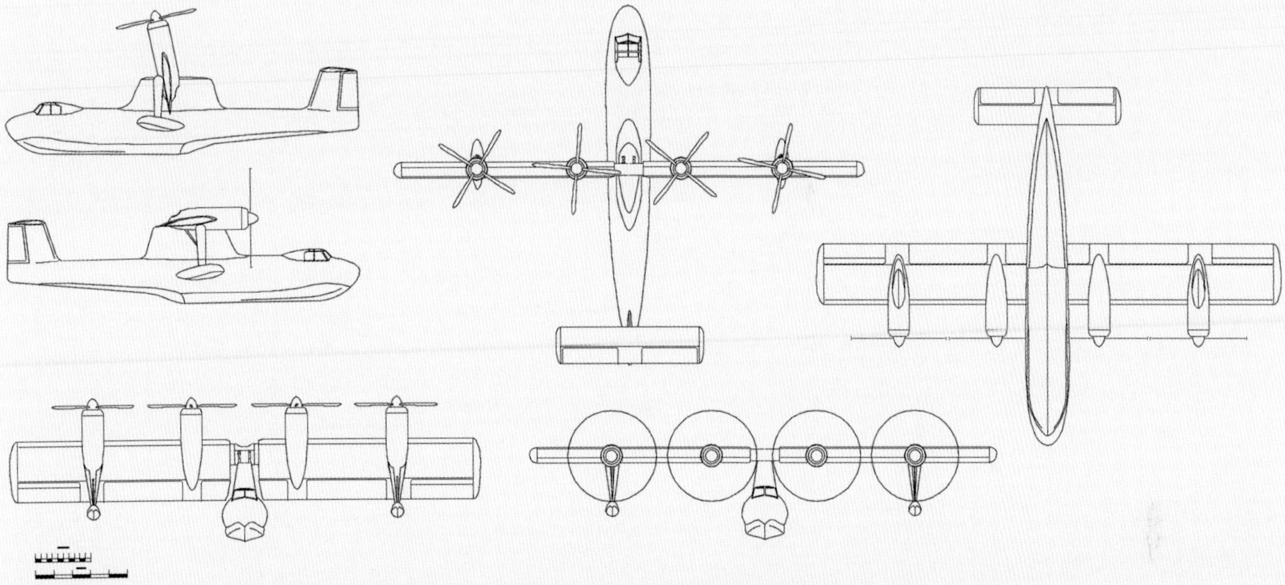

(Jens Baganz)

SARO P.539

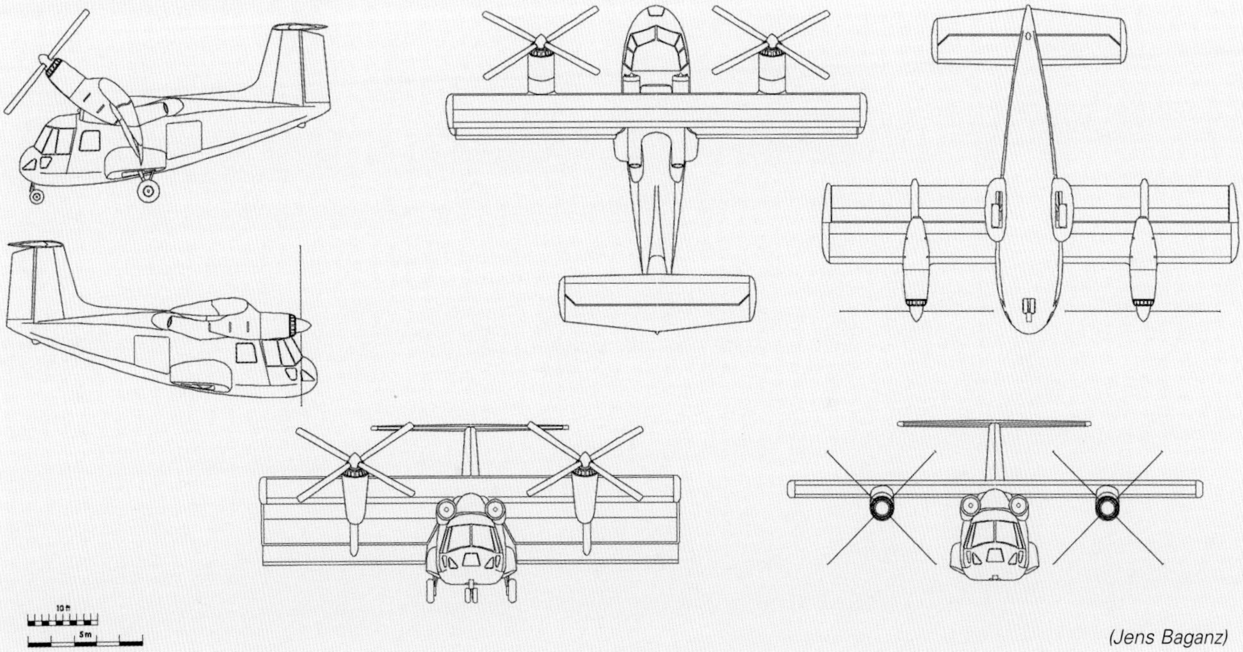

(Jens Baganz)

Westland WG21

Under contract from the Royal Air Force (RAF), Westland began in 1966 to conceive a fighter with tilting wings, the WG21. The plane's design changed much in the course of development, since the RAF requirements of a speed of 0.85 Mach (ca.1,000kph) with the originally planned layout with flat wings, a turret with an MK and four-bladed rotors could not be fulfilled.

The final design thus had slim, tapered wings, a stretched fuselage with an MK mounted rigidly in the nose, and six-bladed rotors. The takeoff weight was to be about 9,760kg, and two Lycoming LTC-4-V1 propeller turbines of 5,000 HP each were to provide the power. Westland was convinced that the WG21 would have been able to outmaneuver all the fighters of its time, but for reasons of cost, this concept too was not followed up.

The original Westland design of the WG21
with turret and untapered wings.

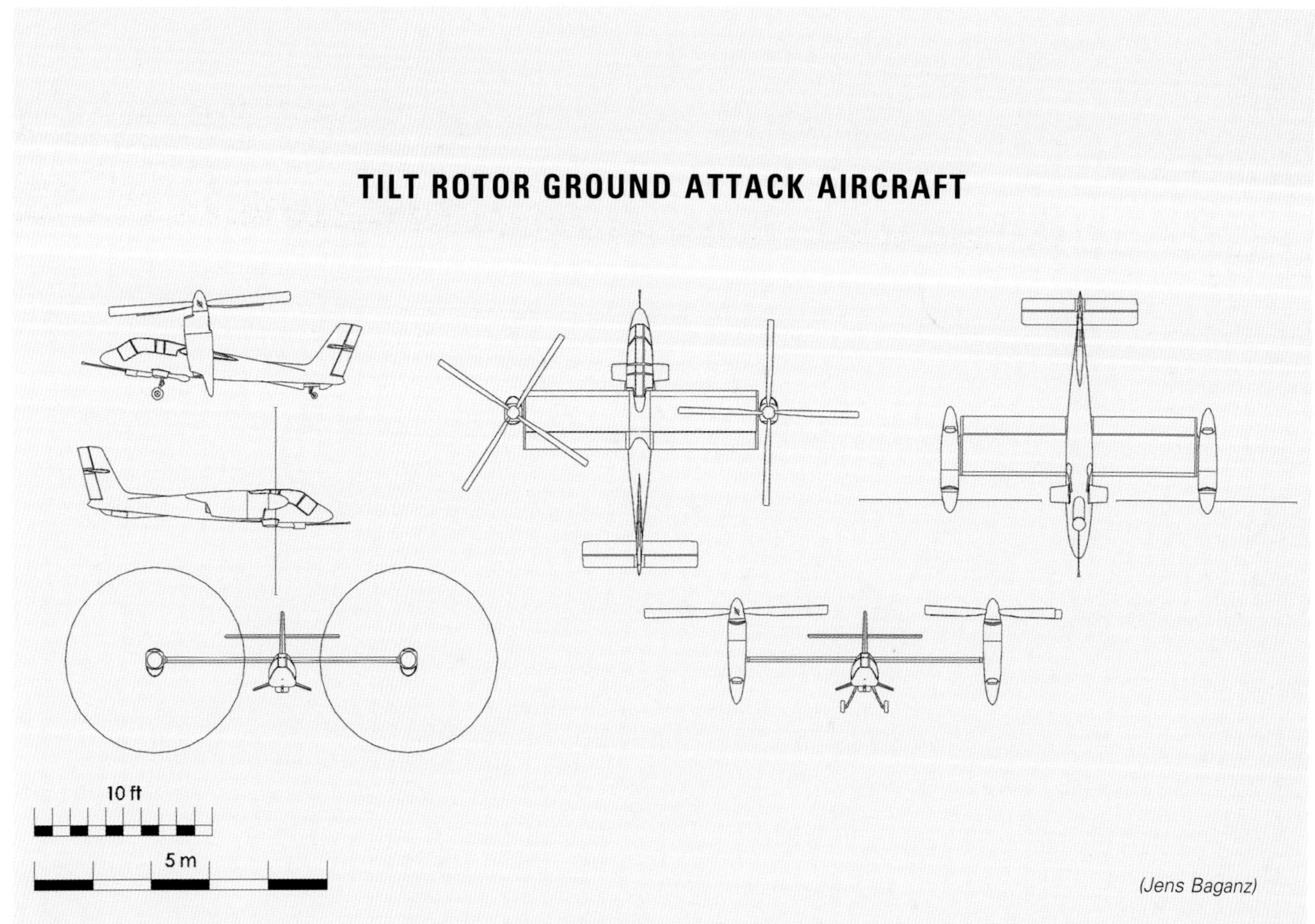

The WG21 was an ambitious fighter
study from the late-1960s.
(AgustaWestland via HMB)

Westland O.R. 358

In the course of governmentally desired restructuring of the British aircraft industry, Fairey Aviation became a part of Westland in 1960. Fairey's former chief designer for helicopters, O.L.L. Fitzwilliams, designed a tiltrotor airplane in 1962 as an answer to the Navy's O.R. 358 description. This craft was to be used as a patrol, submarine hunter and transporter, and be able to attain 840kph at 7,620 meters of altitude. The fuselage length and wingspan (without tilting engine nacelles) were each to be about 15.5 meters long, the height about 5.1 meters. The design showed some interesting design features, such as rotors with variable blade length. In cruising flight the rotor diameter was 13.71 meters, for hover-hold this was raised to 19.81 meters by extending the blades to achieve less circular area pressure. In addition, the wings were foldable so that the plane could be housed on aircraft carriers. Despite these innovations, a prototype was never built.

The O.R. 358 was the concept of a patrol plane and transport for the Royal Navy.

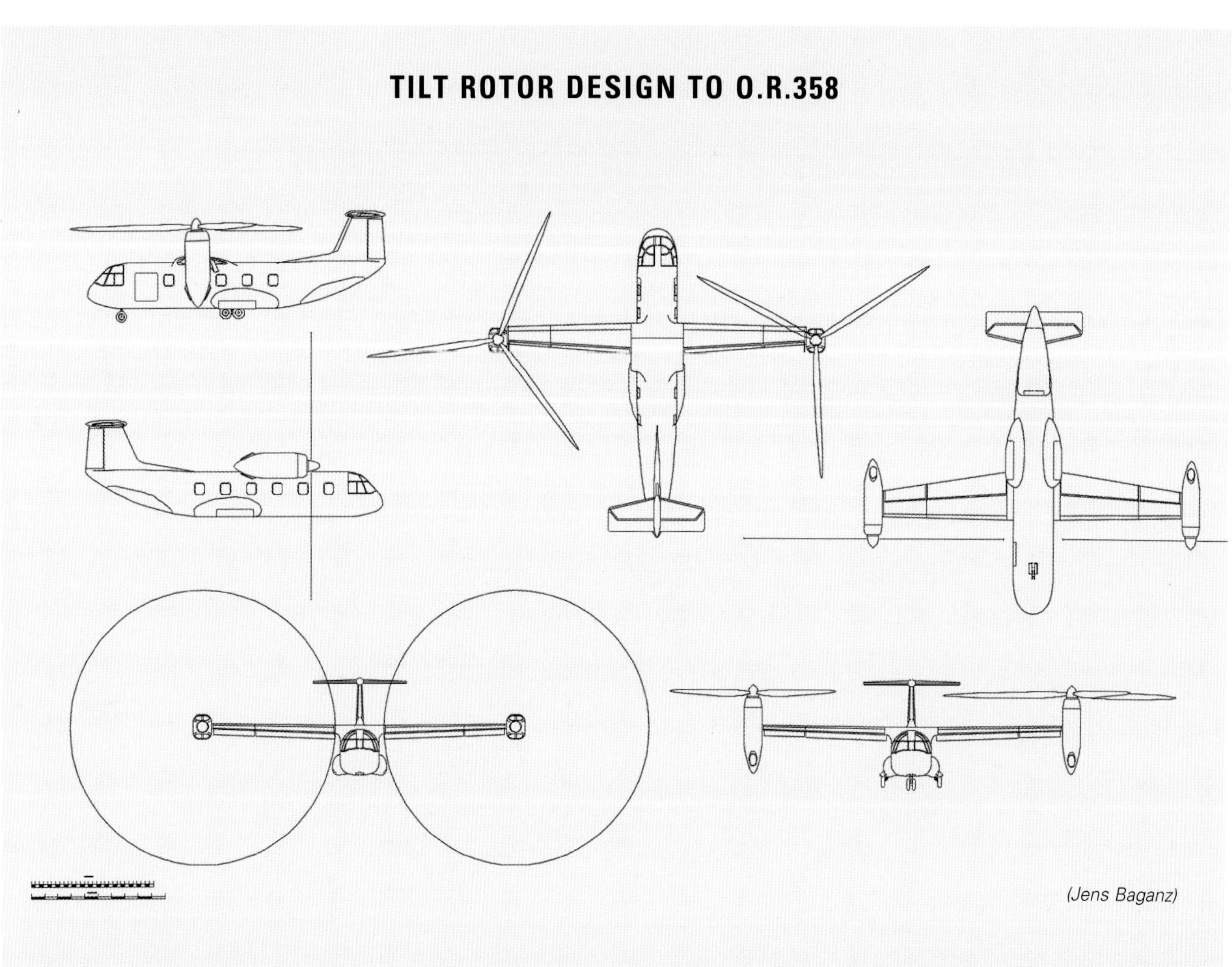

Aerfer Tilting-Propeller Project

As an answer to the NBMR4 (NATO Basic Military Requirements 4) request for a VTOL transport plane in the class of the C-130 "Hercules," published in 1961, the aircraft builder Aerfer, belonging to the Finmeccanica firm, designed a tiltrotor aircraft. It was supposed to have a lowering rear loading ramp and two pairs of very narrow tandem wings, with a four-bladed tilting propeller mounted at the end of each. Four turbine engines of an unknown type were installed in the upper fuselage and drove the airscrews via shafts. Further information was not available.

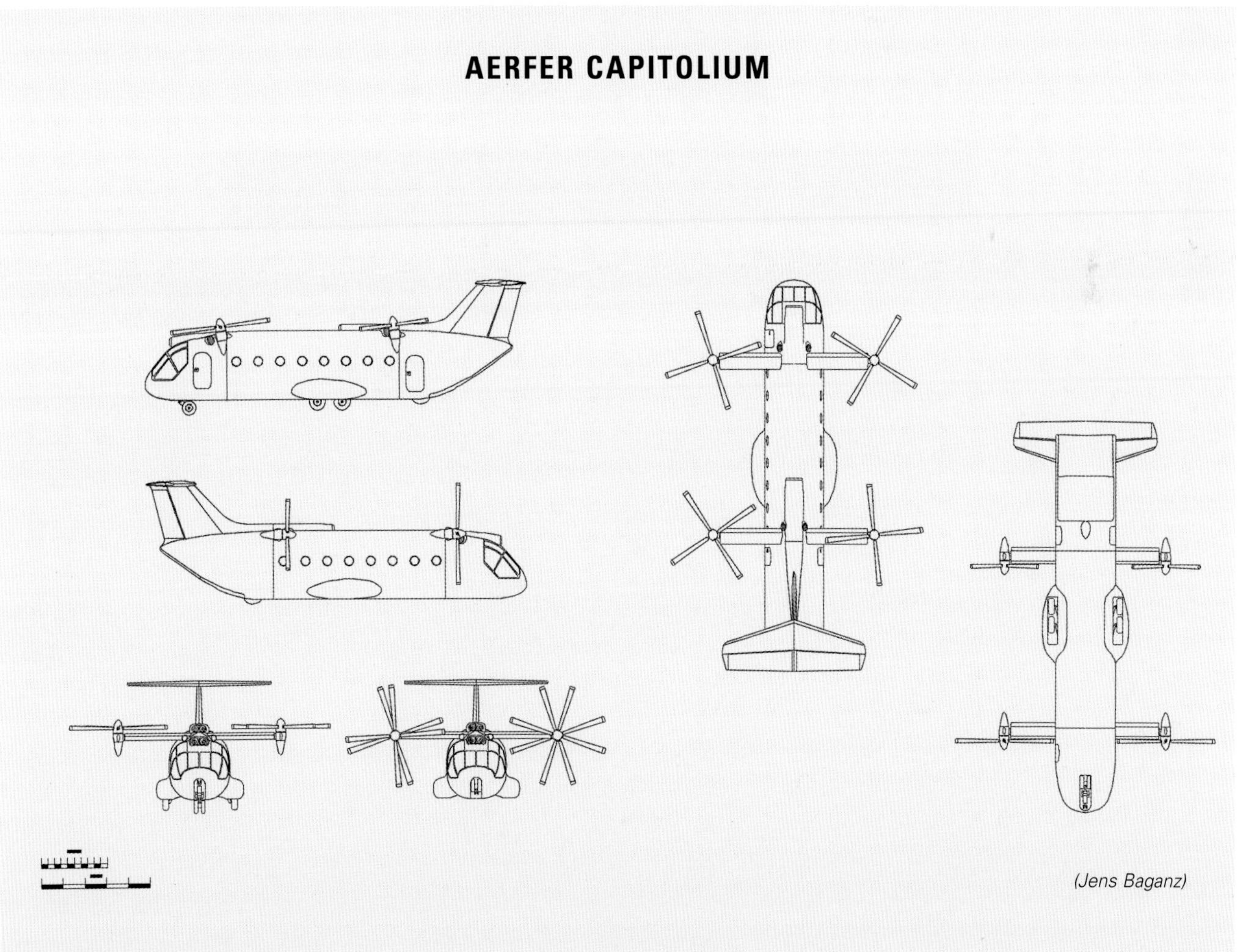

(Jens Baganz)

Agusta A 119

Also as an answer to the NBMR4 challenge, Agusta designed an unusual transporter with tilting puller and pusher propellers. The propellers were mounted on the front and back of the double rudder carriers, with the forward pair tilting upward and the rear pair downward. The four powerplants were obviously to be mounted in pairs in the front part of the rudder carriers.

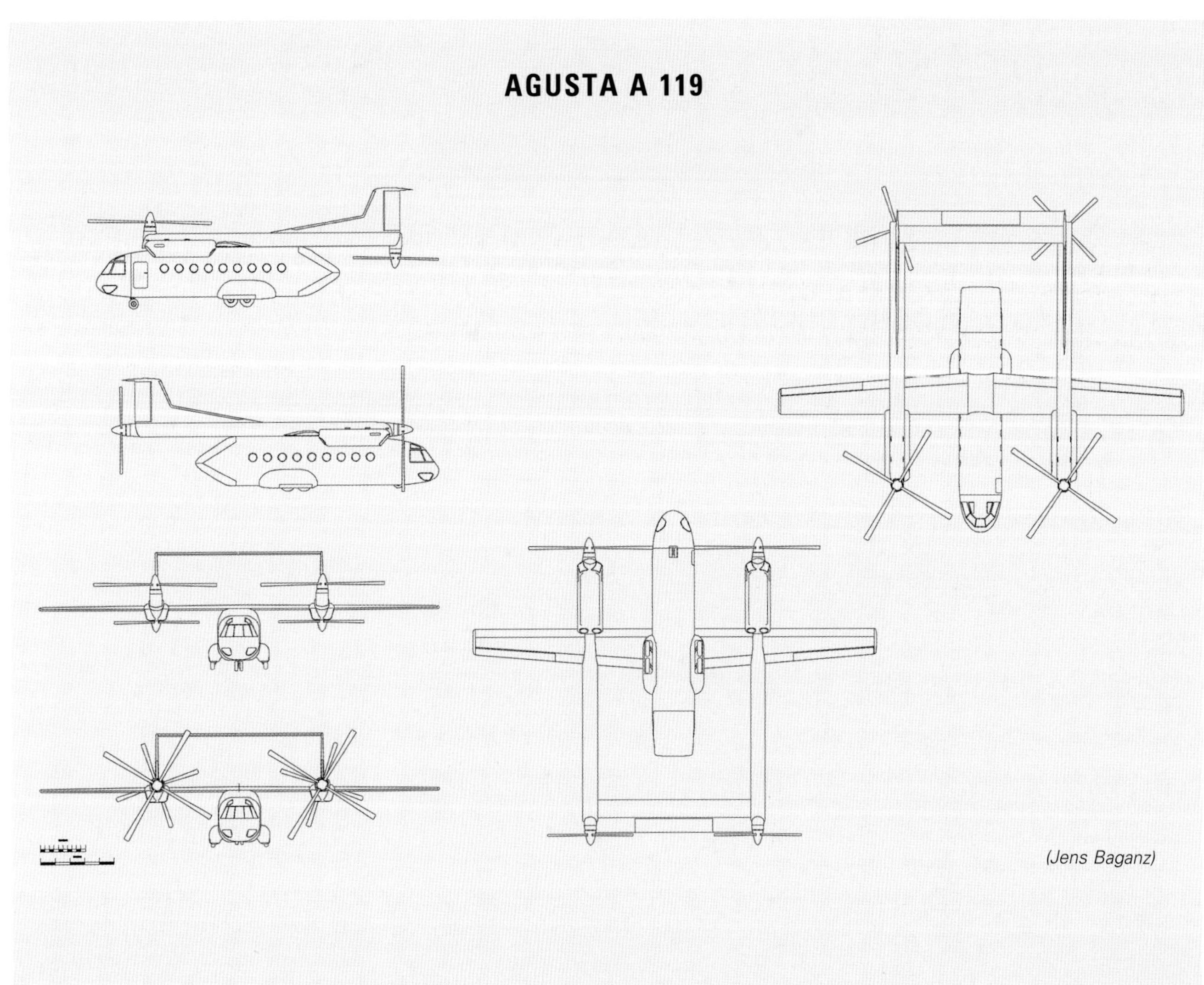

(Jens Baganz)

CANADA

Canadair CL-84 "Dynavert"

Canadair, located in Montreal and founded by the Canadian government in 1944, became a branch of the U.S. firm of General Dynamics in the 1950s. Canadair had already, since the start of the 1950s, been involved with VTOL concepts and designed a whole series of tiltwing planes, such as the CL-43 in 1953 and the twin-engine CL-73 and CL-74, to mention only a few of the projects that came from its drawing boards.

When NATO published a challenge (NBMR4 = NATO Basic Military Requirements 4) for a VTOL transport plane in 1961, Canadair answered with the CL-62, a tiltwing plane with an empty weight of some twenty-four tons, but it was never built.

After Canadair had spent more than ten years on research and developmental work, the Canadian Ministry of Defense granted the firm a contract in 1963 to build a larger version of the CL-73. This new tiltwing plane was designated CL-84 and had a conventional fuselage 12.81 meters long, tapering sharply to the rear. At the back a ramp was installed to give direct access to the cargo space.

Three-side view of the CL-84 from a Canadair sales brochure. *(Canadair via HMB)*

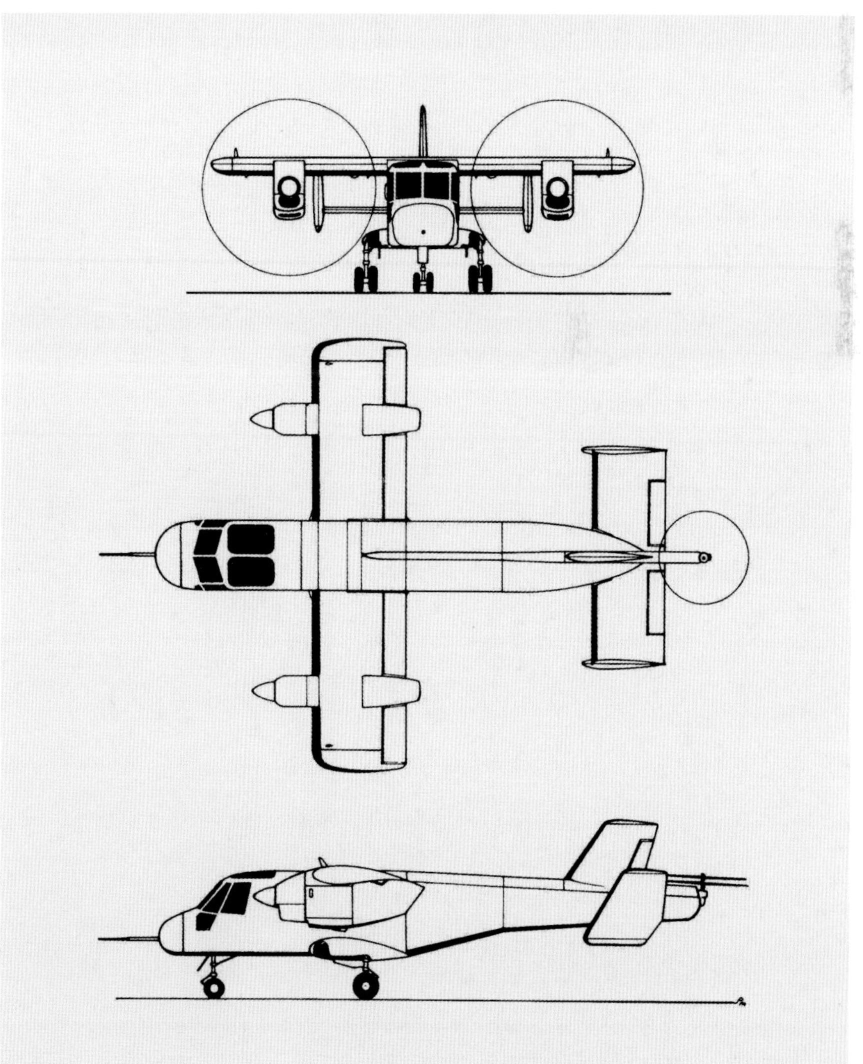

In the cockpit at the front, two pilots had seats side by side and could steer the plane conventionally by means of steering knobs, rudder pedals and gas levers. The only unusual feature was the lever for tilting the wings. An automatic stabilizing system brought all the steering commands together and coordinated them automatically according to the flight situation. In hover-hold an opposed double tail propeller took over the controls on the transverse axis, while steering on the longitudinal axis was done by modifying the propeller setting, and that on the vertical axis by differential activation of the transverse rudder. In horizontal flight the tail propeller was blocked and conventional rudders took over the steering.

The rectangular wings of the CL-84 had a very large profile depth and were attached to the top of the fuselage. Their wingspan measured 10.16 meters. On 45% of the profile they were attached so that they could be tilted 100 degrees. This allowed the CL-84 to hover even in a 55kph tailwind or fly backward at 55kph in no wind. The tilting process itself took ten seconds. Krüger flaps on the leading edge of the wings and large landing flaps on the trailing edge were automatically linked with the tilting movement of the wings so that optimal lift was always created and the plane could not suffer any slipstream shear, even during the transition. The power source consisted of two Lycoming T53 propeller turbines, each of 1,400 HP, which drove the opposed four-bladed propellers, 4.27 meters in diameter. The airscrews were located so that practically the entire wing was constantly in the propeller slipstream. The engines were connected with the tail propeller by gears and shafts and laid out so that if one turbine failed (or was turned off), all three airscrews would be supplied with power.

The long-legged tripod running gear was designed so that it could handle rough landings. The front wheel was retracted into a shaft on the fuselage, while the two main pairs of wheels lay partly covered in side housings. The steering consisted of a wide elevator with end fins and a rudder in the middle. On short takeoffs the elevators were tilted forty-five degrees along with the wings.

Drawing of the CL-84, also from a Canadair sales brochure. *(Canadair via HMB)*

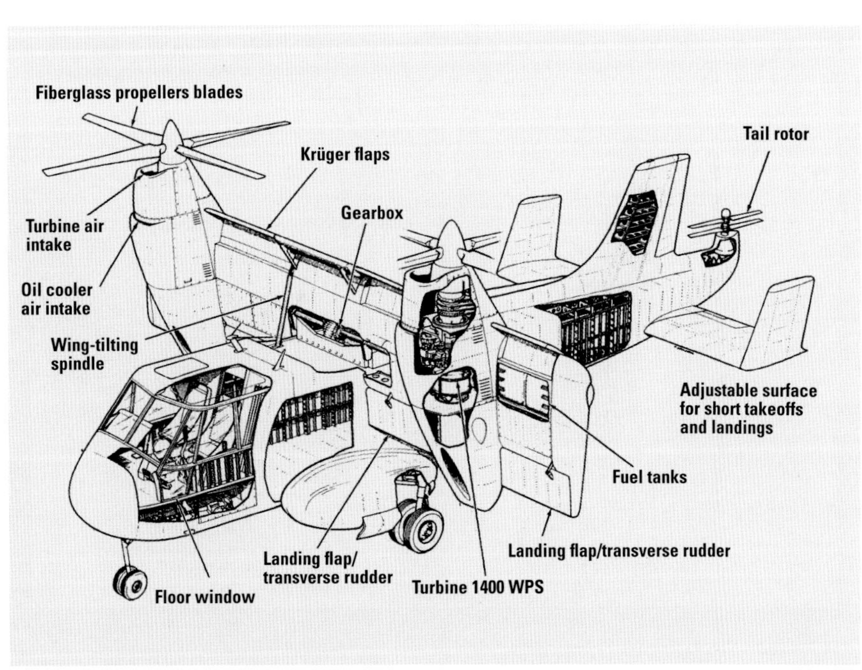

Canadair works photos of the CL-84 in different flight phases. *(Canadair via HMB)*

The empty weight of the CL-84 was 3,405kg. In VTOL mode it was able to carry a payload of 681kg. This value increased to 1,634kg in short takeoffs with wings tipped forty-five degrees. To get over a fifteen-meter barrier the plane required a takeoff run of some 150 meters.

The CL-84 was finished in December 1963 and subjected to ground and rolling tests until the end of April 1964. The first hover-hold of the CL-84, registered CF-VTO-X, took place on May 7, 1965, and a good seven months later the plane made its first short takeoff, plus its first full transition on January 17, 1966. By September 1967 the CL-84 had been flown by sixteen civilian and military pilots, including members of the American and British forces. The CL-84 accrued a total operating time of 405 hours and a pure flight time of 145 hours. It carried out simulated rescue missions with and without a winch and transported various loads, including those suspended under it.

Above | CL-84 in hovering flight.
(Canadair via HMB)

Left | During its testing, the CL-84 also carried out simulated rescues.
(Canadair via HMB)

The plane proved to be very maneuverable and without basic defects. It was so stable that the pilots could even take their hands off the steering knob in hovering flight. When CF-VTO-X was on its 306th flight on September 12, 1967, though, there was an accident. The plane was flying at 277kph at a height of some 975 meters when it suddenly became uncontrollable and crashed. Luckily both crewmen were able to save themselves by using the ejection seats. A later investigation showed that a bearing in the propeller steering system had most likely failed and thus caused the crash.

The CF-VTO-X had already completed its flight tests without problems at that point, so the program was evaluated as a success by Canadair and the Defense Ministry. Thus the Ministry ordered three more, slightly modified planes (designated CL-84-1) in February 1968; they were to be given military suitability tests. These three planes were called CX-84 by the Canadian Air Force and bore tail numbers CX8401, 8402 and 8403.

The first CL-84-1 made its maiden flight on February 19, 1970, and essentially corresponded with the CF-VTO-V prototype, but had a fuselage that was 1.6 meters longer, 7% stronger engines, additional electronics, improvements to various individual parts, double steering controls in the cockpit, an increased internal fuel capacity, and the ability to attach external loads.

The CL-84 made 305 flights without problems before crashing on its 306th flight, on September 12, 1967.

CAF
FORCES ARMÉES CANADIENNES
402
401

In VTOL action the CL-84-1 was able to carry 725kg of fuel and a payload of 1,136kg. A headwind of 65kph allowed the payload in a vertical takeoff to be increased to 2,272kg, since the wings only had to be tipped forty-five degrees then.

Shortly after the evaluation of the CX8401 by the Canadian forces had begun, the model also drew the interest of the U.S. forces. So the CL-84-1 demonstrated its capabilities impressively in February 1972 when it landed on a small platform outside the Pentagon and took off again. In addition, the plane showed its potential at Edwards Air Force Base and the Marine bases at Norfolk and Patuxent River. Finally a group of VTOL and STOL actions were flown from on board the helicopter carrier USS Guam. CX8401 finished these tests without an error and showed that it was useful not only for transport tasks but also for (simulated) submarine hunting and radar surveillance.

Between 1972 and 1974, CX8401 and 8402 were tested intensively by pilots of the U.S. Air Force and Navy, as well as Canadian and British forces. It showed that it was suitable for a long list of uses, such as a light transport for up to twelve soldiers or a corresponding amount of freight, a search-and-rescue aircraft, a reconnaissance and communications plane, or a civilian short-flight craft. It was also found to be capable of armed actions such as close air support, protection of its own helicopters or fighting enemy ones, as well as submarine fighting.

During this testing by pilots from three countries, there was an accident on August 8, 1973, when the gears of the left propeller of CX8401 failed. Again the two pilots were able to save themselves with the ejection seats, but the plane was lost. Testing in the USA was then continued with CX8402, which suffered an engine failure during the program, but thanks to the connection between the two engines by a cross shaft, it was able to land without problems.

In June 1974, the testing was finished without CX8403 ever having been flown. The two CL-84-1 planes that were flown had made over 700 flights with forty civilian and military pilots from three countries by that time. Although Canadair tried to interest not only the USA, but also various West European countries, including the Federal Republic of Germany, in the CL-84-1, there were no series contracts. Thus the whole program was ended for financial reasons. The two existing CL-84-1 planes are now in museums. The restored CX8402 is in the Canada Aviation Museum in Ottawa, while the fuselage of the never-flown CX8403 spends a rather sad life in the Western Canada Aviation Museum on Winnipeg.

The restored Canadair CL-84-1 CX8402 is now at the Canadian Aviation Museum.
(Adam Hunt, PD)

Canadair CL-84-1

Crew	2
Empty weight	3,827kg
Takeoff weight	5,715kg (VTOL),
	6,576kg (STOL)
Length	14,410mm
Height	4,340mm
Wingspan	10,160mm
Powerplant	2 Lycoming T53-LTC1K-4C
	propeller turbines,
	1,500 HP each
Top speed	518kph
Maximum altitude	unknown
Range	520km (VTOL with max. payload),
	547km (STOL with max. payload

Officially the CL-84 bore the exotic name of "Dynavert." This name was based on Canadair's being at that time a branch of General Dynamics, and the firm's marketing department that all products, if possible, should have names beginning with "Dyna." The second part of the name, "Vert," indicated "vertical." Within Canadair, though, the name "Dynavert" was never used, but rather regarded with scorn.

Canadair designed various variants on the basis of the CL-84, but they never left the drawing board. The CL-84-1C was practically unchanged but was to be fitted with 1,825 HP Lycoming T53 LTC1S-2 turbines to allow a higher takeoff speed. The CH-84-1D was a special version for close-range air support. It had a tandem cockpit in the style of a combat helicopter and was equipped with a 7.62mm minigun in a bow turret. Rocket launchers and other weapons could be carried on stump wings. The CH-84A, a further-developed CH-84-1D, was Canadair's contribution to the U.S. Army's AAFSS competition. The CH-84E was a VTOL reconnaissance and observation plane and was also offered in vain to the U.S. Army. Finally, the CL-84-8 was a special variant for submarine fighting which was developed at the beginning of the 1970s. The U.S. Navy's "Sea Control Ships" (SCS) was considered as the place of action for the CL-84-8. This low-cost little carrier was to use VTOL or STOL airplanes. It was planned to equip the CL-84-8 with considerably stronger engines (GE T64, each with some 3,000 HP) to allow a greater load and range. After the U.S. Navy discarded the idea of the SCS, the CL-84-8 project was also dropped.

In all, one can call the CL-84 the most successful airplane of its time that, mainly for financial and political reasons, never received a contract for series production.

Bratuchin Tipping-Wing Transport

In 1955 and 1956 a study of a transport plane with tipping wings was carried out at the Central Aerohydrodynamic Institute (ZAGI) in Moscow. The leader of the team was Ivan Bratuchin, one of the USSR's helicopter pioneers. Bratuchin's design had a typical fuselage for a transport plane, with a lowering loading ramp at the rear, plus conventional control surfaces. The intended powerplants were two Kusnetzov NK-12 turbines, each of 12,000 HP, which were also used in the Tupolev Tu-95 and Antonov An-22. The wings could tip ninety degrees and were mounted high on the fuselage. Bratuchin calculated a takeoff weight of some thirty tons for his plane with a five-ton payload, a top speed of 700kph, and a range of some 1,250km. Further data on this project are not known.

Ivan Bratuchin designed this tipping-wing plane in 1955-56. *(Vincent Bourguignon)*

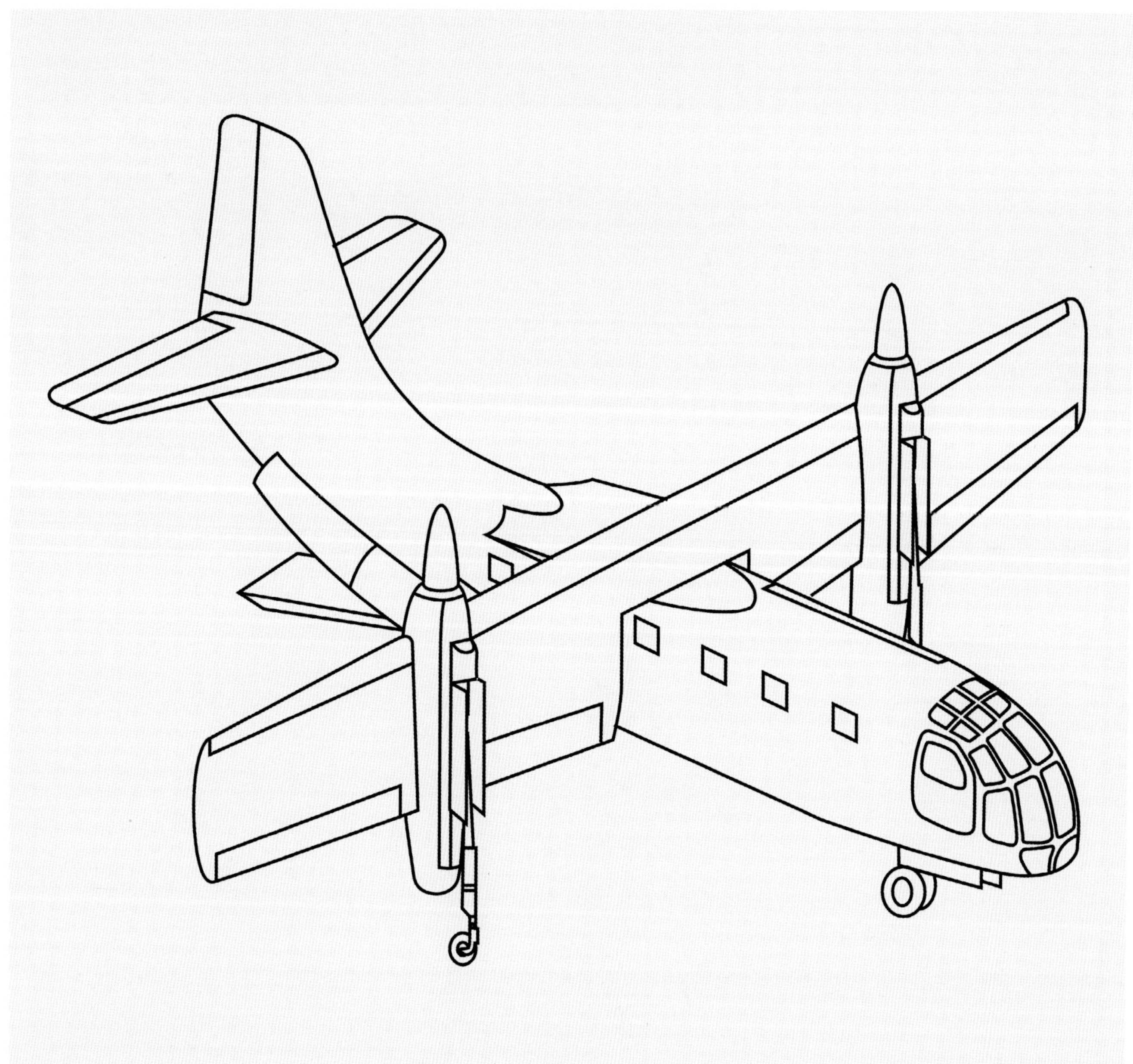

Be-32	
Crew	2
Empty weight	unknown
Flying weight	31,000kg
Powerplant	4 propeller turbines,
	4,250 HP each
Top speed	640kph
Length	19,300mm
Height	7,500mm
Wingspan	12,000mm (without rotors)
Service ceiling	unknown
Range	max. 2,100km
Range with max. 5-ton payload	650km

Beriev Be-32

Between 1965 and 1970 the Beriev design bureau studied, under project name Be-32 (not to be confused with the conventional turboprop airplane of later date), various concepts for a VTOL transport plane. Besides various designs with jet propulsion, a tilting-propeller plane was also suggested in 1965. This design had a pair of high-mounted tandem wings, with a pair of coaxial contra-rotating four-bladed propellers at their outer ends. The fuselage had a lowering rear ramp. Four propeller turbines mounted at the forward wing tips and the sides of the side fins supplied the power.

Three-side view of the Beriev Be-32.
(Vincent Bourguignon)

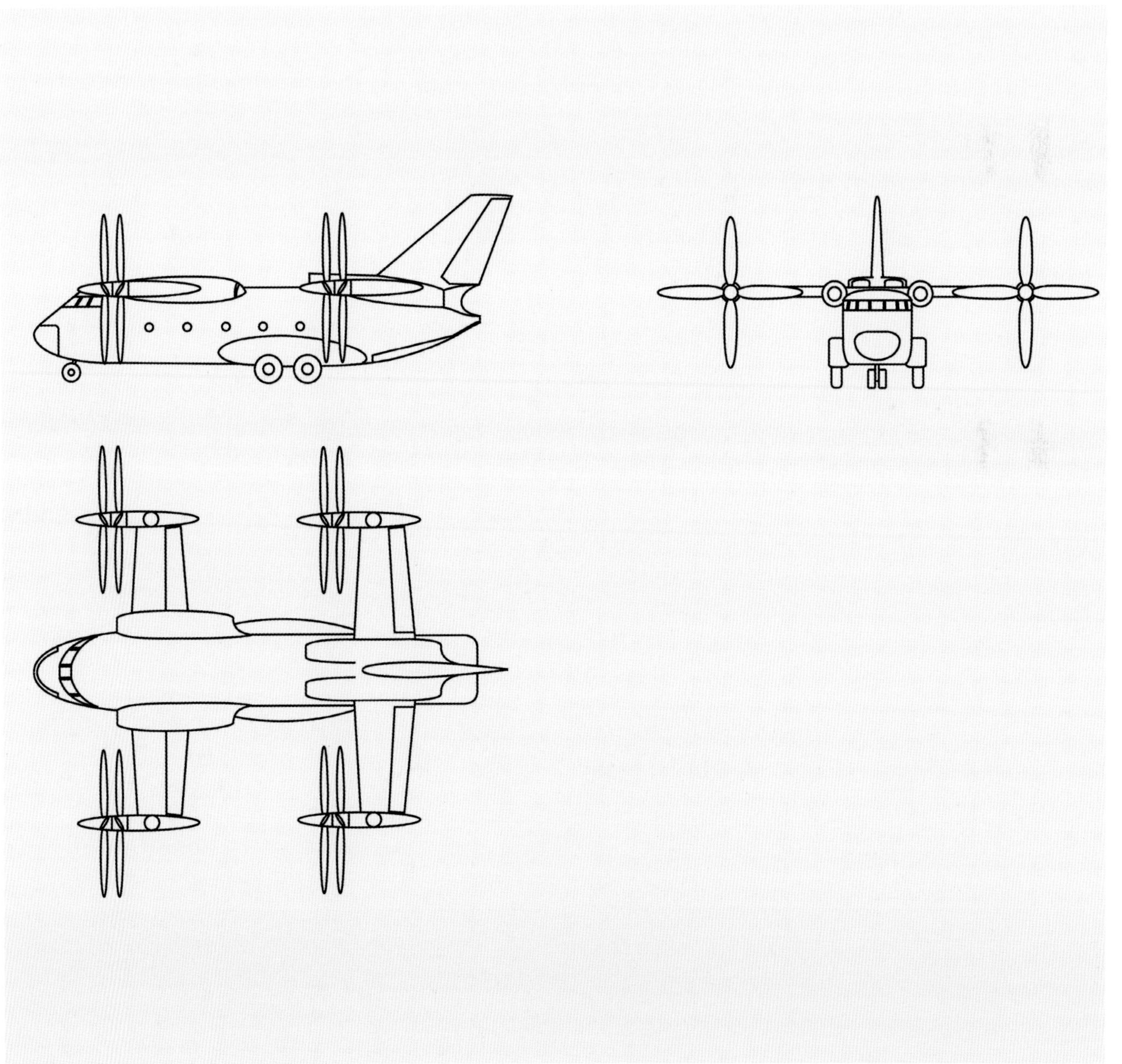

Myasischev M-12

In competition with Beriev, the Myasischev design bureau also worked on the design of a VTOL transport, designated Project M-12, between 1965 and 1970. Myasischev suggested several variants, most of them with jet engines. One version of the M-12, though, was to have two large tiltrotors, with their powerplants mounted in tilting nacelles on the wings. Unfortunately, no further data on this design or on an M-80 tiltwing project of the mid-1990s is available.

Three-side view of the Myasischev M-12.
(Vincent Bourguignon)

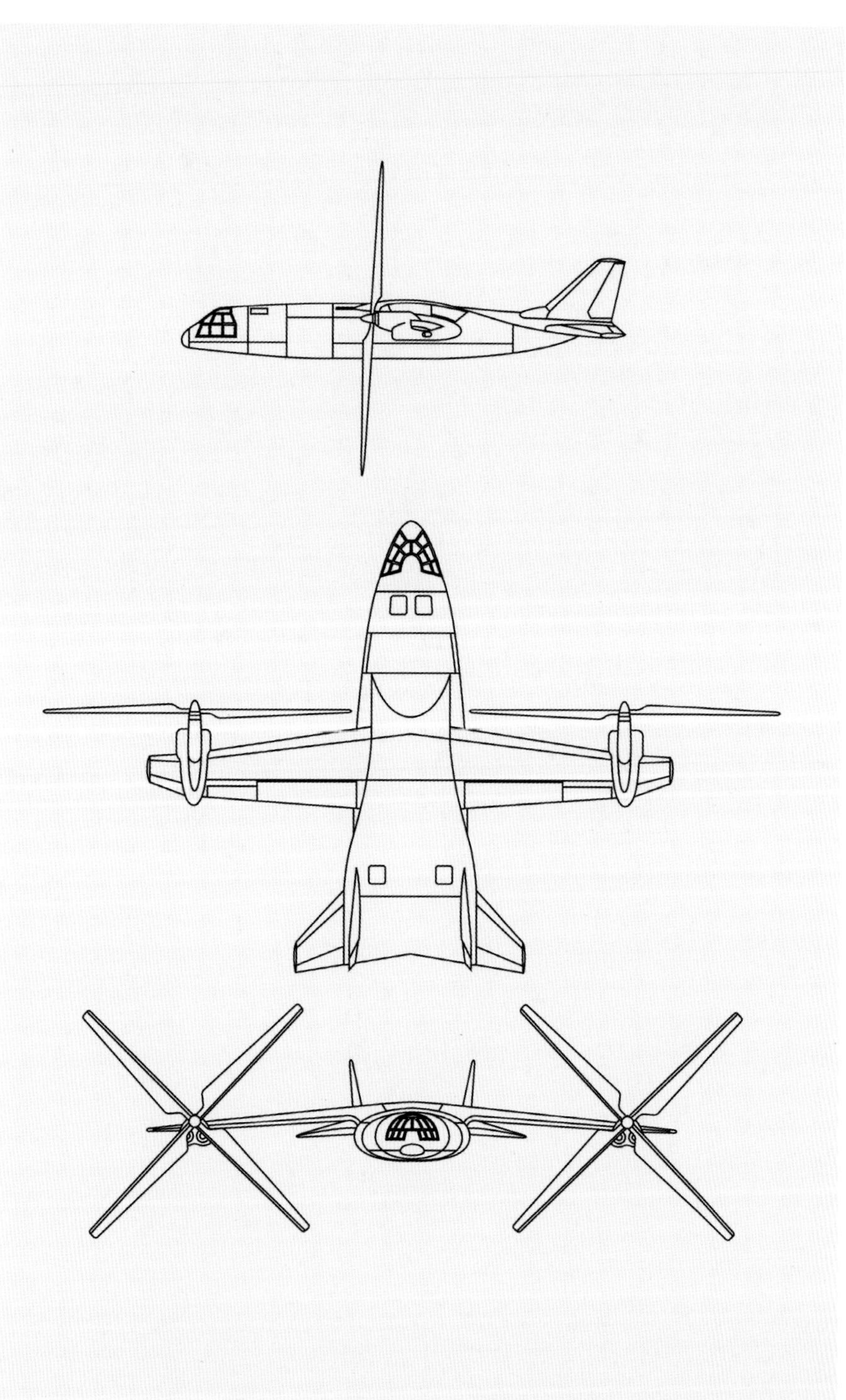

Mil Mi 30 "Vintoplan"

Mil, the largest helicopter producer of the former Soviet Union, began as of 1977 to design a tiltrotor airplane without government support. It was to carry a payload of two tons or nineteen passengers and be the successor to the Mi-8. The intended power sources were two Klimov TW3-117 turbines, each of 2,000 HP, which operated four-bladed tiltrotors of eleven-meter diameter. The takeoff weight was to be some 10,600kg, the top speed 500 to 600kph, and the range ca.800km. Work on this plane, called "Vintoplan" by Mil, at first progressed only slowly; this changed only when the Soviet government officially encouraged the design of a tiltrotor airplane for civilian and military use in the summer of 1981. The Russian literature indicates that the Red Army's action in Afghanistan since the end of 1979 encouraged promotion of an aircraft that had a higher speed, range and maximum altitude than the available helicopters. Because of the differing civilian and military requirements, Mil reworked its original design several times during the 1980s. The appearance, dimensions, takeoff weight, loads and engines changed at various times. The Mil engineers even considered a plane with a thirty-ton takeoff weight at that time. At the beginning of 1991 three different variations were finally settled on, the Mi-30S, Mi-30D and the smallest type, the Mi-30L.

Three-side view of the Mi-30S.
(Vincent Bourguignon)

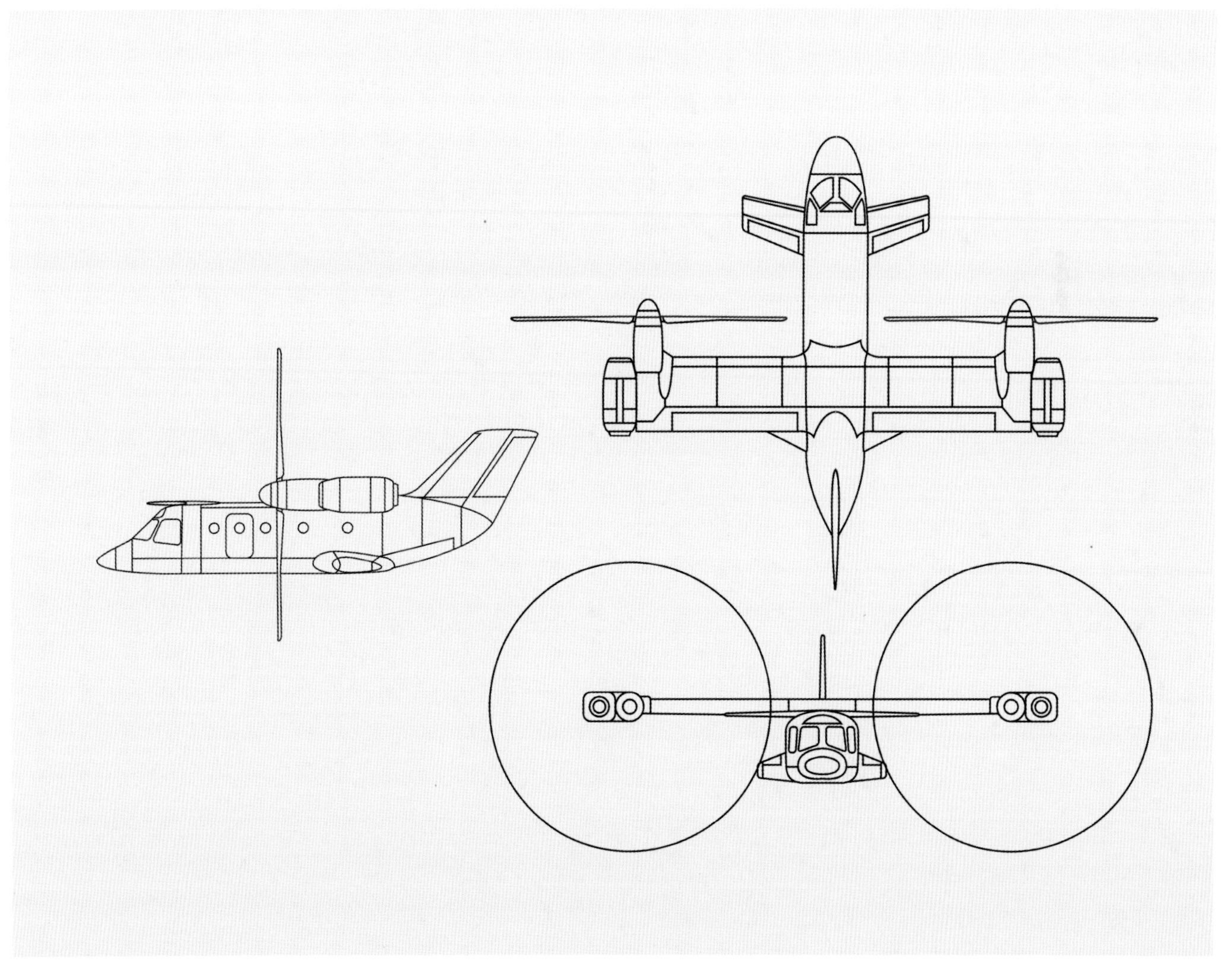

The Mi-30S was to carry a payload of 3.2 tons or twenty passengers and be fitted with two Klimov TW3-117 engines, each of 2,000 HP, in tilting nacelles at the ends of the wings. But information has already turned up saying that TW7-117 turbines with a power of 2,800 HP each were planned for. The Mi-30S had no conventional elevators, but was designed in canard form, with the elevators located in front of the actual wings. The conventional-looking fuselage had small coverings on the sides for the main landing gear, plus a rear-loading ramp. The takeoff weight was to be thirteen tons.

The Mil-30D was a slightly smaller version of Type S and, like it, had TW3-117 (or TW7-117) turbines and canard wings. It was to carry 2.5 tons of freight or eleven persons. It seems, though, that no rear-loading ramp had been planned for the Mi-30D, and its elevators were located at the nose.

The Mi-30L had conventional end-tab stabilizers and was considerably smaller and lighter. Its takeoff weight was to be only some 3.75 tons, and its payload about 950kg of freight or seven passengers. Two Lyulka AL-34 turbines of unknown power on or in the sides of the upper fuselage were foreseen as its powerplants. In the Mi-30L too, the main landing gear retracted into coverings on the sides.

Besides these three transport versions, military variations were also to be considered, but more precise data and pictures are not available.

The three versions of the Mi-30 were included in the USSR's "13th Five-Year Plan" beginning in 1991. According to this, a first prototype was to be tested in 1996. Although extensive studies and wind-tunnel tests were made, only a small remote-control model was built, with which the flight qualities of the design were tested. The end of the Soviet Union at the end of 1991 also meant the end of the Mi-30 program. As far as is known, Mil has not made any more attempts to continue the development of this project.

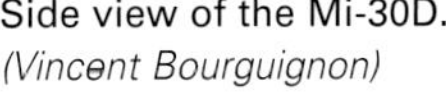

Side view of the Mi-30D.
(Vincent Bourguignon)

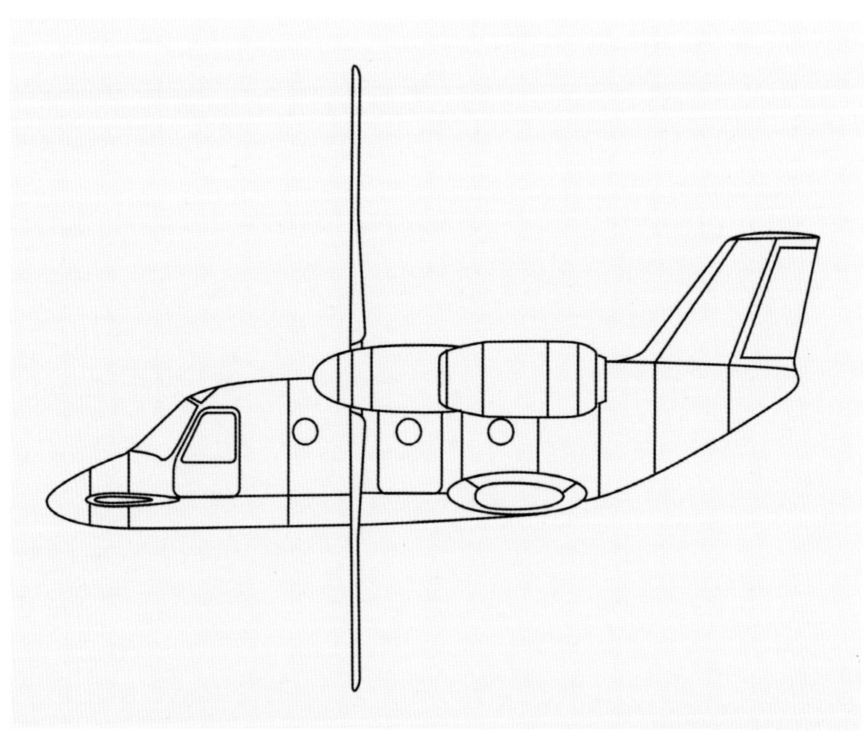

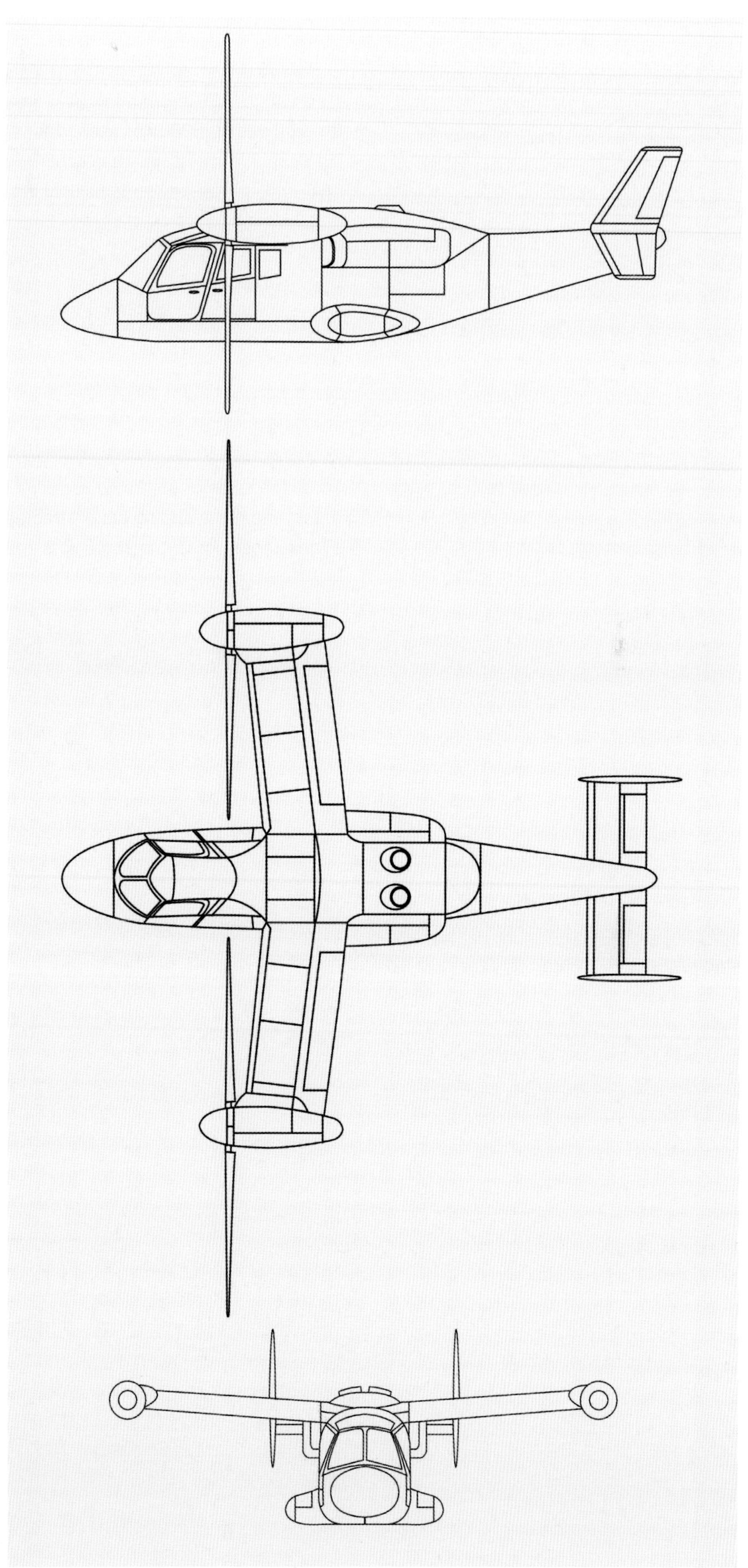

Three-side view of the Mi-30L.
(Vincent Bourgignon)

CIVILIAN PROJECTS AND PROTOTYPES SINCE 1945

Chapter 6

In 1929, George Lehberger was already writing in his patent application for a tiltrotor airplane (see Chapter 2) that the gain in time that air travel brings was being negated by building airports far outside cities. Therefore he suggested that vertically taking-off and landing airplanes be used, which could land on small airports in city centers or even on the roofs of large buildings. In eight decades this idea had lost none of its timeliness. Today in many cases, the drive to the airport takes longer than the flight itself. In view of the overused main airports of today as well, Lehberger's idea cannot be rejected offhand.

Business travelers who could fly by air directly from firm to firm, from appointment to appointment, would certainly know how to cherish this kind of travel – and would save much time, and therefore money, in this way. Surely helicopters have been used for these tasks for decades, but their limited speeds and ranges allow their use only for short runs. The use of vertically taking-off airplanes in search-and-rescue missions and by the police would be even more practical. Their speeds, considerably higher than those of helicopters, could save lives.

Aircraft able to do such things could enjoy outstanding opportunities on the market. Attempts to build such aircraft are thus numerous. Some of them arose as branches of military projects, but often they were considered for civilian purposes. Yet only in the last few years does this dream seem able to become reality. The Bell/Agusta BA609 promises to be the first civilian tipping-rotor airplane in series production.

But in the realm of private flying the idea of VTOL airplanes also has branches. To be able to take off and land with your own airplane on a small field behind your house has a strong allure. In recent years a series of projects therefore arose for the building of such private planes, but whether they will ever be realized remains questionable.

EUROPEAN COMMUNITY PROJECTS

Financed by the European Commission, the first feasibility studies for a European tipping-rotor airplane began in 1987. Leading aviation firms from all of Europe took part, including Agusta, Westland, CASA, MBB and Aerospatiale. As a result of these studies, the "EuroFar" (European Future Advanced Rotorcraft) project finally emerged at the beginning of the 1990s, for a civilian tiltrotor airplane for thirty passengers, with a planned takeoff weight of fourteen tons. It was notable that the powerplant nacelles mounted on the wings could not be tilted completely, but only the rotor hubs.

Despite several wind-tunnel tests with models and a full-size rotor, the design work only crawled along.

Only when Bell and Boeing announced at the end of 1996 that they wanted to build a civilian tiltrotor airplane were efforts in Europe intensified again. In 1997, Agusta, Eurocopter and Westland decided, on the basis of the EuroFar program, to develop a tiltrotor airplane for nineteen or twenty passengers, with a takeoff weight of ten tons, a top speed of 610kph, a maximum altitude of over 7,620 meters, and a range of ca.1,400km. It was hoped that a prototype would be ready in 2004-05 and the first production planes would be delivered in 2008.

The EuroFar Project was the first joint European attempt to design a tipping-rotor airplane.

EUROFAR
(EADS/AGUSTA/WESTLAND)

The new program was given the temporary name "Eurotilt." Besides use as a passenger and business plane, uses in search-and-rescue (SAR) missions and deliveries to offshore oil platforms were planned. In addition, testing its utility for military use was contracted for by the French Defense Ministry. In 1999, the number of cooperating firms had grown to thirty-three from nine European countries.

In the same year, Agusta suggested a further study for a tiltrotor airplane that was to be developed in cooperation with Saab, Israel Aircraft Industries, Aermacchi and others. This "Erica" (Enhanced Rotorcraft Innovative Concept Achievement) design showed size and power similar to that of the "Eurotilt" project (twenty passengers, ten-ton takeoff weight, 650kph top speed, range over 1,200km), and the intended use areas also overlapped.

Seen technically, there were several differences between these two designs. The designers of "Erica" planned that the outer parts of the wings should tilt with the rotors (as had those of the Weserflug P1003/1 sixty years before) to minimize the disturbing influence of the wings. In this way the rotor was to be made so small that the plane could take off and land with the rotors tilted only five to seven degrees. Agusta described the design as a mixture of tiltrotor and tiltwing planes and hoped to be able to present the first prototypes by 2001.

The Eurotilt project initiated jointly by Agusta, Eurocopter and Westland in 1997 finally resulted in a program called "2Gether" to build a European tiltrotor airplane.

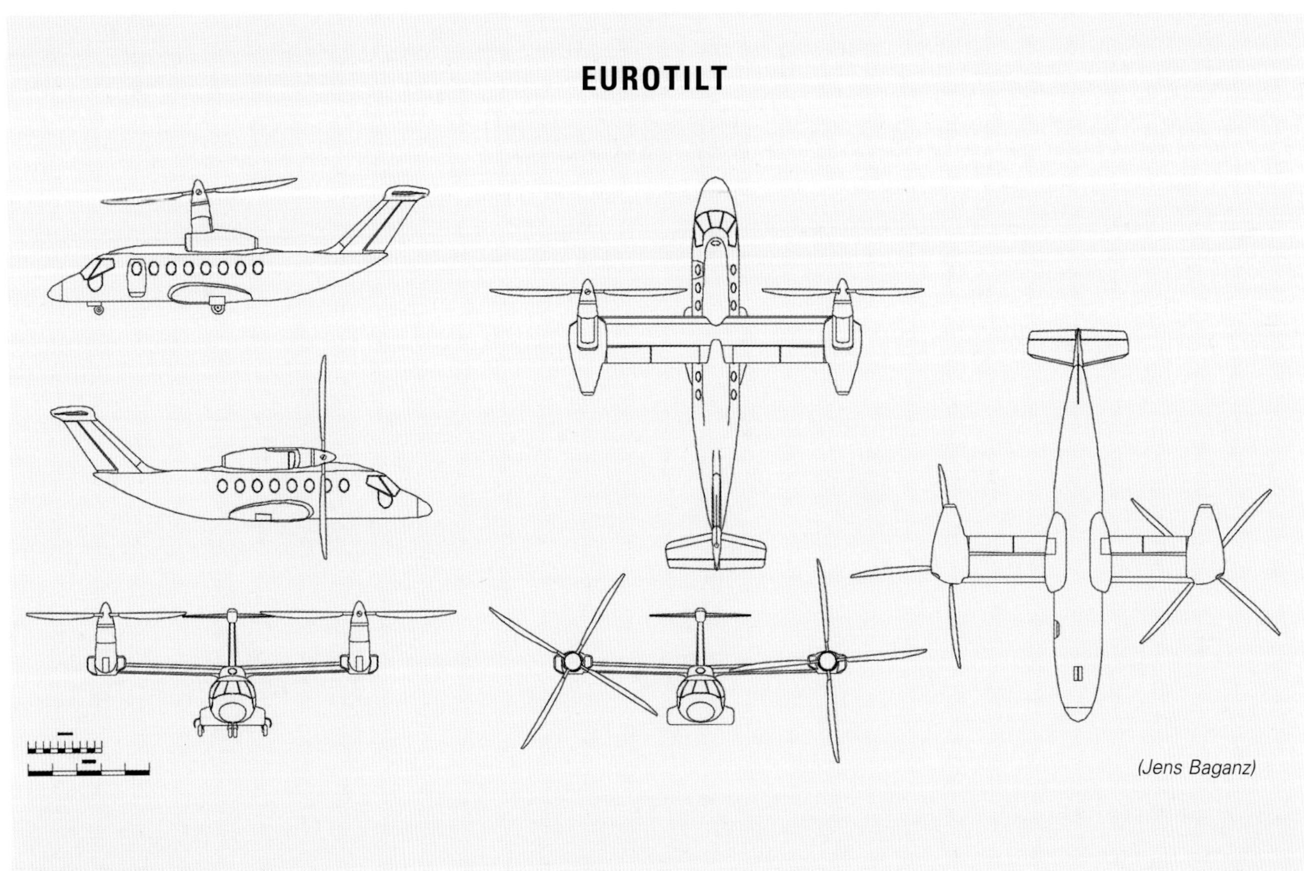

EUROTILT

(Jens Baganz)

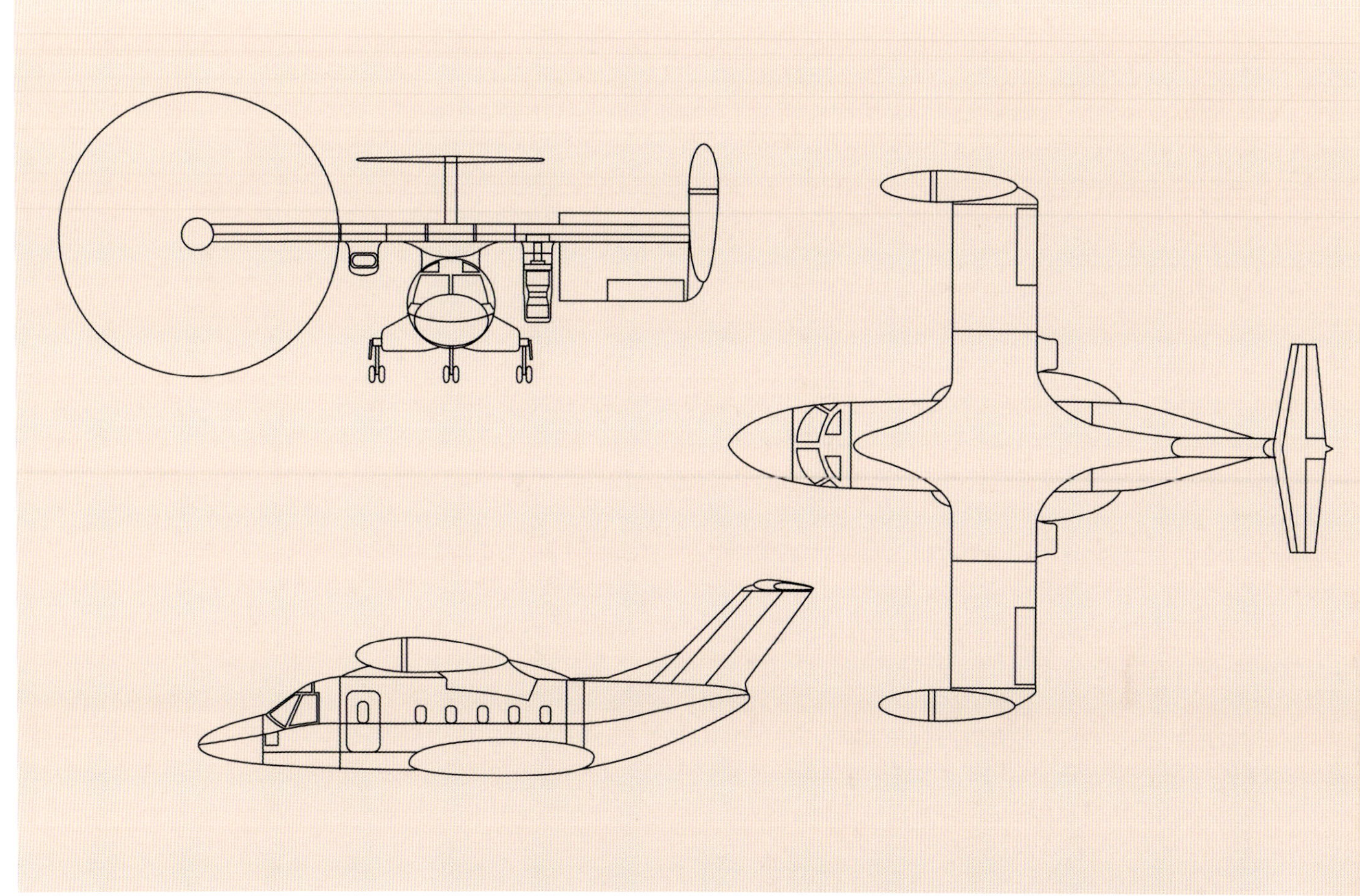

The Agusta "Erica." *(Vincent Bourguignon)*

The EU hesitated, though, to promote the development of two practically identical tiltrotor airplanes, and insisted in October 1999 on cooperation of the involved firms. Thereupon Eurocopter, Agusta and Westland (which had merged into AgustaWestland in July 2000) submitted to the EU in March 2000 a joint project under the name of "2gether" (second-generation European tilting highly efficient rotorcraft). Because of the too-high costs and lack of innovative features, this offer was rejected at first, and only after significant improvements by the industry was it approved in April 2001. The schedule for the project foresaw that flight-testing should begin in 2005 and series production in 2010. Eurocopter, though, came to the conclusion during the course of the program that the tiltrotor technology was too complex and costly for commercial use. There were also too many problems concerning the operation, such as certification and air traffic management, that had not yet been cleared up. Therefore Eurocopter halted all work on a European tiltrotor airplane at that time (summer 2009). But Agusta continued the work on the "Erica" project.

BTZ Concepts

Helmut, Count von Zborowski, was a leading member of the aircraft branch of BMW during World War II. Zborowski was also the inventor of the ring-wing concept that was still used in 1945 for two Heinkel studies ("Wespe," Wasp, and "Lerche," Lark). Research had shown that a propeller cab become some 25% more effective through the Bernoulli effect if it is surrounded by a mantle.

Since airplane building in Germany was banned after the war's end, Zborowski went to France in 1948. There in 1950 he founded the "Bureau Technique Zborowski" (BTZ), to which Prof. Heinrich Hertel (former development leader of the Junkers Flugzeugwerke) and the aerodynamicist Dr. Wilhelm Seibold also belonged. During the next few years BTZ designed a series of futuristic aircraft, all equipped with ring-wing or mantled propellers.

(Jens Baganz)

Among them was also the "Lucane" (Hirschkäfer) study, a small VTOL passenger plane, of which BTC conceived two versions. The first type had two large tilting mantled propellers, to be driven by two 1,000-HP-class turbines, which were located in the nacelles before the mantled propellers. The propellers themselves were to have four blades and rotate in opposite directions.

The other version had two fuselages, set to the left and right of a big tilting mantled propeller. Power was to come from four coupled turbines in a nacelle in front of the four-bladed propeller. Besides a two-man crew, this version would also carry sixteen passengers. But both of these concepts were not followed further.

BTZ LUCANE
(double fuselage)

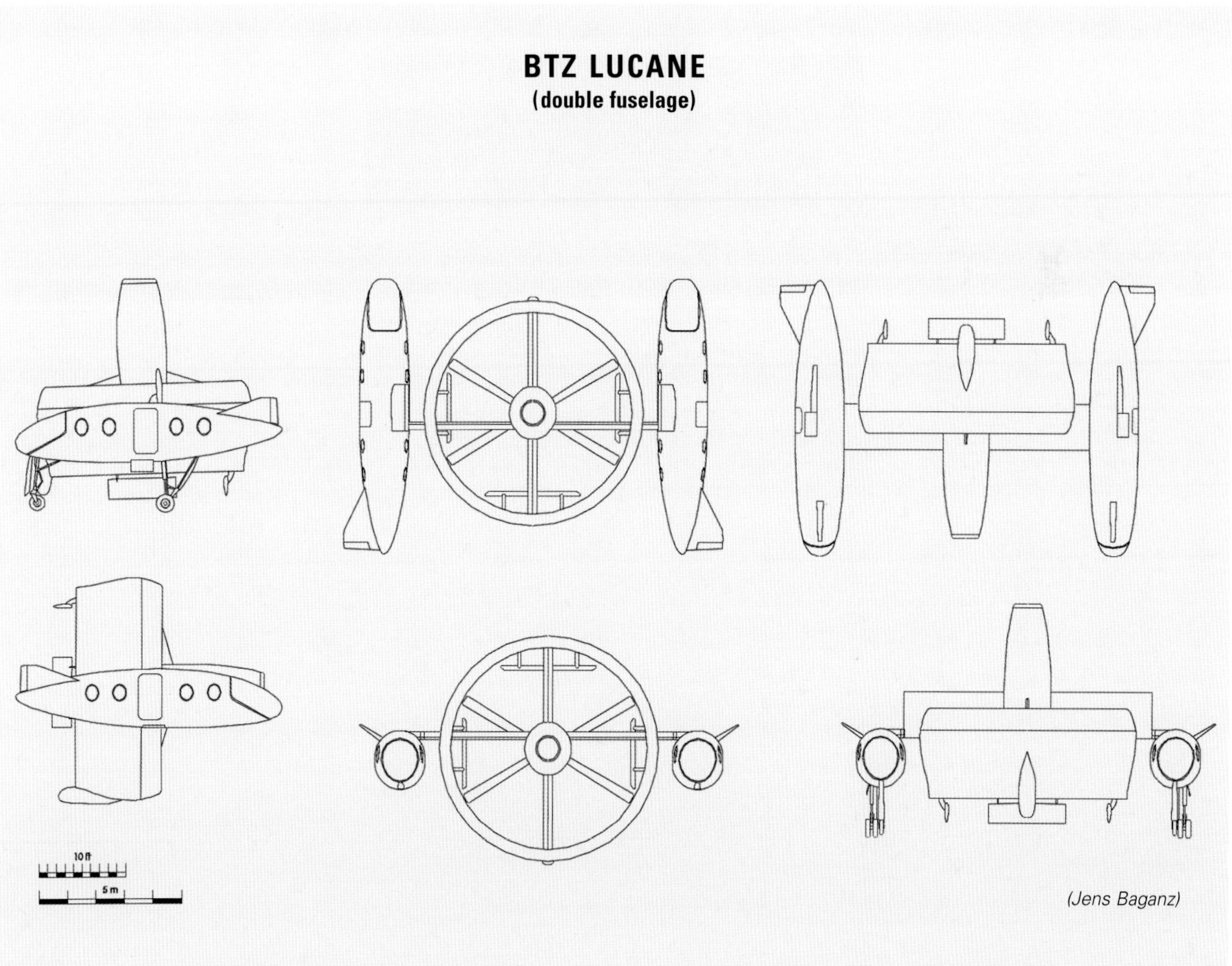

(Jens Baganz)

Nord Passenger Plane Concepts

A further Nord study was also numbered N 501 (see Chapter 5), but this time it was the design of a passenger plane for eight passengers and a two-man crew. Except for a few technical details, no further information for this plane has been found.

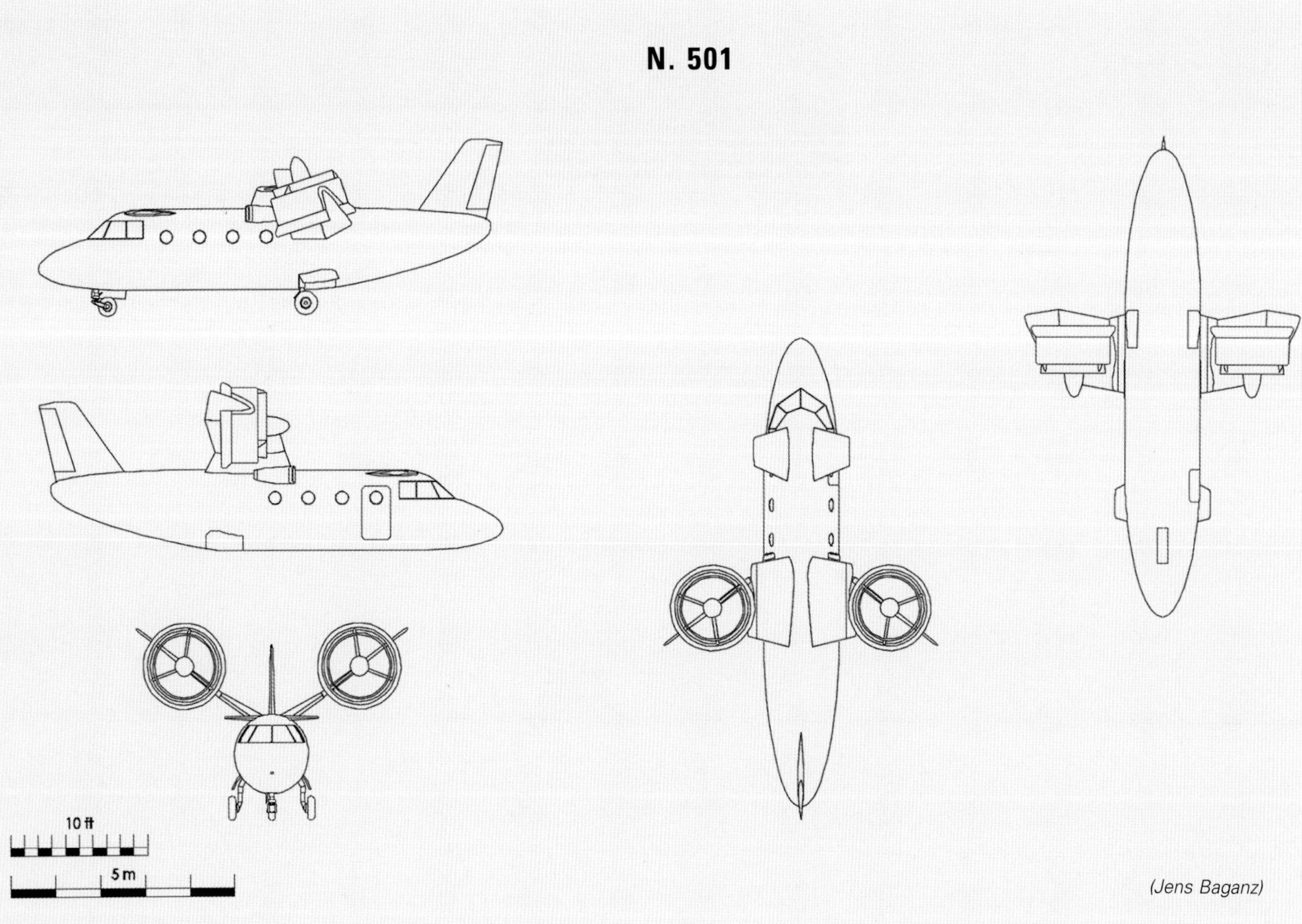

(Jens Baganz)

Nord "Rocade" (transport plane)

Crew	2
Empty weight	9,450kg
Takeoff	weight 15,700kg (VTOL)
Powerplant	4 Turbomeca Turmo-IIIC turbines, 1,000 HP each
Top speed	over 540kph
Length	18,400mm
Height	6,900mm
Wingspan	19,500mm
Service ceiling	unknown
Range	unknown

Under the somewhat strange name of "Rocade" (roundabout), Nord designed a VTOL transport for forty passengers. Its two large tilting mantled airscrews were to be driven by four Turbomeca Turmo IIIC turbines, each producing 1,000 HP, mounted in a high structure on the fuselage. The arrangement of the wings on this structure and their attachment by struts to the fuselage were reminiscent of flying boats of the 1930s and 1940s, such as the Dornier Do 18 or Consolidated PBY "Catalina" and were necessary to be able to tilt the big mantled propellers (external diameter 5.46 meters, internal 4.7 meters) ninety degrees without problems. A prototype of the "Rocade" was already being built when the program was broken off in 1970.

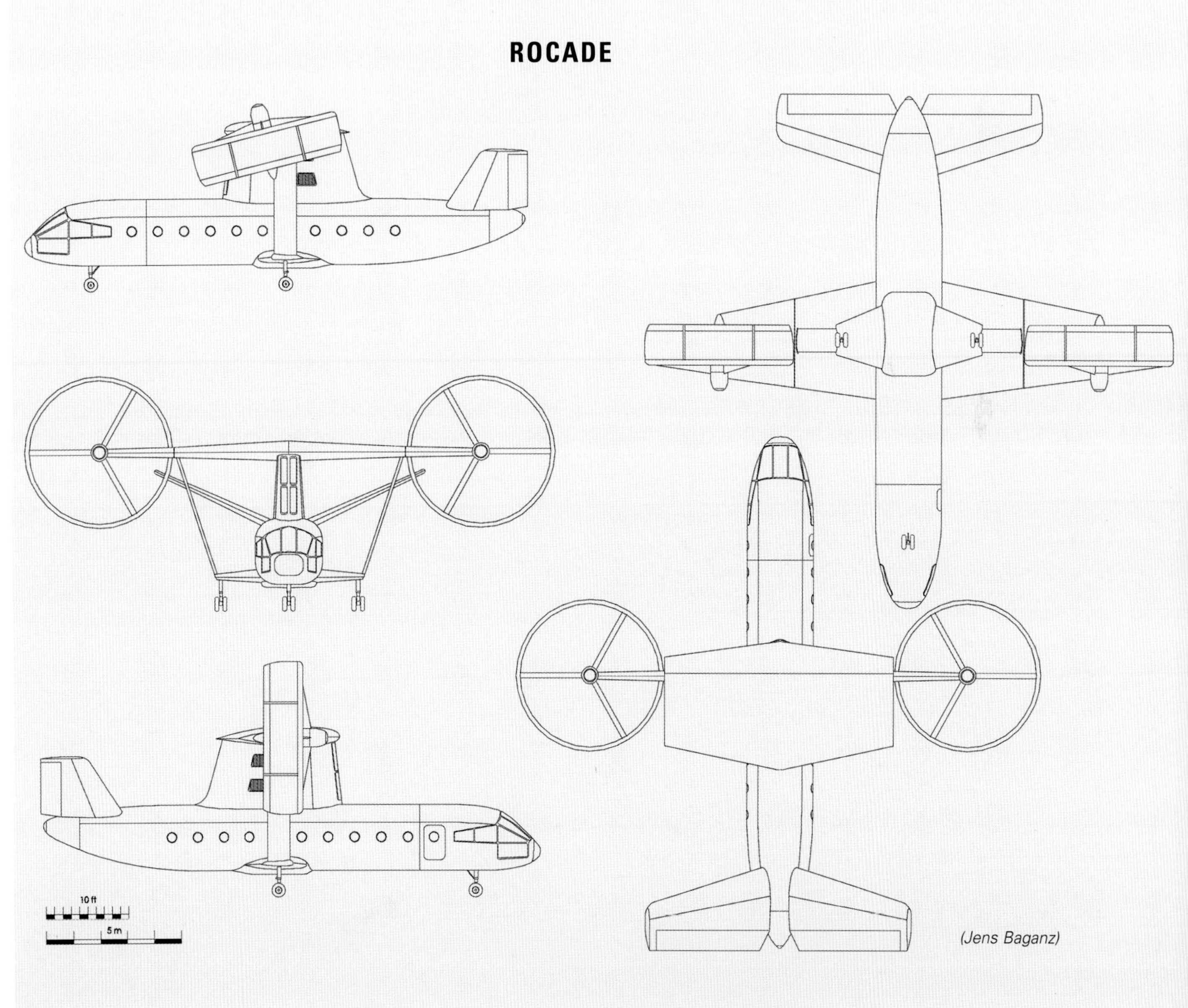

Aerospatiale X 910

Crew	2
Empty weight	1,640kg
Takeoff weight	2,455kg
Powerplant	2 Turbomeca Arriel turbines,
	850 HP each
Top speed	517kph
Length	6,700mm
Height	3,820mm
	(rotors in vertical position)
Wingspan	7,640mm
Service ceiling	unknown
Range	800km (with four passengers)

Aerospatiale X 910

In January 1970, Nord Aviation and Sud Aviation merged to become the Soci-ete Nationale Industrielle Aerospatiale, or "Aerospatiale" for short. The new firm threw out the earlier designs of vertical takeoff planes with tilting mantled propellers and instead turned to the tipping-rotor technology. The X 910 looked similar to the Bell XV-15 that appeared at the same time, but showed several significant differences. The two Turbomeca Arriel turbines, each of 650 HP, were not located in the tilting nacelles at the wing tips, but were mounted at an angle of twenty-five degrees in the fuselage behind the passenger cabin, and drove the two three-bladed rotors via shafts and gears. To avoid a catastrophic loss of thrust in hover-hold, the rotors were also linked by a cross shaft. The engine air intakes were located at the roots of the wings. The rotors had a diameter of only five meters and thus could be in a horizontal position, even on the ground. Besides a two-man crew, the passenger cabin offered space for up to six persons.

Wind-tunnel tests with a 1/5-scale model were carried out as of 1974, and with a full-size rotor with tipping mechanism in 1975-76. In April 1977, Aerospatiale announced that a prototype would make its maiden flight in 1981, but the program was ended in 1977.

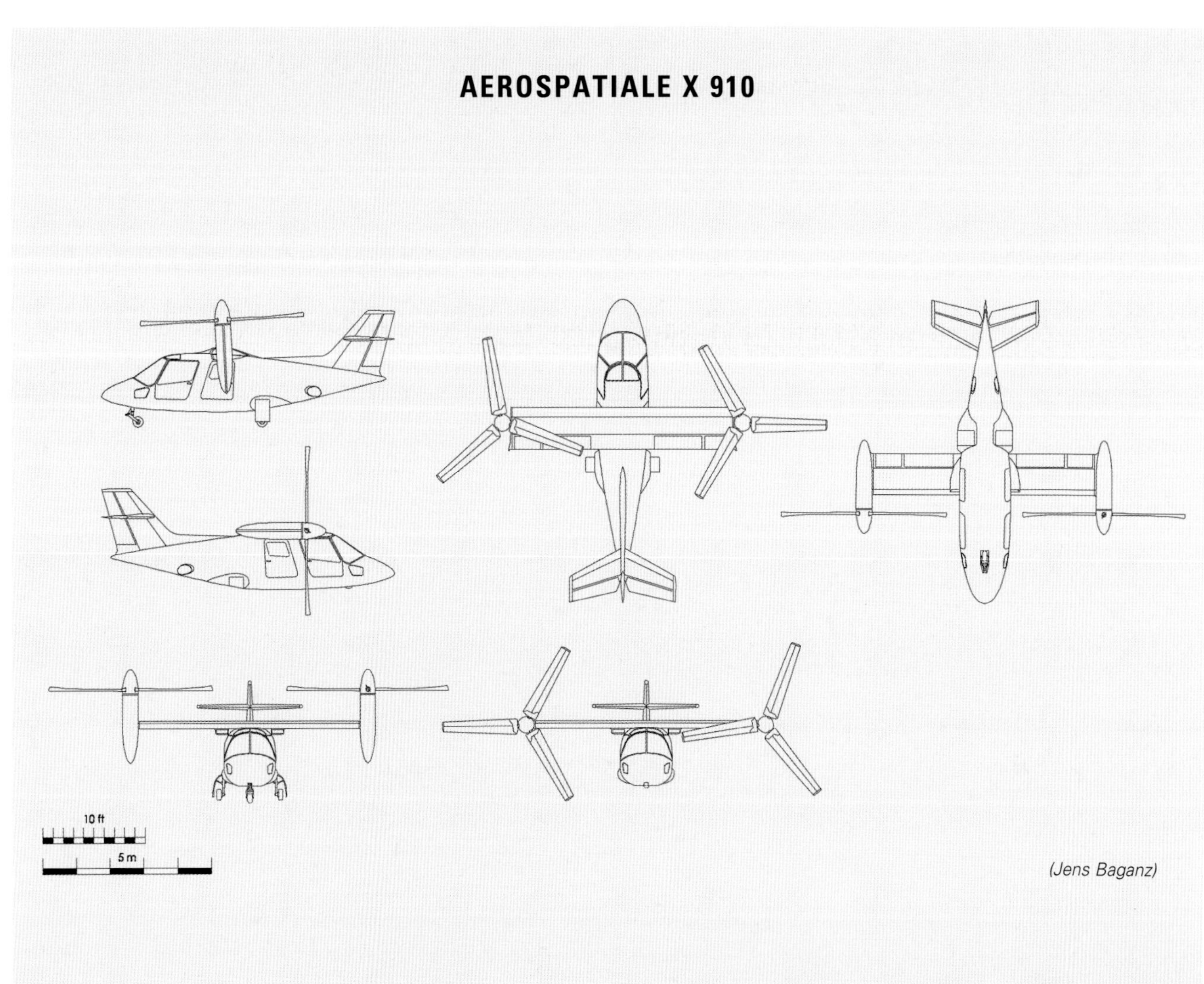

(Jens Baganz)

Bristol 199	
Crew	3
Empty weight	16,011kg
Takeoff weight	27,215kg
Powerplant	4 Rolls-Royce Tyne turbines, 4,000 HP each
Top speed	over 640kph
Length	20,100mm
Height	7,900mm
Wingspan	unknown
Service ceiling	unknown
Range	1,300km

GREAT BRITAIN

Bristol 199

The Austrian-born British helicopter pioneer Raoul Hafner, development leader in the helicopter Department of the Bristol Aeroplane Company since the end of 1944, designed a tiltwing plane, the Bristol 199, in 1955-56. This large transport craft for fifty passengers was to be driven by two Rolls-Royce Tyne twin turbines located in nacelles at the wing tips. The diameter of the four-bladed rotor was 14.63 meters, so that landings and takeoffs with the wings not tilted would have been impossible. Bristol's studies went no further than the drawing board.

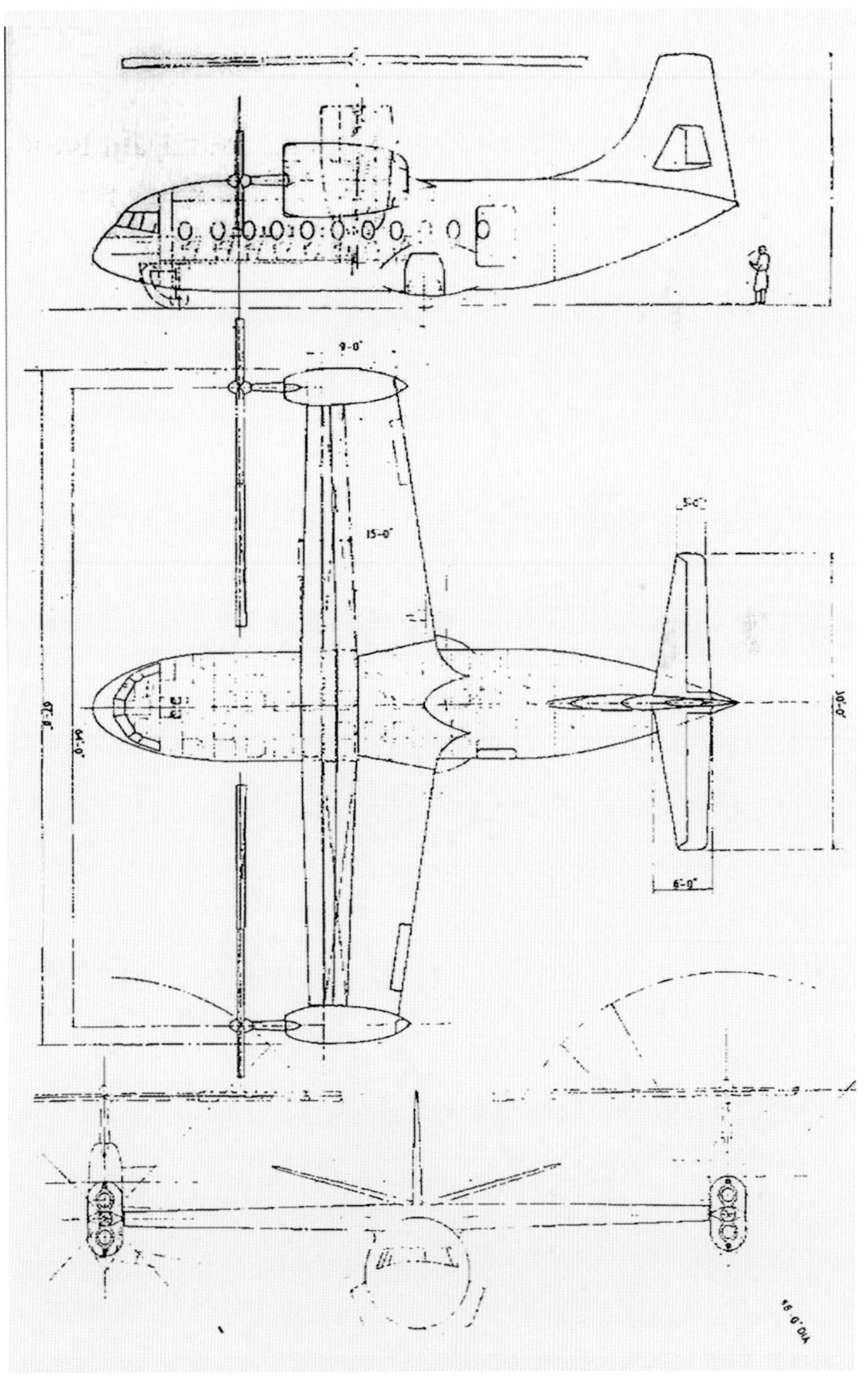

Works drawing of the Bristol 199.
(BAe via Jens Baganz)

Westland WG15

Bristol's helicopter department was bought by Westland in 1960, and Raoul Hafner, now chief designer at Westland, made a number of studies for the new company, in which he placed special value on a low circular-area pressure, thus they were all equipped with large-diameter rotors.

Among Hafner's studies there were also those that dealt with the Vickers "Viscount" and "Vanguard" airliners. The study of a vertically lifting and landing "Vanguard" finally developed in 1965 into Westland Project WG15 (WG = Westland Group), a tiltwing craft with a calculated takeoff weight of 68,100kg and rotors of ca.28-meter diameter.

Since they had the possibility of cyclical and collective blade adjustment, an additional tail rotor to control the pitching movements, as with the XC-142A or CL-84, could be omitted. In 1966, the British Technology Ministry requested that the country's aviation industry prepare studies of possible VTOL passenger airplanes, and published a recommendation in 1967 stating which performance criteria these planes should fulfill (Transport Aircraft Requirements Committee," TARC), so that their development could be advanced with government funds. In September 1969 Westland thus suggested a further developed version of the WG15 that corresponded to those criteria. The plane was laid out for 100 passengers, with a takeoff weight of ca.50,000kg, a top speed of 720kph, and a range of 1,000km.

Drawing of a WG15 from a Westland sales brochure. *(Westland via HMB)*

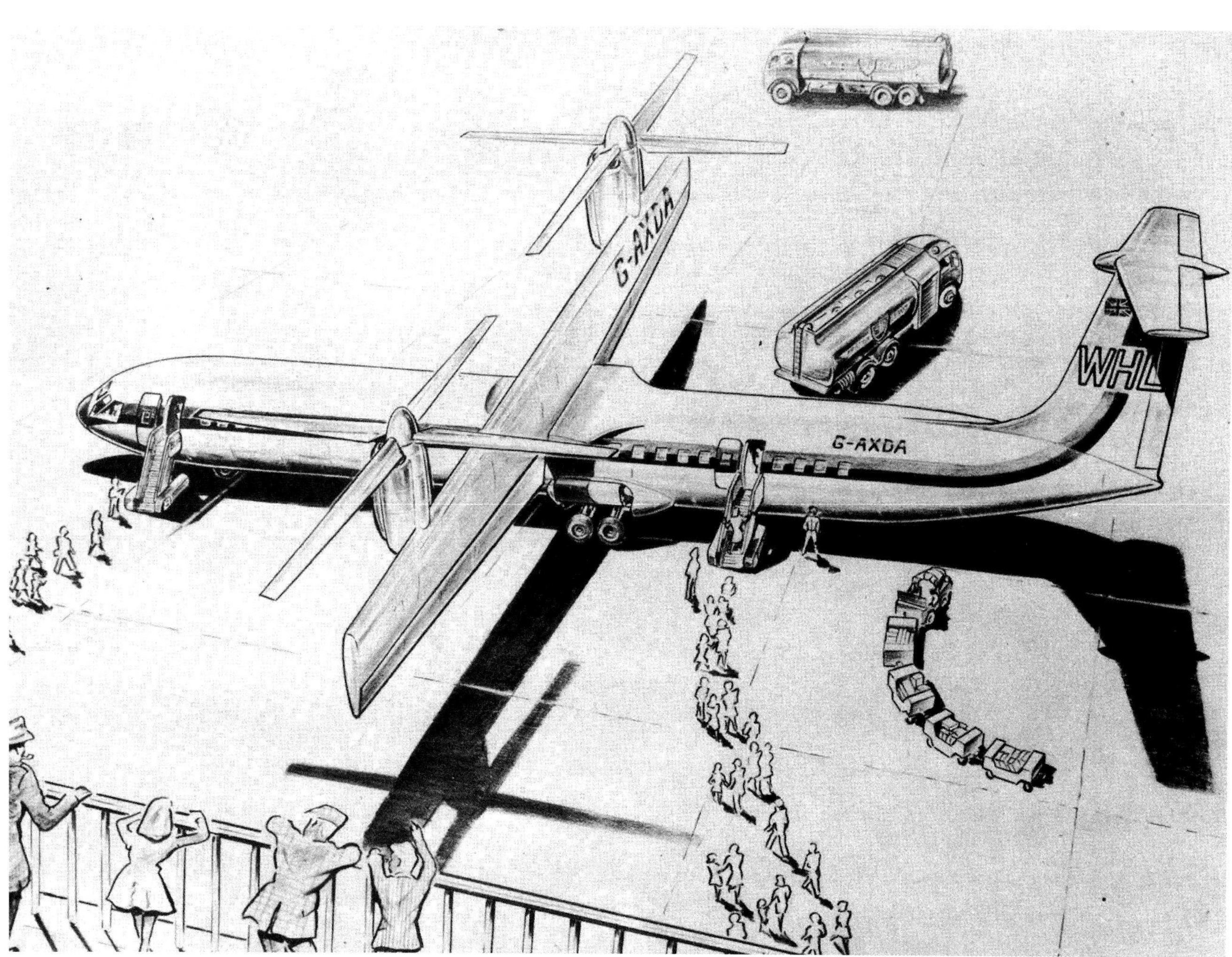

WG. 15

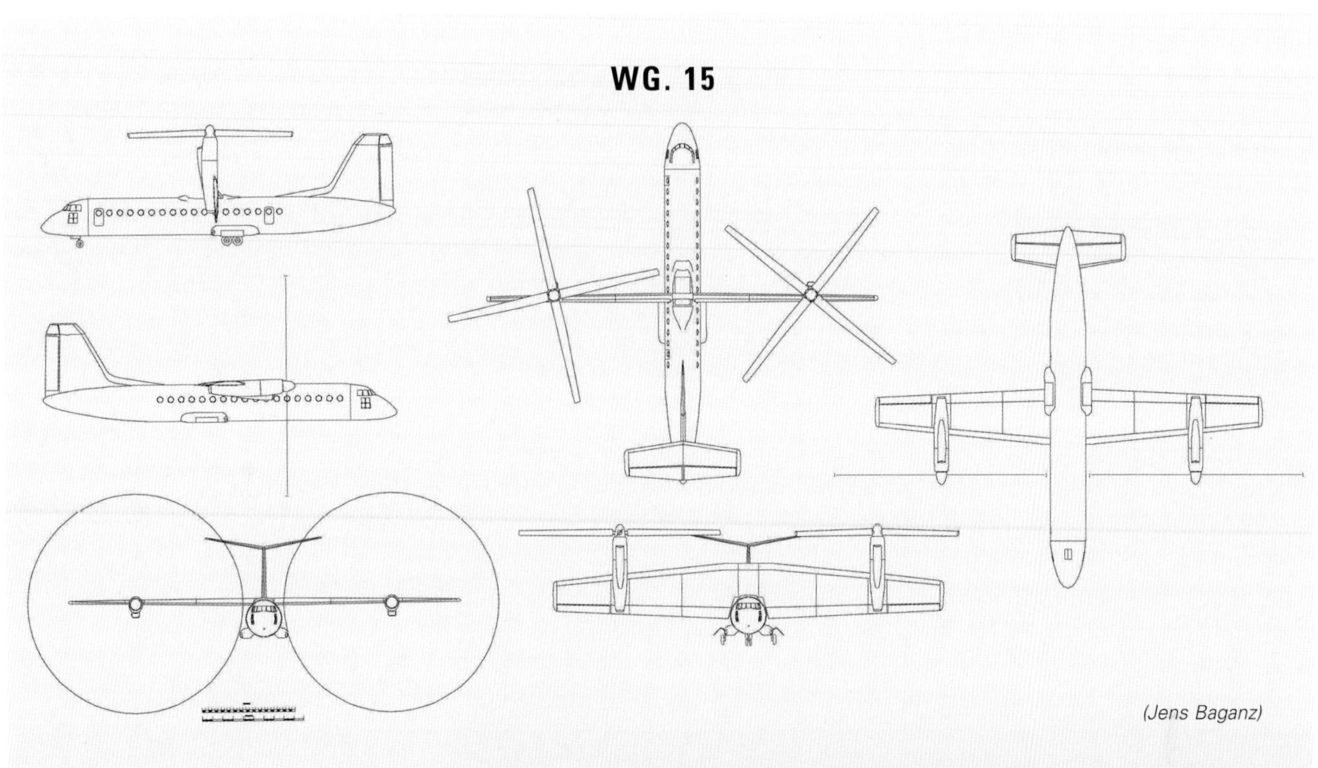

(Jens Baganz)

This further-developed version of the
WG15 was planned for 100 passengers.
(Westland von HMB)

235

Westland WG22

Another tipping-wing plane conceived within the bounds of this request was the WG22. In this type, a specially developed wing was to avoid problems that occurred in the transition with the large rotors preferred by Westland, and help the plane achieve especially high efficiency.

Model of the WG22. *(Westland via HMB)*

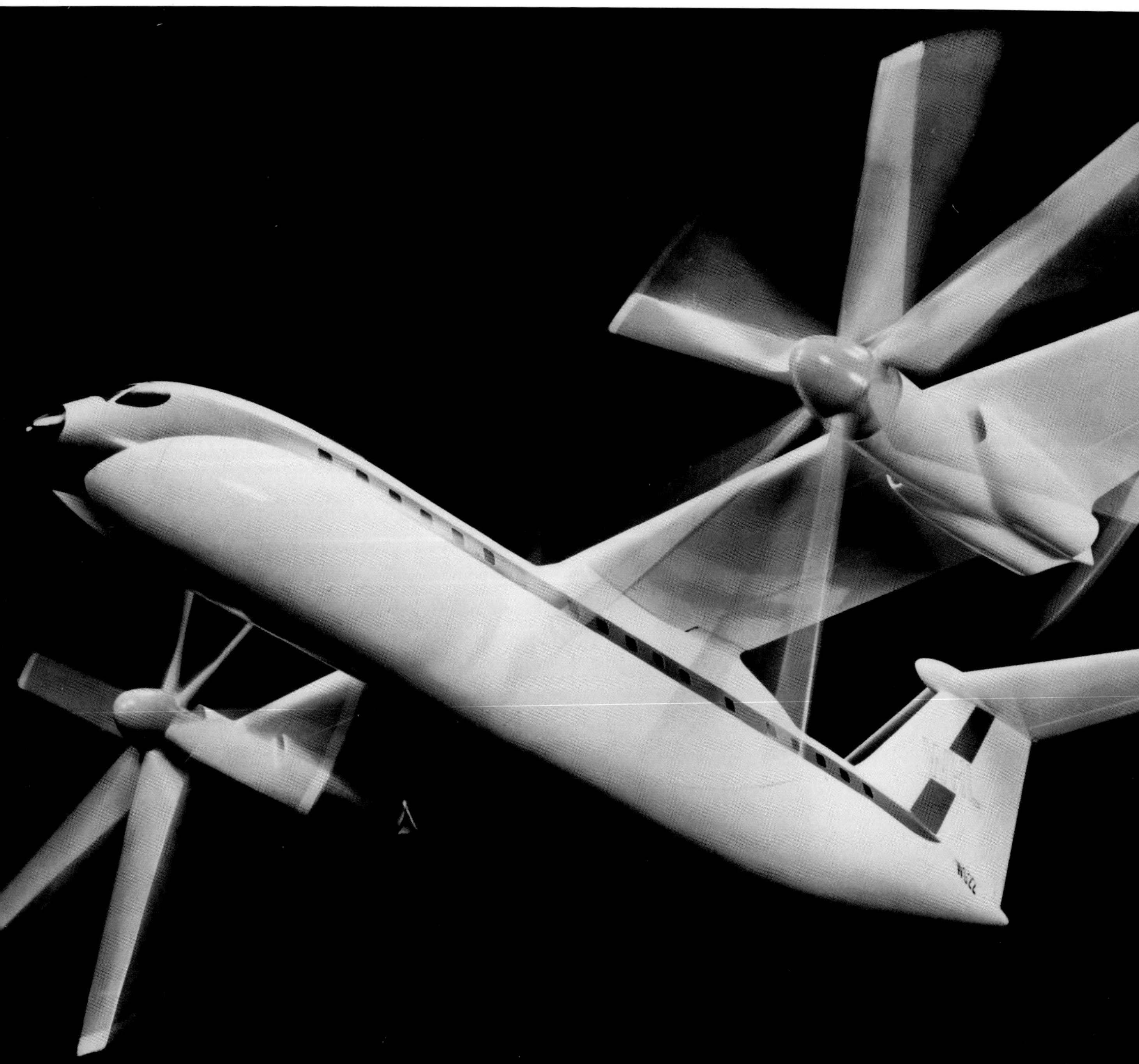

The WG22 was to carry 100 passengers in a pressurized cabin, be 28.04 meters long, and have a wingspan of 30.82 meters. Four Rolls-Royce RB 411-01 or Lycoming LTC4V-4 turbines with a takeoff power of 9,450 HP each drove two six-bladed rotors of 14.78-meter diameter. The turbines were mounted in two large engine nacelles in pairs that drove a common gearbox, so that the WG22 looked like a twin-engine plane. A cross shaft linked the two rotor gearboxes to prevent thrust loss in case of engine failure. The wings could be tilted 100 degrees hydraulically. In the end, neither the WG15 nor the WG22 succeeded in attracting contracts, so development was halted.

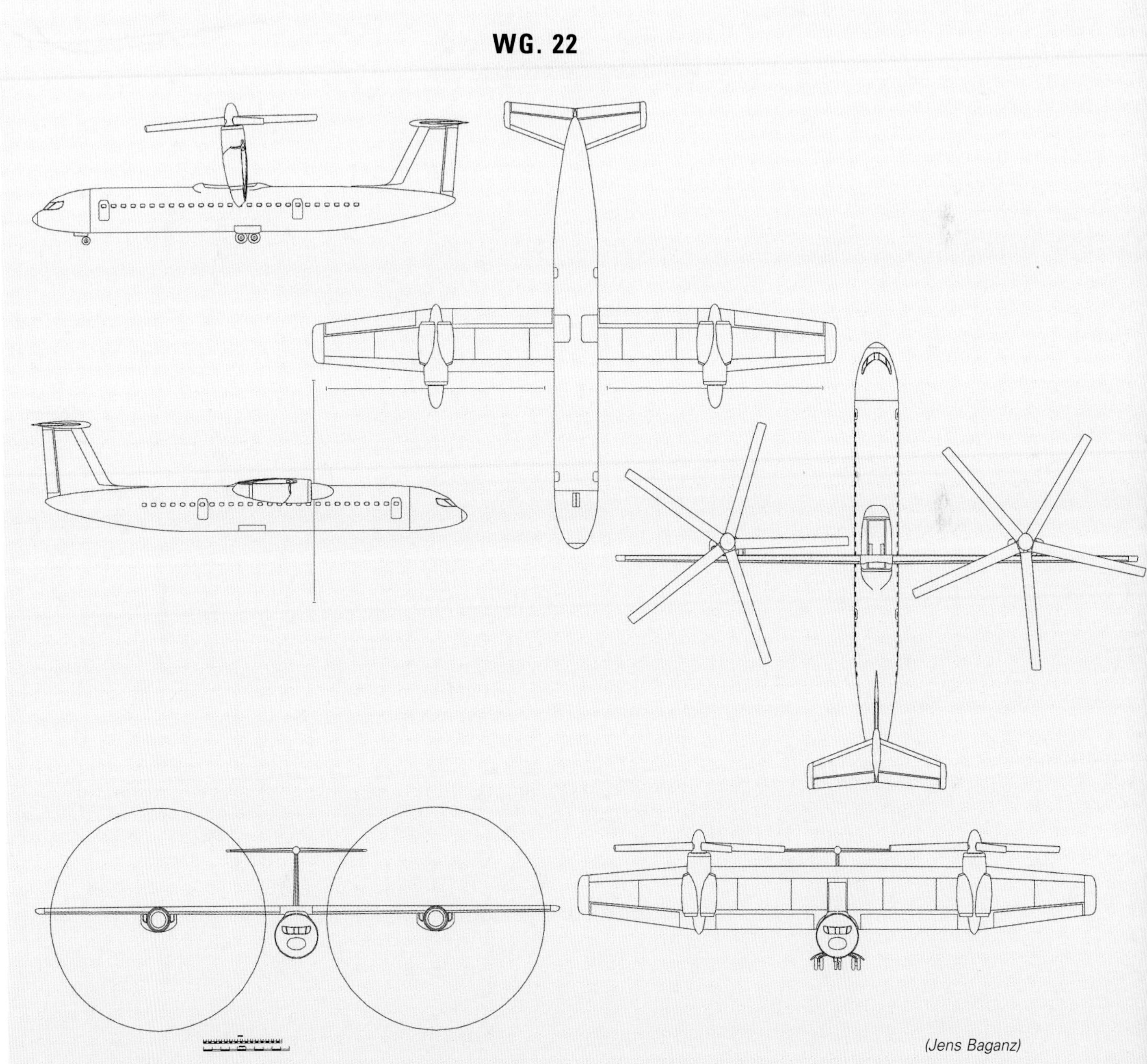

(Jens Baganz)

Westland WE01 (1968)
Crew   1+5 passengers
Empty weight   2,450kg
Takeoff weight   3,400kg
Powerplant   4 Allison T63 turbines,
                                     370 HP each
Top speed   434kph
Length   9,750mm
Height   3,050mm
Wingspan   12,500mm
Service ceiling   unknown
Range   400 km (with 5 passengers)
One-way range   (2,044km)

Westland WEO1

In 1966, Westland began to design a small six-seat tiltrotor airplane for military and civilian use, the WEO1. Four Allison T63 turbines, of 250 HP each, were mounted in pairs in nacelles at the middle of the wing and drove contra-rotating four-bladed rotors of 5.94-meter diameter, which were connected by a shaft.

At the 1967 air show in Le Bourget, Westland presented a full-scale mockup of the WEO1 and showed a functioning full-size model of the wing gondola with tilting mechanism and rotor. The first flight was announced for 1971.

In the course of development, the data and appearance of the WEO1 changed. For instance, the powerplant nacelles moved to the wing tips and the plane was given a slightly modified fuselage with two small forewing-like strakes under the cockpit.

Westland also designed two larger versions of the WEO1 for ten and twenty passengers, with takeoff weights of 6,435 and 7,990 kilograms. The twenty-seat plane, according to calculations, was supposed to have a top speed of 500kph and a range of 500km.

Although Westland carried out thorough wind-tunnel tests and built a rotor test rig, no prototype of the WEO1 was built.

Artistic portrayal of the WEO1 from a Westland brochure. *(Westland via HMB)*

Westland WEO2

The WEO2, conceived at the same time, was considerably larger. It was also intended for military and civilian use. This tiltrotor design was laid out for eighty passengers or a corresponding payload, and was to attain 610kph.

Four T64-GE-16 turbines, linked as two sets of twins with an expected 3,485 HP from each, were to power two contra-rotating rotors with18.28-meter diameters and six blades. The takeoff weight was calculated to be 30,410kg and the payload 10,442kg. While the tilting engine nacelles were at first mounted about halfway out the wings, they were finally moved to the wing tips during the course of development. The control surfaces also changed during the design work. At one time a threefold tailfin was considered necessary, but this arrangement was soon dropped.

An enlarged version, the WEO2B, was to transport eighty-four passengers and weigh 34,731kg when it took off. Westland hoped to be able to finish a prototype of the WEO2 by 1975. But all the conceived versions of the WEO2 shared the fate of the WEO1 and thc other Westland projects of this kind: Neither military nor civilian buyers showed an interest in the designs, thus the development was finally stopped.

Enlarged version of WE01 for twenty passengers.

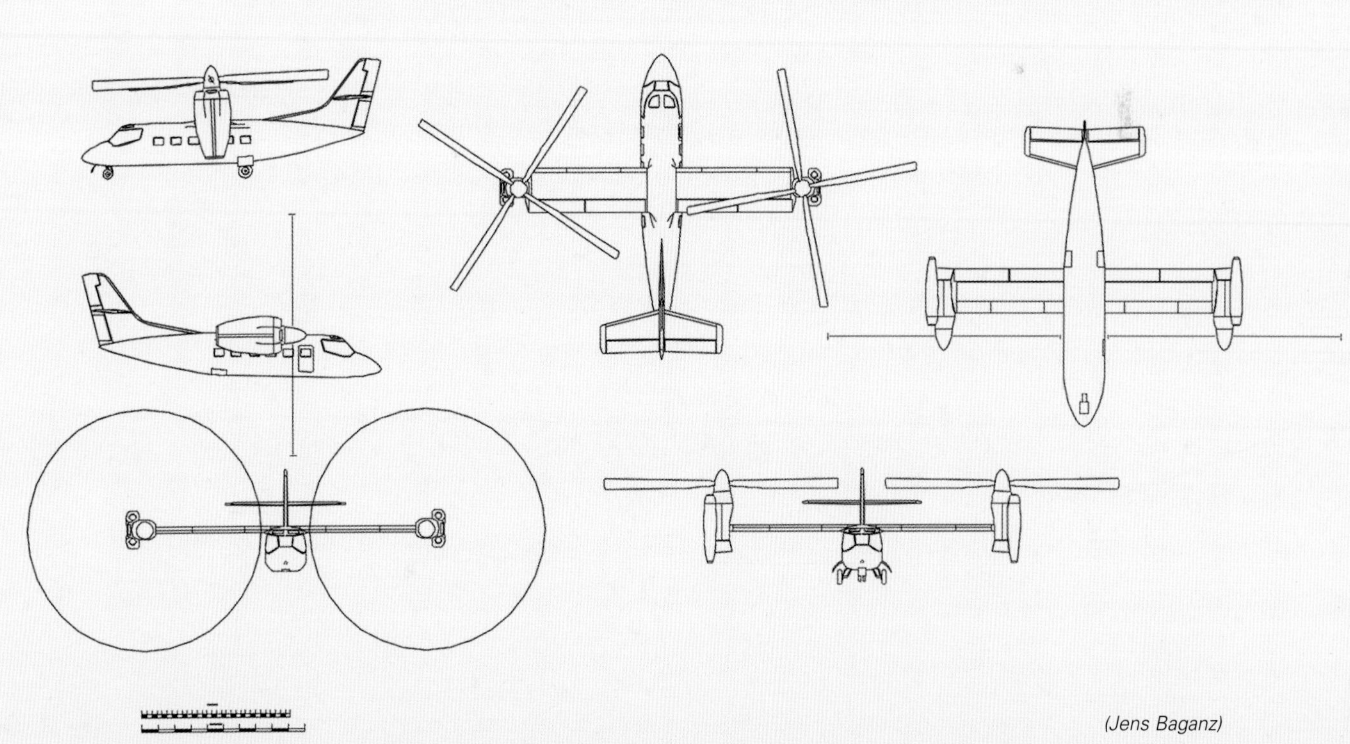

Although this model of the WEO2 was painted in Royal Air Force colors, the design was conceived primarily as a passenger liner. *(Westland via HMB)*

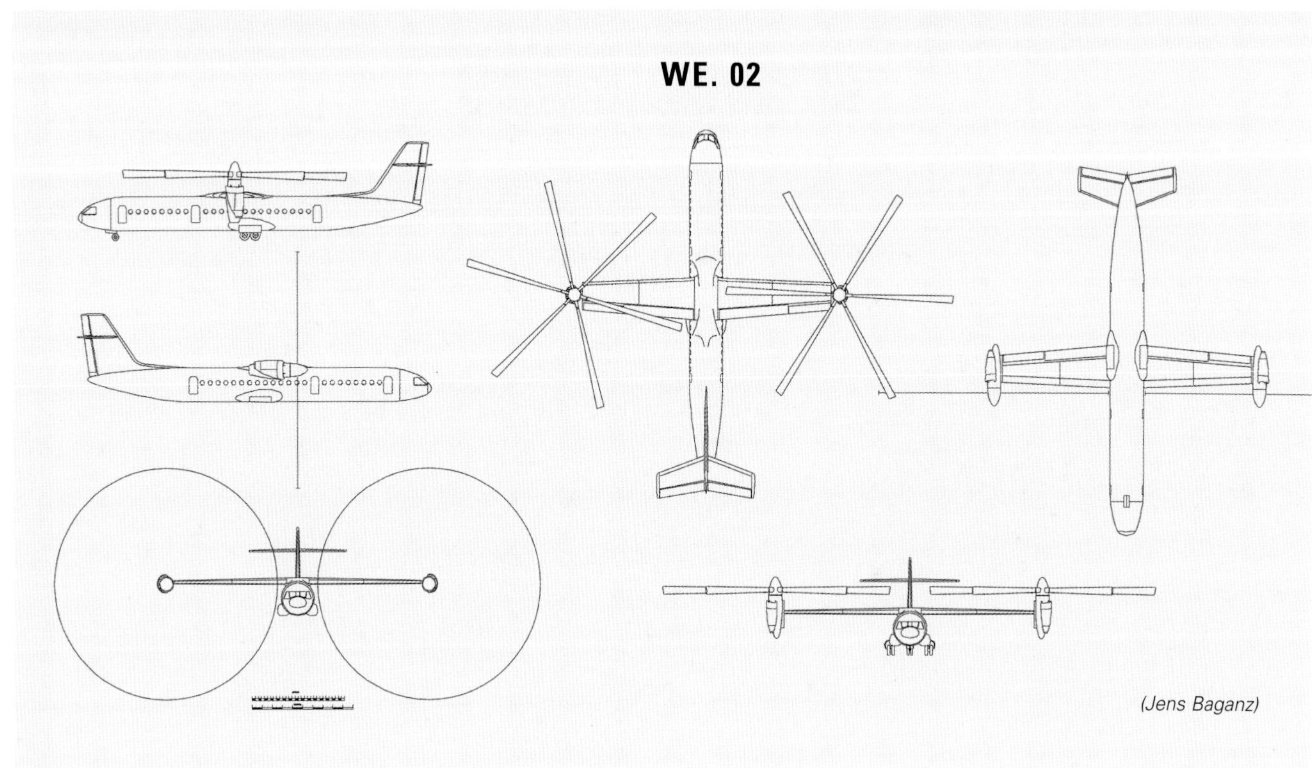

Design of the WEO2 with powerplants at the wing tips. *(Jens Baganz)*

240

Ishida Aerospace TW-68

The Japanese Ishida Foundation conducted extensive surveys in the 1980s about delivery and short-haul air traffic, and came to the realization that a turboprop plane with tipping wings would be ideal for these uses. To have such a craft designed, Ishida did not go to a Japanese firm, but founded a branch, the Ishida Aerospace Research, Inc., which was located, surprisingly, in Fort Worth, Texas, and worked to a large extent with American personnel.

The development of the TW-68 began in 1987, and during the following years its looks and performance data changed slightly several times. Basically, though, the TW-68 was a tiltwing plane planned for fourteen passengers and luggage, with two twinned engines and a takeoff weight of ca.8,600kg. Ishida Aerospace turned back in its design to data that had been gained in the designing of the Canadair CL-84. In this way they were sure that the first prototype would be displayed as early as 1994 and series production would start in 1997. These dates were later postponed to 1995 and 1999.

Four-side view of the TW-68 from an Ishida sales brochure. *(Ishida via HMB)*

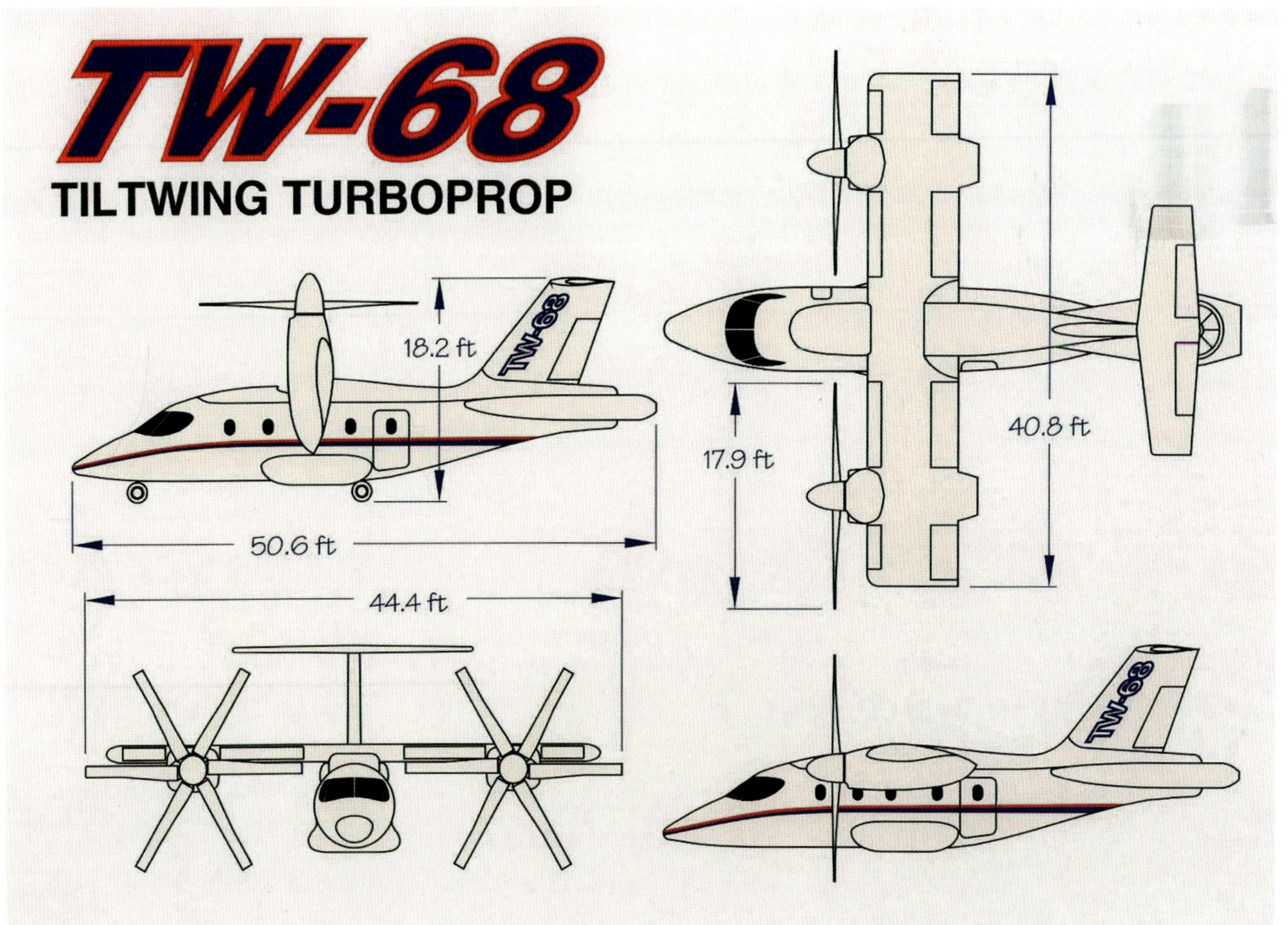

The wings of the TWE-68 could be tilted 100 degrees. The two engine nacelles under the wings each held two PT6B-67R turbines (1,000 HP each), which drove, through a joint gearbox, two six-bladed propellers 5.46 meters in diameter. By the installation of four engines the designers hoped for greater safety, since the hovering ability would be preserved safely despite the failure of one unit. The gears were also connected by a shaft. The TW-68 was supposed to be able to rise to 7,620 meters, fully loaded, in nine minutes, and still be able to hover at 1,500 meters.

The steering in hover-hold was to be done by a mantled propeller at the tail (pitching), adjustment of the propeller-setting angles (rolling) and differential activation

Artistic portrayal of the TW-68 as a delivery plane for oil-drilling platforms.
(Ishida via HMB)

Ishida Aerospace TW-68 (1993)

Crew	2+14 passengers
Empty weight	5,623kg
Takeoff weight	8,626kg
Powerplant	4 Pratt & Whitney Canada PT6B-67R turbines, 1,000 HP each
Top speed	574kph
Length	15,423mm
Height	5,547mm
Wingspan	12,436mm, 13,533mm with propellers
Service ceiling	8,840 meters
Range	1,400km (with 14 passengers), 1,700km (with 9 passengers)

Ishida was very sure at the end of the 1980s and the beginning of the 1990s as to what the future of the TW-68 would be.
(Ishida via HMB)

of the rudder (yawing). In level flight conventional rudders took over these tasks. In 1992, the building of a full-size mockup began in Fort Worth, and in a brochure published in the spring of 1993, Ishida Aerospace was still very confident that the TW-68 had its best chance on the commercial market. At the same time, the plane would have been splendidly suitable for police and border guarding work, search-and-rescue missions, MEDEVAC flights, plus deliveries to oil-drilling platforms. In July 1993, though, the Ishida Foundation announced that work on the TW-68 would be interrupted for the time being. Since that time, nothing more has been heard of the project.

Platt-LePage PL-16

Dr. Wynn Laurence LePage and Haviland H. Platt formed the Platt-LePage Aircraft Company in 1938. Shortly before that, Platt had traveled to Germany and had negotiated unsuccessfully for the licensed production of the Focke-Wulf Fw 61, so that Platt and LePage decided to build their own helicopter. The XR-1, first flown on May 12, 1941, resembled the Fw 61 externally, and also had two contra-rotating rotors mounted on side struts. In 1945-46 the firm developed the concept of a passenger airplane with tiltrotors, the PL-16, about which not much is known. The takeoff weight was supposed to be some 24,000kg, and the rotors mounted on the wings had a diameter of twenty-four meters and were supposed to be tilted ninety degrees.

Financial difficulties in August 1946 led to the end of the Platt-LePage firm, and thus of all their projects. To be sure, many of the company's patents and designs were taken over by the McDonnell Aircraft Company. In July 1950, Haviland H. Platt finally submitted patent documents for a tiltrotor design and was issued the applicable patent in February 1955. Platt's patent foresaw a radial engine mounted in the center of the fuselage and driving both rotors. In a factory development, the possibility of autorotation was foreseen, and the rotors were supposed to be adjustable smoothly between their vertical and horizontal positions. Interestingly, certain details of the XV-3 showed an astonishing similarity to this patent, so that Bell later had to pay patent fees to Platt.

Platt LePage PL-16. *(NASA)*

Drawing from Platt's patent application for a tiltrotor airplane.

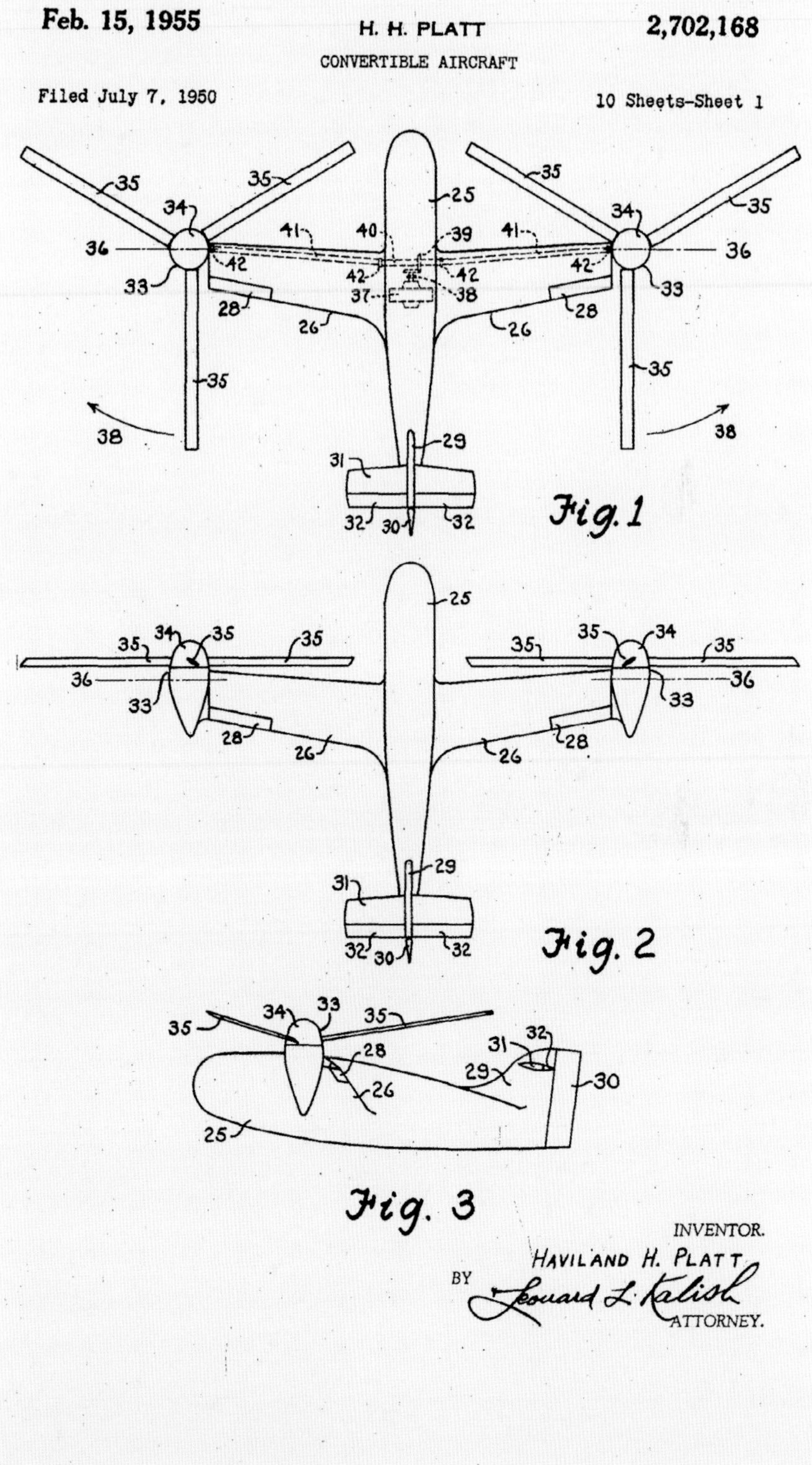

Yorkopter, 1956

The American C.H. York displayed a tiltrotor craft in 1956 that he called the Yorkopter and that was probably the first example of a craft developed for private flying. Practically nothing is known of the aircraft itself. Whether the craft ever flew cannot be verified. York's machine had similar dimensions to the Transcendental 1-G, but had an open cockpit and rigid three-point landing gear. At each end of the wings was a two-bladed tiltrotor.

C.H. York displayed this tiltrotor machine in 1956. Whether it ever flew is not known. *(via HMB)*

Bell Projects

Since the 1950s, Bell has carried out a scarcely imaginable number of studies for civilian passenger aircraft with tilting-mantle propellers and tiltrotors. Usually, scarcely anything is known of them except for a sketch or a picture. The extent of the studies reaches from business-trip planes to large airliners. These concepts were often variants of military designs, such as the D-2239 and D-2240 proposed by Bell in 1965, which were based on the technology of the D-2064.

On the basis of the D-266, developed at the end of the 1960s for the U.S. Army, Bell conceived civilian variations with seats for thirty, or in a larger version, sixty passengers. The larger version was to be 27.33 meters long and 6.86 meters high, and its wingspan was to be 22.4 meters. Its four-bladed rotors were to allow a maximum cruising speed of 651kph. Bell calculated its takeoff weight as about 23,400kg.

Artistic portrayal of the Bell D-2240.
(Bell via HMB)

The successful testing of the XV-15 led Bell to initiate a great many new projects for military and civilian airplanes with tiltrotors at the end of the 1970s. In the civilian realm, the D-326 concept was developed for an airplane for thirty passengers at the most. The "Clipper" was displayed in 1980 and followed the usual Bell format. Its three-bladed rotors had a diameter of 11.73 meters. Besides delivery services and short scheduled flights, the D-236 was also to fly personnel to and from oil-drilling platforms.

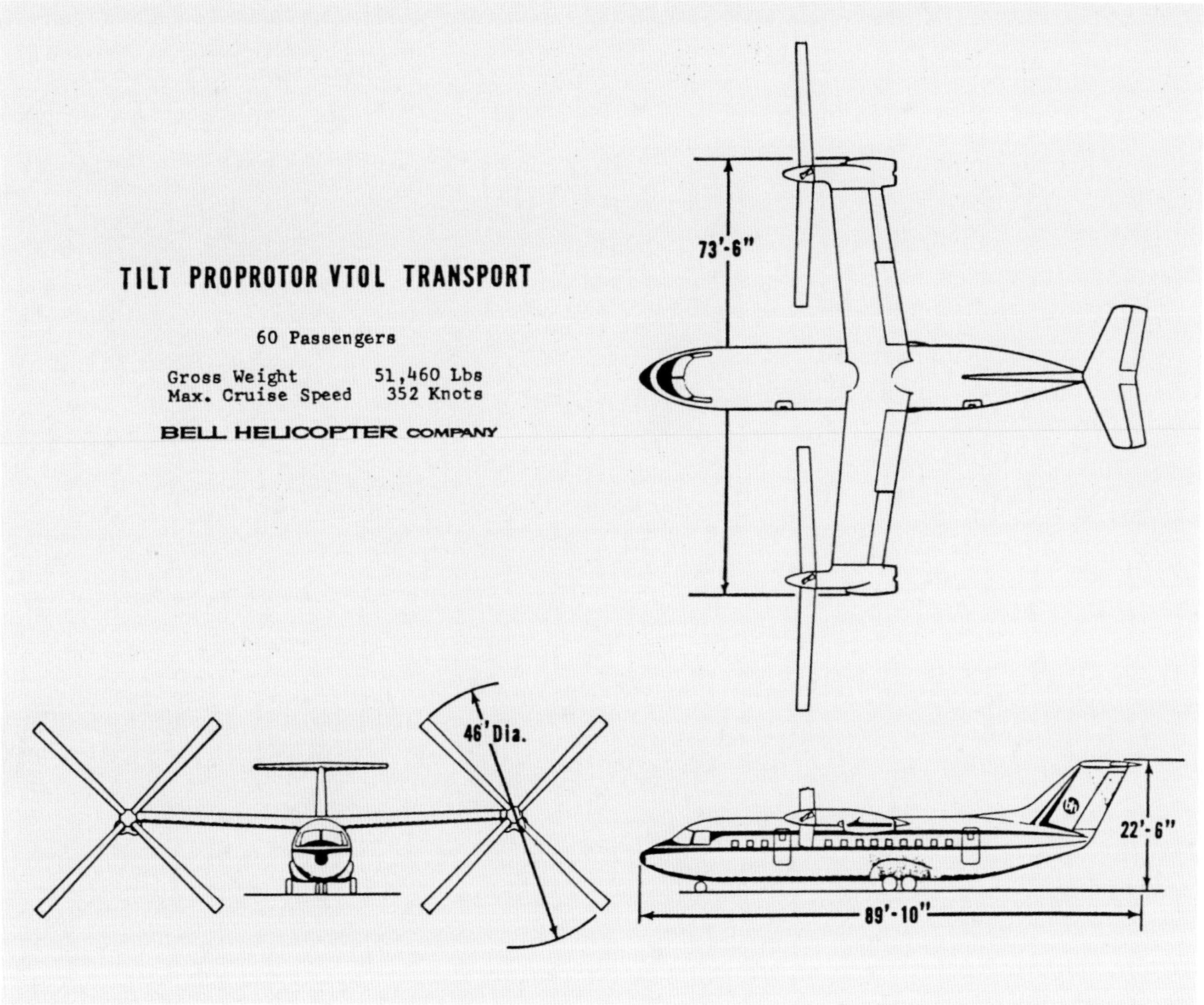

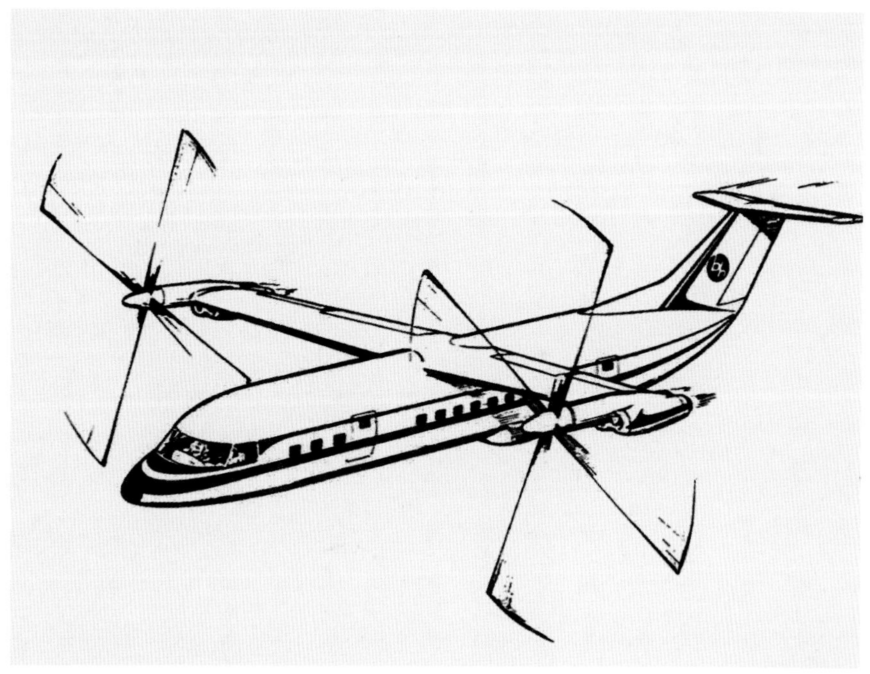

Above | Three-side view of the D-266 passenger version. *(Bell via HMB)*

Right | Passenger version of the D-266. *(Bell via HMB)*

Bell D-326 "Clipper"

Crew	2
Empty weight	16,783kg
Takeoff weight	19,050kg (VTOL), 22,680kg (STOL)
Length	7,210mm (rotors tipped vertically)
Wingspan	26,520mm (with rotors)
Powerplant	2 General Electric CT64 propeller turbines, 5,000 HP each
Top speed	611kph
Service ceiling	unknown
Range	1,110km with 30 passengers, 2,464km with 16 passengers.

Building on their experience with the XV-15 and V-22, Bell projected in 1987 a number of civilian tiltrotor airplanes. Among them were: one that was very similar to the V-22, but without the turning-folding mechanism for wings and rotors, an enlarged version of the V-22 with pressurized cabin, and a smaller craft that was to serve as a light passenger and business-trip airplane. This design had wings strongly angled forward and an elevator on the nose. The neat design of this study lets one conclude that Bell sought as high a cruising speed as possible, so as to move into the market of the established business-trip planes, and possibly even representative jets.

On the basis of their cooperation with Boeing to build the V-22, joint studies were also made at the end of the 1980s for various passenger planes. This even happened, in part, under official contracts and cooperation from NASA.

A study of a passenger airliner with tiltrotors, carried out jointly by Bell, Boeing and NASA. *(Bell via NASA)*

Boeing-Vertol Projects

Just like Bell, the helicopter department of the Boeing firm also made a large number of studies of passenger craft in tiltwing and tiltrotor configurations, which were often offshoots of military designs. At the end of the 1960s Boeing published the concept of a four-engine craft with tipping wings, based on the LIT design made for the USAF at the same time. The plane was laid out for ninety passengers and was to attain a cruising speed of 724kph.

At the end of the 1960s Boeing published studies for passenger aircraft with tipping wings. *(Boeing via HMB)*

251

Duncan Aviation "Xantus"

Terry Duncan, proprietor of Duncan Aviation in Michigan, USA, began in the early-1990s to design the lightest tiltwing airplane for private users. The fuselage of the "Xantus" (named after a kind of hummingbird) offered space for two people and their luggage. Two tandem wings were designed so that their outer halves could be tilted ninety degrees for takeoffs and landings. At the end of each of the four wings was a piston engine producing 125 HP, which drove a three-bladed propeller. Besides vertical takeoffs, the "Xantus" was also to be able to make short takeoffs, so as to increase its payload. The fuel capacity of 303 liters was to allow a range of 1,480km, at a speed of 460kph.

On July 7, 1999, the plane first made a bound flight, and was shown in public for the first time at the "AirVenture" in Oshkosh, Wisconsin at the end of July 1999. Duncan intended to begin systematic flight-testing as of the autumn of 1999, but no news has come from "Xantus" since then.

Duncan "Xantus"	
Crew	2
Empty weight	681kg
Takeoff weight	1,090kg (VTOL),
	1,362kg (STOL)
Length	unknown
Height	unknown
Wingspan	unknown
Powerplant	4 piston engines,
	125 HP each
Top speed	519kph
Service ceiling	7,620 meters
Range	1,480km

The "Xantus" at Oshkosh in 1999.
(Dave Mangham)

Moller M400 "Skycar"

Dr. Paul Moller has worked some four decades on the development of VTOL aircraft without any of them reaching series production. The model now in development, the M400, offers space for four people and is driven by eight Wankel motors. These engines, according to Moller International, are especially low in wear and emissions as well as reliable, and operate four tilting mantled propellers that are to give the M400 VTOL ability.

Moller markets the M400 as a "flying auto" that should be affordable for almost anyone and revolutionize personal transport. Moller declares that the purchase price with a series production of a million should be about $100,000. The Moller M400 was originally to be equipped with an automatic flight and navigation system, so that passengers are flown, fully automatically and without their subsequent intervention, to any place (within its range) that was previously pro-

Moller M400 with tilted mantled propellers.
(Moller International)

Moller M400 "Skycar"	
Crew	1+3
Empty weight	unknown
Takeoff weight	1,088kg
Length	5,900mm
Height	2,300mm
Wingspan	2,600mm
Powerplant	8 Wankel motors, 90 HP each
Top speed	579kph
Service ceiling	10,973 meters
Range	1,200km

grammed into the system. Of this ambitious goal, though, there is no longer any mention. Moller now states that a pilot's license will be required for the M400. The M400 should also be able to fly and hover in case one of the eight motors fails. For safety, the "Skycar" is designed so that in time of danger a parachute will bring the entire craft safely to the ground.

A first prototype made a tethered hover-hold lasting a few seconds in 2003. Since then, Moller has postponed the date of an actual flight repeatedly; the date now (announced summer 2009) is to be in 2012. The pictures and graphics published by Moller show a picture of the M400 that has changed slightly again and again over the years. The lasting delays in the program and his overly ambitious goals have caused many experts to predict the failure of the project.

Bell/Agusta BA 609

Since Bell foresaw the best chances for marketing a small passenger and business-trip plane, the first design work for such a craft, designated D-600, began at the end of 1994. In August 1996 Bell and Boeing agreed to cooperate in developing the type (now called Bell Boeing BB609), and in November of that year they announced their joint work on a civilian tiltrotor airplane.

In June 1997, Bell and Boeing displayed a mockup of the BB609 at Le Bourget. It was also seen at the 1998 ILA in Berlin. But in the spring of 1998 Boeing had already withdrawn from the project.

A mockup of the BA609 at the 1998 ILA. There the Aero Dienst Nürnberg made a pre-contract for the BA609 and was thus the sixty-seventh potential customer for the plane. *(Roland Oster)*

The prototype of the BA609, built in the USA, on a test flight.

In August 1998, Bell and Agusta (today AgustaWestland) made known that they would carry on the development of the plane, now called BA609, together and wanted to build four prototypes at first: two in the USA and two in Italy. Bell, though, is clearly the leader of the team. AgustaWestland has only a 25% share in the project, and is responsible for only the design and building of the gearboxes and control surfaces. There is actually a third partner: the cell of the production plane is to be built by Fuji Heavy Industries Ltd. in Japan. Fuji is also responsible for the design of the cabin, cockpit and rear fuselage. The final assembly, to be sure, would be done at the Bell works in Amarillo, Texas (where the V-22 is already being built) and at Agusta in Italy.

Like the cockpit of the larger V-22, the cockpit of the BA609 is dominated by color monitor screens. *(AgustaWestland)*

The skin of the BA609 consists of CFK and GFK, but the inner structure is made of aluminum. The pressurized fuselage offers space for two pilots and, depending on its use, six to nine passengers. The BA609 can be flown from either pilot's seat and has a digital glass cockpit with three-color monitor screens (MFD), weather radar, and electronic "fly-by-wire" steering.

In hover-hold it is controlled by the cyclical and collective adjustment of the proprotors. Unlike the V-22, the BA609 has a lever for collective blade adjustment. Since the craft has no side rudder, steering on the vertical axle in straight flight is done by means of the different settings of the propeller-adjusting angle.

The wings of the BA609, like those of the XV-15 and V-22, are angled slightly forward. The two-engine gondolas (which can tip ninety-five degrees) each hold an electronically controlled (FADEC) Pratt & Whitney of Canada PT6C-67A turbine, with 1940 HP driving a three-bladed proprotor. The opposed proprotors are also made of composition material, are strongly twisted, and have a diameter of 7.92 meters. The BA609 reaches a cruising speed of 465kph and is thus twice as fast as most helicopters. The cabin of the BA609 measures 4.08x1.47x1.42 meters and generally offers space for six to nine persons (plus baggage) or a 2,500kg payload.

Interior views
of the mockup
of the BA609
displayed at
the ILA in 1998.
(Roland Oster)

BellBoeing 609
TEXTRON

Because of the difficulties in the V-22 program, the finishing of the first BA609 prototype was delayed until the end of 2002. It finally began its ground tests on December 6, 2002, and took off on its maiden flight on March 6, 2003. After a total flight time of fourteen hours in helicopter mode, the flights were interrupted and the plane, in a ground test bench, began to tilt its engine nacelles.

The flight-testing was restarted only in June 2005, as new software for the "fly-by-wire" system had to be programmed and the controls surfaces had to be made more secure against being struck by birds. On July 22, 2005, Prototype No.1 took off at the Bell works in Arlington, Texas and carried out its first full transition. In this flight the plane reached 350kph in airplane mode.

Prototype No.1 in horizontal flight. *(Bell)*

By November 2006 the BA609 had accrued 100 hours of flight time in all. On November 9, 2006, the second prototype, built by Agusta in Italy, finally took off on its fifty-two-minute first flight at Cameri (near Milan), and in June of the next year it was displayed in flight at the Le Bourget air show. The two BA609s spent a total of 365 hours in the air by October 2008 without any problems being known. The BA609 built in Italy was also on display at Farnborough in July 2008 and at Le Bourget again in June 2009. According to the manufacturers, prototypes Nos.3 and 4 should be finished by the end of 2009.

The development of the BA609 was and is characterized by numerous delays. Though the authorization of the U.S. authorities (Federal Aviation Administration, FAA) was expected in 2001 for 2003, the date of 2005 was already postponed to 2008. In 2007 the manufacturers finally mentioned 2010, and now (summer 2009) it is said that the BA609 will be authorized for the end of 2011 or the beginning of 2012.

Despite that, a number of orders for the BA609 have been waiting for several years. According to the manufacturers, eighty planes have been pre-ordered by forty customers from twenty countries. A definite price has not been determined, but experts expect it to be ten to fifteen million dollars per plane.

The ability of the BA609 to take off and land like a helicopter, and then to fly with the speed of a turboprop at altitudes that remain uninfluenced by the weather, may bring Bell/Agusta a goodly number of orders despite the high price – if the BA609 is authorized in the foreseeable future.

The manufacturers do not see the BA609 as only a light passenger plane or a business-trip craft that brings managers from the roof of their headquarters to an airport or heliport of another business. It was also intended as an SAR and MEDEVAC plane, a craft for police and border patrols, and a delivery craft for oil platforms.

BA609
Tilt Rotor

Above | The possible uses Bell and Agusta see for the BA609 can be seen in this drawing from a company brochure. *(Bell/Agusta via HMB)*

Left page | Thanks to its VTOL ability, the BA609 can land on small surfaces in city centers and bring their passengers to their destination at twice the speed of a helicopter.

Bell/Agusta also hopes for the development of military variants, such as a trainer for the V-22, a multipurpose version for transport, communications and observation, and an armed model for combat tasks. The U.S. Coast Guard actually was interested in the BA609 for its "Deep Water" program. Because of the delays in developing the plane, the Coast Guard backed out in 2001. Bell and Agusta are also developing the concept of an enlarged version with twenty-six seats and four engines in tandem with the BA626. Obviously, this design is not being followed up any more.

Prototype No.2 on a test flight over northern Italy. The authorization of the BA609 is expected for 2011-2012 after several delays. (AgustaWestland)

Bell/Agusta BA609

Crew	2
Empty weight	4,765kg
Takeoff weight	7,600kg
Powerplant	2 Pratt & Whitney of Canada PT6C-67A turbines, 1,940 HP each
Top speed	509kph
Length	13,410mm
Height	4,570mm (upper edge of side fins)
Wingspan	10,050mm, 18,280mm with rotors
Service ceiling	1,300km
Range	1,300km

BA609 prototype No.2 in ground testing.
(AgustaWestland)

DRONES

Chapter 7

The drones, or UAVs (Unmanned Aerial Vehicles), have gained significance strongly in the most recent years, especially for military use. For the most part they are used as low-cost reconnaissance and observation craft, with no pilot being endangered if they are lost.

There are decisive advantages for VTOL drones, especially for action near fronts, in built-up areas, or from ships. Takeoff and landing strips or the catapults often used for drones, or landing and catching apparatus (parachutes, nets, air pillows) can be dispensed with. Drones with tiltrotors (also called VTUAV/VTOL UAV: Vertical Takeoff and Landing Ummanned Aerial Vehicles) can also linger over the object to be observed via their hovering ability, and are as a rule more mobile than conventional drones.

AUSTRALIA

AVT "Hammerhead"

The first considerations for the design of a small, unmanned tiltrotor airplane with electric drive were begun in 1993 by the Australian firm of AVT (Advanced VTOL Technologies). To be sure, only as of 2003 was the necessary technology available, especially in the realm of batteries, to allow the design to commence. Flight-testing of the "Hammerhead" prototype with canard wings began on February 25, 2006, and is being continued in 2009.

The control of the pitching and yawing movements in hover-hold is done via an electrically powered blower located in the rear of the fuselage; rolling movements are steered by the opposed propellers. For takeoffs and landings, the airscrews can be tilted 100 degrees, but the "Hammerhead" can also make short takeoffs. The payload in VTOL mode is some 3.5kg.

AVT has decided on electric motors for power, since they create less vibration and noise than piston engines. The present model, though, is purely a test plane for testing the concept and the flight capability. For series production, the use of other engines and enlargement of the dimensions would be possible if their action required them.

The prototype of the "Hammerhead" is driven by electric motors. *(AVT)*

AVT "Hammerhead"

Crew	none
Empty weight	10.5kg
Takeoff weight	14kg
Powerplant	2 electric motors, unknown performance
Top speed	167kph
Length	2,500mm
Height	unknown
Wingspan	2,000mm
Service ceiling	unknown
Range	200km

The "Hammerhead" in hover-hold tests.
(AVT)

Chiba University QTW-UAS FS4

Prof. Kenzo Nonami of the University of Chiba has, in cooperation with the Japanese firm of GH Craft, developed an electrically powered drone for military and civilian uses. The craft, called QTW (Quad Tilt Wing), has tilting tandem wings with electric motors installed at their tips and driving three-bladed propellers of 70cm diameter. The payload of the small craft is five kilograms, its steering is done by the differential adjustment of the four propellers and their performance. The development of the QTW began in 2004, and the drone made its first automatically steered flight with full transition in February 2008.

The QTW-UAS FS4 designed by Prof. Kenzo Nonami of the University of Chiba is also driven by electric motors.
(GH Craft/Chiba University)

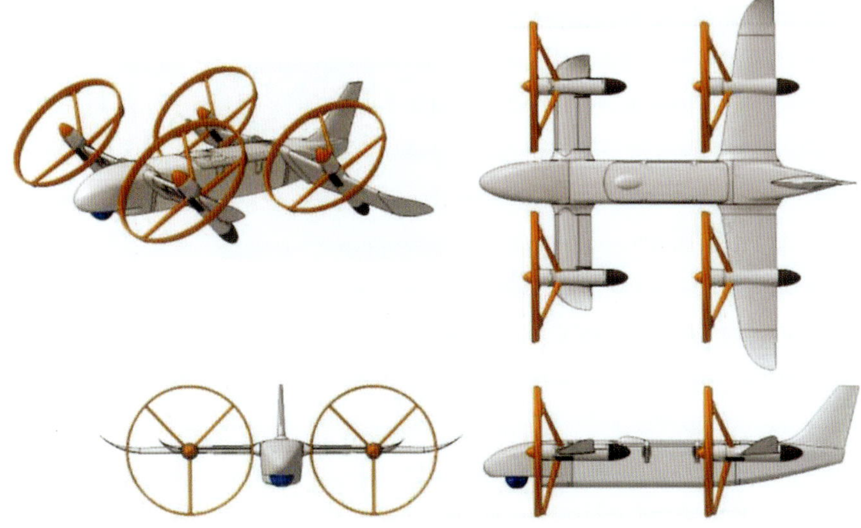

The QTW-UAS FS4 tiltwing drone developed by the University of Chiba and GH Craft (shown here as a model) made its first fully autonomous flight in February 2009. (GH Craft/Chiba University)

QTW-UAS FS4

Crew	none
Empty weight	25kg
Takeoff weight	30kg
Powerplant	4 electric motors, 2kw each
Top speed	150kph
Length	1,863mm
Height	619mm (wings vertical)
Wingspan	1,800mm
Service ceiling	unknown
Range	maximum 1 hour of flight

First flight of the "Smart" on November 30, 2007. *(Korean Aerospace Research Institute)*

SOUTH KOREA

"Smart" UAV System

In 2002 the Korean Aerospace Research Institute (KARI), along with the "Smart UAV Development Center" set up by the South Korean Economic Ministry, began to develop an unmanned tiltrotor airplane similar to the Bell "Eagle Eye." The design of the drone for civilian and military uses came about in the course of a program initiated by the Korean government and running until 2012 with a funding of 109 million dollars.

On November 22, 2007, a concept demonstrator about two meters long, with a wingspan of 1.8 meters, made its first flight in Goheung, Jeolla Province. The final prototype is to be some five meters long and have a wingspan of about four meters. Its production was expected in mid-2009, with its first flight that autumn. As of the summer of 2009, though, there were no further reports.

The "Smart" strongly resembles the Bell tiltrotor drones in its structure. *(Korean Aerospace Research Institute)*

Yakovlev "Albatross"

In the mid-1990s the design bureau of A.S. Yakovlev set up a concept for an unmanned reconnaissance airplane with tiltrotors, designated "Albatross." The "Albatross" has a wide, flat fuselage with short, rounded wings in shoulder-decker configuration, on each end of which is a tilting nacelle with a three-bladed rotor of 2.2-meter diameter. A butterfly control surface inclined downward serves as part of the running gear and complements a single central wheel mount that is retracted into the fuselage. Under the fuselage is a turning cupola with TV and infra-red cameras, whose signals can be sent immediately over distances of up to 100km. As far as is known, no prototype has yet been built.

Three-side view of the "Albatross."

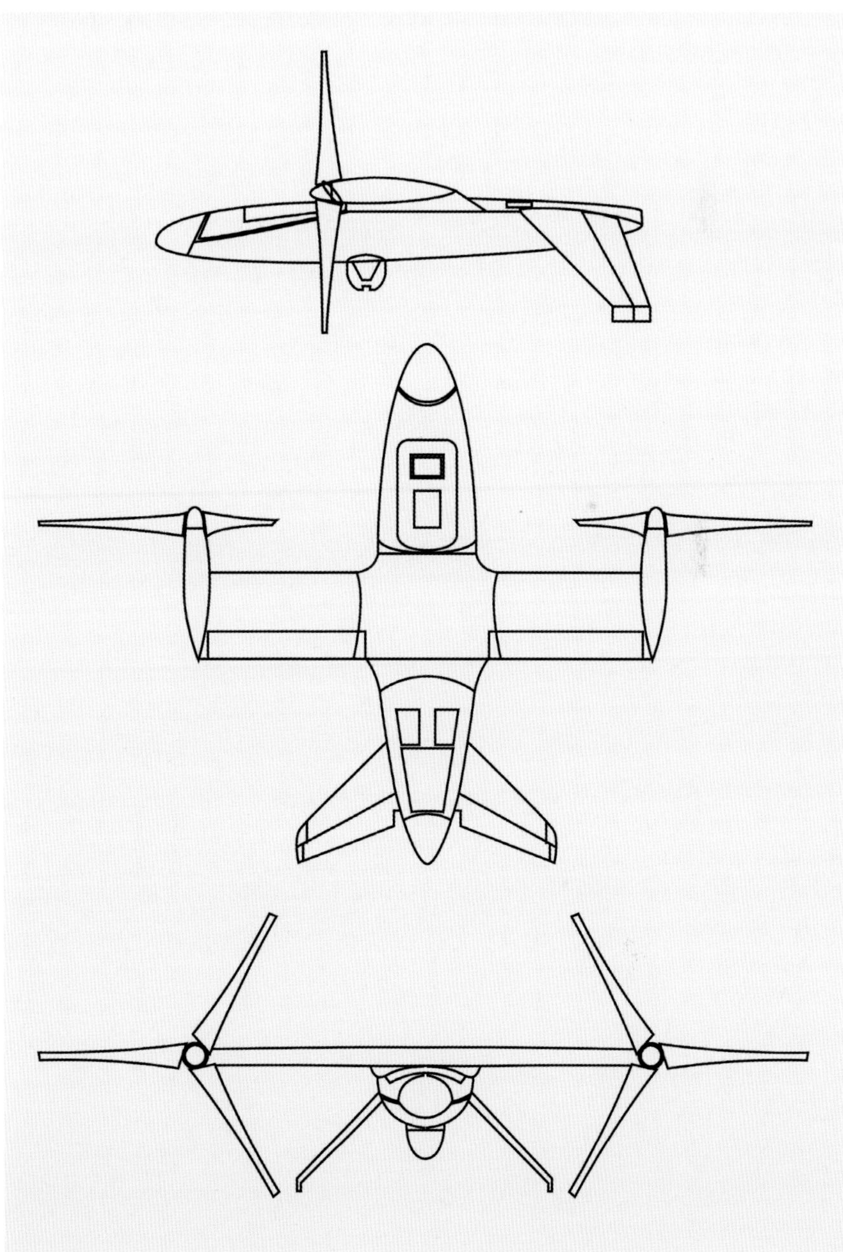

Yakovlev "Albatross"	
Crew	none
Empty weight	unknown
Flying weight	450kg
Powerplant	160 HP piston engine
Top speed	300kph
Length	4,800mm
Height	2,200mm
Wingspan	8,000mm (with rotors)
Service ceiling	350 meters
Range	maximum 7 hours flight time

Bell-Boeing D-340 "Pointer"

Crew	none
Empty weight	185kg
Flying weight	250kg
Powerplant	95 HP Suzuki piston engine
Top speed	297kph
Length	4,060mm
Height	1,670mm
Wingspan	3,250mm
	(5,610mm with rotors)
Service ceiling	2,750 meters
Range	maximum 7 hours flight time

Bell TR-916 "Eagle Eye"

Crew	none
Empty weight	unknown
Flying weight	unknown
Powerplant	1 Pratt & Whitney
	PW200/55 turbine, 641 HP
Top speed	370kph
Length	5,563mm
Height	1,880mm (vertical rotors)
Wingspan	4,318mm,
	7,336mm with rotors
Service ceiling	6096 meters
Range	1,480km or maximum
	6 hours flight time

USA

Bell-Boeing D-340 "Pointer"

The development of the "Pointer" began in 1986 as an offshoot of the V-22 program. The structure of the drone consisted completely of composition materials. A 95 HP snowmobile motor made by Suzuki and mounted in the middle of the fuselage drove two tilting three-bladed rotors of 2.36-meter diameter mounted on the wing tips. The fuselage and the flight regulating system were designed by Boeing, the power and rotors by Bell. The "Pointer" was first displayed in public at the Farnborough air show in September 1988; the first flight took place at the end of that November. Shortly after that Boeing left the program and Bell continued the development alone.

Bell "Eagle Eye"

After the testing of the "Pointer," Bell developed an improved drone named "Eagle Eye" as part of the Pentagon's UAV program, and commissioned the Scaled Composites firm to build two test planes in 7/8 scale. The planes were made extensively of composition materials and were fitted with an Allison 250 C-20 turbine (420 HP) in the fuselage, driving two tiltrotors, mounted on the wing tips, via shafts.

The first hover-holds of this prototype, designated TR-911X, took place early in 1992. In the summer and autumn of 1993 the two TR-911X were tested by the U.S. forces at the Yuma Proving Ground in Arizona. The planes fulfilled all their set tasks and made forty-five flights, with fifteen hours of flight time, without having any problems. In 1994 the program was ended on the part of the Pentagon, and Bell decided to continue the development at its own cost.

Because the U.S. Navy was interested, a two-stage test program was carried out as of April 1998. Part one of the program took part on land; part two was completed on a ship at the end of 1999. Although one of the two prototypes crashed during these tests, the TR-911X fulfilled or exceeded all of the Navy's requirements.

Yet this successful testing led to no contract from the Navy, but the U.S. Coast Guard (USCG) contracted with Bell in their "Deep Water" program in July 2002 to develop a model, called TR-916, with IR and radar sensors, that could carry an internal payload of 91kg.

In October 2007, the Coast Guard broke off the program before a single one of the planned "Eagle Eye" craft was taken over. The USCG also considered in 2009 whether the acquisition of the TR-916 was to be taken up again or another, less costly drone should be purchased.

In 2005 Bell announced the development of a model called TR-918 for the U.S. Marine Corps, which made its first flight on January 26, 2006. On April 5 of that year the prototype crashed but was repaired. The main difference between the TR-916 and TR-918 is their equipping with different sensors, and the latter has slightly larger dimensions, but 95% of all their components are identical.

Since the summer of 2004 Bell has tried, in partnership with Sagem and Rheinmetall, to market the "Eagle Eye" in Europe and Asia, but so far without success.

Three-side view of the "Pointer."

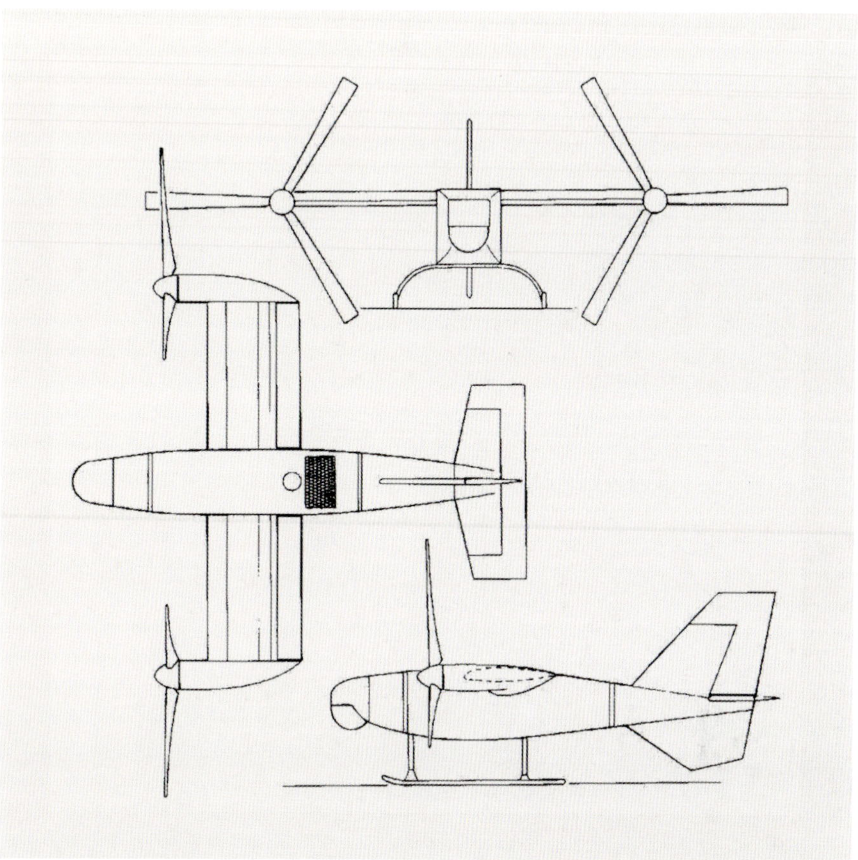

The acquisition of the "Eagle Eye" for the U.S. Coast Guard was postponed for an unspecified time for reasons of cost. Whether the program will ever be taken up again is more than questionable. *(USCG)*

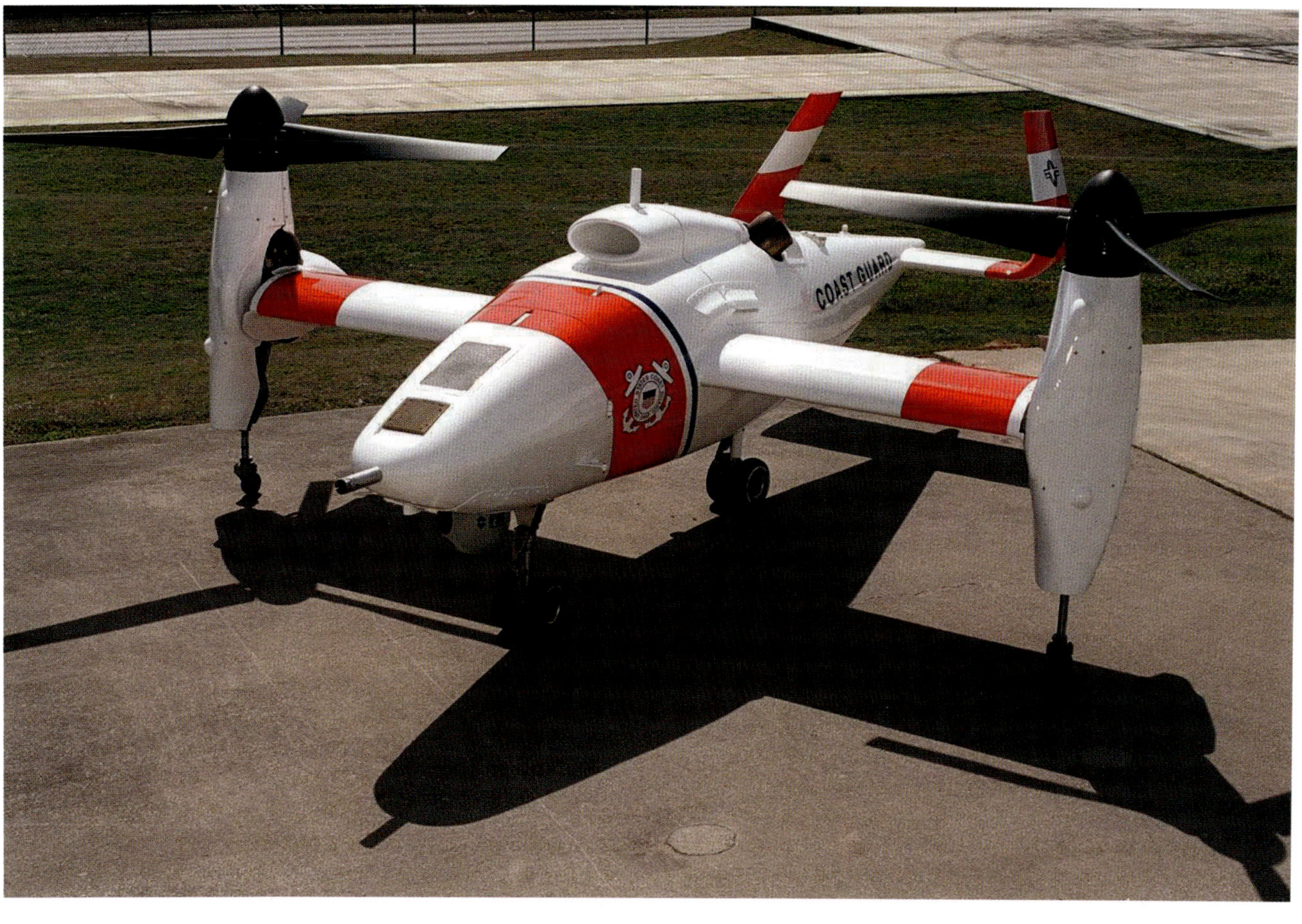

FUTURE DEVELOPMENTS

Although neither the V-22 nor the BA609 can finally be evaluated as a success, tiltrotor technology (and the related concepts) may be used in the future. The advantages that a combination of helicopter and airplane offer are too great.

In particular, the reawakened interest of the U.S. forces in VTOL aircraft may lead to tiltrotor craft being designed and built in the near future.

The Air Force, Army and Marine Corps need replacements in foreseeable time for their C-130 "Hercules" transport planes or CH-47 "Chinook" helicopters. While the USMC is in favor of further development of the esteemed old CH-53 as the CH-53K, the Army has more ambitious goals. In 2005, the U.S. Army made known that it was seeking a new vertical takeoff and landing transport that must be capable of transporting an eighteen-ton load at a speed of 463kph. In answer to this "Joint Heavy Lift" (JHL) specification, proposals on two tiltrotor craft were received: the Bell Boeing QTR and Karem TR-65-190.

The Bell Boeing QTR (Quad Tilt Rotor), as its name indicates, has two pairs of wings in tandem order and four tilting engine nacelles. The QTR is largely based on the technology of the V-22, and thus is unofficially called "V-44." Its front wings are taken completely from the V-22, while only the outside parts of the rear wings match the wings of the "Osprey." The engines, four Rolls-Royce AE 1107C Liberty turbines of 6,150 HP each, also come originally from the V-22. They drive four tilting proprotors of 15.24-meter diameter. Since all of the steering (also in straight flight) is to be done by the four proprotors, the design had no lateral or vertical rudders. The fuselage of the QTR is close to that of the C-130 in size. The cargo space is 18.97 meters long and carries 110 fully equipped paratroops, or over eighteen tons of cargo. The cruising speed is to be 519 to 546kph and the range with a maximum payload is 925km (in VTOL mode). Bell and Boeing received a contract in September 2005, valid through March 2007, for further development of the concept. During this time extensive tests were made in the NASA wind tunnel at Langley, Virginia.

In May 2007 the contract was lengthened by the Army, but the requirements had changed so much by that time that the original QTR could no longer fulfill it. Now the Army required a payload of twenty-seven to twenty-nine tons. Bell and Boeing reworked and extended the design appropriately in 2007-08. Among the variants now considered is also a "Big Boy" version, with cargo space 20.7 meters long and proprotors measuring 16.76 meters that would be capable of transporting an armored wheeled vehicle of the "Stryker" type. This version would have to be equipped with higher-performance powerplants, which are not yet available in 2009.

Artistic portrayal of the Bell Boeing QTR.
(Bell Boeing)

Five-side view of the QTR design by Bell on its patent application. *(Bell)*

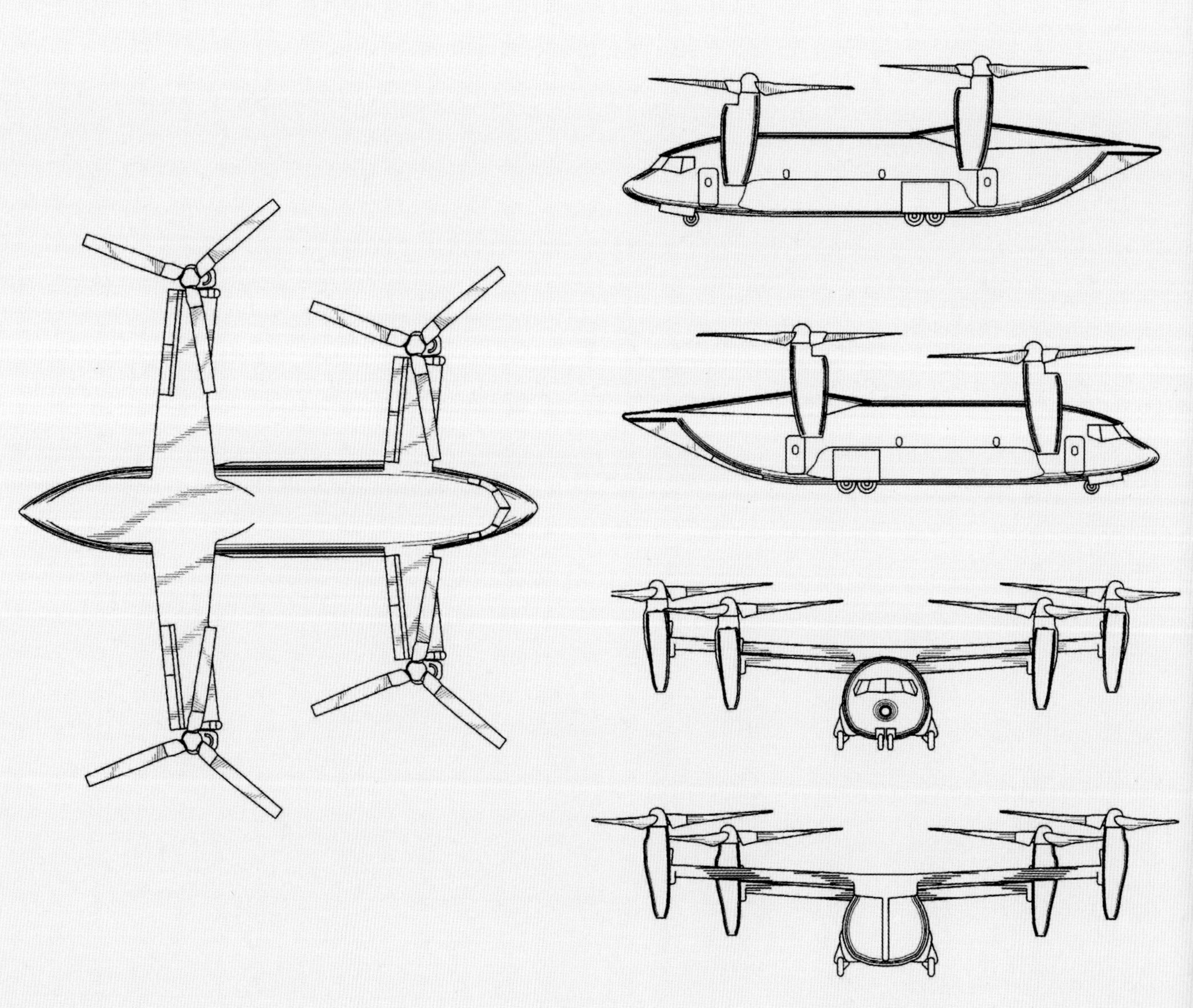

Left | Model of the QTR in the Langley wind tunnel. *(NASA)*

Below | Artistic portrayal of a possible use of the Bell QTR. *(Bell)*

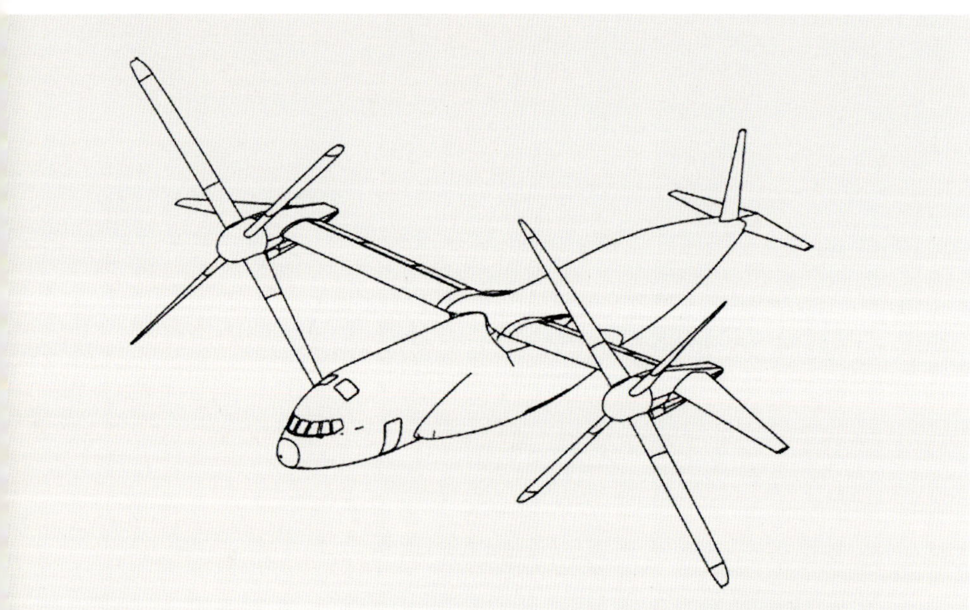

The Karem TR-65-190 was designed by Karem Aircraft Inc., a small firm located in California. Like Bell Boeing, Karem Aircraft also received a contract in 2005 for further development of the design. Karem says that the TR-65-190 should be able to attain a cruising speed of up to 639kph and an altitude of over 12,000 meters. Its range with a full payload in VTOL mode would be 1,200km. In one-way flights the plane, with 120 passengers and auxiliary tanks, should be able to cover 10,600km.

These astounding achievements are based, Karem says, on an "Optimum Speed Tilt Rotor" (OSTR) technology. In simple terms, the power is configured by an electronically controlled gearbox so that both 19.8-meter rotors always run optimally (meaning faster or slower speeds) in hover-hold and cruising speed.

The stated empty weight of 28,100kg is also astonishingly light for a craft the size of the C-130; the VTOL takeoff weight Karem states as 50,400kg. In STOL use a payload of up to thirty-six tons is to be possible. Karem also had to rework the TR-65-190 because of the new requirements of mid-2007, and in 2008 they cooperated with Lockheed-Martin for further development of the model. In the same year Karem introduced a civilian variant which was designated TR53 "AeroTrain." Its cruising speed is stated as 720kph.

The USAF too, in their search for a successor to the C-130, likewise issued a description (Advanced Joint Air Command System – AJACS) shortly before 2000. Unlike the Army, the Air Force required no VTOL action, but called for the ability to operate from an extremely short takeoff and landing strip (SSTOL – Super Short Take Off and Landing). In addition, a thirty-ton load was to be transported over 2,000km.

Computer graphics of the "Aero Train."
(Karem)

Boeing advertisement for the ATT *(Boeing)*

One of the submitted designs was a Boeing concept called "Advanced Theater Transport" (ATT) that had originated already in the 1990s.

This model, also known unofficially as the "Super Frog," owes its amazing STOL ability particularly to its tiltwings. To be sure, they, unlike those of the XC-142A or CL-84, do not tilt completely, but only forty-five degrees. The ATT also has inflated flaps, so that it gets by with a landing distance of 183 meters. According to Boeing, a landing speed of 60 to 90kph and a cruising speed of over 700kph are possible.

The wingspan and fuselage length of the Boeing design are shorter than those of the C-130, but the ATT fuselage is twice as wide and can hold over thirty-six tons of freight.

In 2008, the Pentagon also instructed that the JHL and AJACS requirements be combined for reasons of cost. In 2009 the Army and Air Force were still harmonizing their requirements so that by the end of the year they could issue a new set of requirements for the program, now called "Joint Future Theater Lift" (JFTL).

In May 2008, though, Boeing presented a concept that was to meet the needs of both. This design, called "Joint Common Airlift Systems" (JCALS), foresees that there should be a common fuselage with different wings and the engines attached to them. The USAF variant has two turbofan motors hung under the wings and is SSTOL-capable, while the Army version has engine nacelles and proprotors mounted on the wing tips, giving it VTOL characteristics.

Time will tell how the JFTL program works out and what design finally prevails. Budget cuts, changing priorities, or new requirements could lead to the program being dropped or strongly modified. The fact is, though, that the U.S. forces must find successors to their C-130 and CH-47 fairly soon. As things look now, the requirements for possible successors will bring out further tiltrotor or tiltwing designs.

Farther in the future (as of 2030) the U.S. Army plans to replace its AH-64 "Apache" and UH-60 "Blackhawk" combat and transport helicopters. The Marines will also need new helicopters at that time. Thus the two service arms decided to have a "Joint Multi-Role Rotorcraft" (JMR) successor developed as of 2023. Bell already presented an initial study for such a rotorcraft in 2009. This "Hybrid Tandem Rotor" (HTR) concept has tiltrotors but cannot tip them ninety degrees, like the V-22, but only twenty-five degrees. Through the cyclical adjustment of the rotor blades, another five degrees of tilt should be attainable. Bell states that the design should attain a cruising speed of up to 416kph, more than current helicopters (about 300kph), but less than the V-22.

As already shown, unmanned planes with tiltrotors or tilting propellers have appeared increasingly in recent years. This trend will continue, since the military has recognized the advantages of VTOL qualities for drones. This also applies to the American Dynamics AD-150, which is now being developed into a VTOL-UAV because of the strong interest of the U.S. Navy.

Right | Boeing JCALS study with tiltrotors.
(Boeing)

Below | Bell study of a "Hybrid Tandem
Rotor" (HTR) in multi-use and combat
forms. (Bell)

Above | Computer graphics of the AD-150.
(American Dynamics)

Right | The mantled propellers of the
AD-150 are supposed to be both swingable
and tiltable. (American Dynamics)

The aircraft has two tiltable and swingable mantled propellers driven by a 750-H PW200 turbine mounted in the fuselage. Its takeoff weight is about 1,022kg, and its length 4.42 meters. The drone should attain 555kph and a flight extent of up to four hours. The AD-150 consists mainly of composite materials and Kevlar. It navigates with the help of GPS, flies up to 6,100 meters high, and has an internal shaft for a 227kg payload, and can also carry outside loads. A full-size mockup of the AD-150 was first displayed to the public in Washington, D.C. on August 7, 2007.

In both the military and civilian sectors there may be more work on improving the proprotor. One goal will be to make it more effective in hover hold and cruising speed. To be most effective in hover hold, the proprotors must have a larger diameter, but this is not optimal at cruising speed. A possible solution might be extendable rotor blades, as was already planned by Westland and VFW in the 1960s. Sikorsky is now working on similar concepts.

To increase the speed of tiltrotor planes, there has been the idea since the 1960s of using rotors only for takeoff and landing. At cruising speed they would fold up and be stored; the propeller turbines would then become jet engines. This "tilt-fold" or "stop-fold" concept was already tested thoroughly by Bell early in the 1970s and found to be feasible, but the combination propeller turbine-jet engine in particular was problematic. But Bell never let this concept pass completely out of their minds, and are working harder at this time to realize it, especially in view of the radar signature "Stealth."

Studies were made by Bell in the late-1980s for combat planes with tilting/folding rotors. *(Bell via NASA)*

BILL DALE

VTOL airplanes, including those with tiltrotors, make noise, often more than conventional planes. This is one reason why the establishment of city "Vertiports," airports for VTOL planes, may be objected to. In the future, climbing fuel costs will also play a more and more important role.

The Falx Air firm of North Staffordshire, Great Britain, therefore began around 2000 to develop a small VTOL aircraft, with tilting propellers or wings, that could be equipped with gasoline-electric motors to minimize noise and operating costs. In the most recent years, the outward appearance of the airplane has changed slightly many times. Besides tilting propellers, tilting mantled propellers are seen on the graphics that the company has published.

In the summer of 2009 Falx stated that they wanted to build a prototype in the next twelve months. To what extent this will be possible remains to be seen.

The capability of a helicopter to hover and land in the smallest space is undeniable today. The helicopter itself, though, has come to the boundaries of its capability for aerodynamic reasons. An extension of these boundaries is possible in the foresee-

Falx hopes to be able to build a prototype of its tiltwing craft with hybrid drive in 2010. *(Falx Air)*

able future only through tiltrotor technology and concepts related to it. The XV-15, BA609, and in part also the V-22 have proved that this technology is practicable. Mechanically, airplanes like the XV-15 and BA609 are no more complex than a CH-47. What the future will bring is yet uncertain. If the V-22 proves itself in the long run and the BA609 is accepted on the market, then this type of aircraft can look forward to a very promising future in both civilian and military uses.

Artistic portrayal of possible future tiltrotor and tiltwing aircraft, published by the "Council for Aeronautics Research in Europe." *(ACARE)*

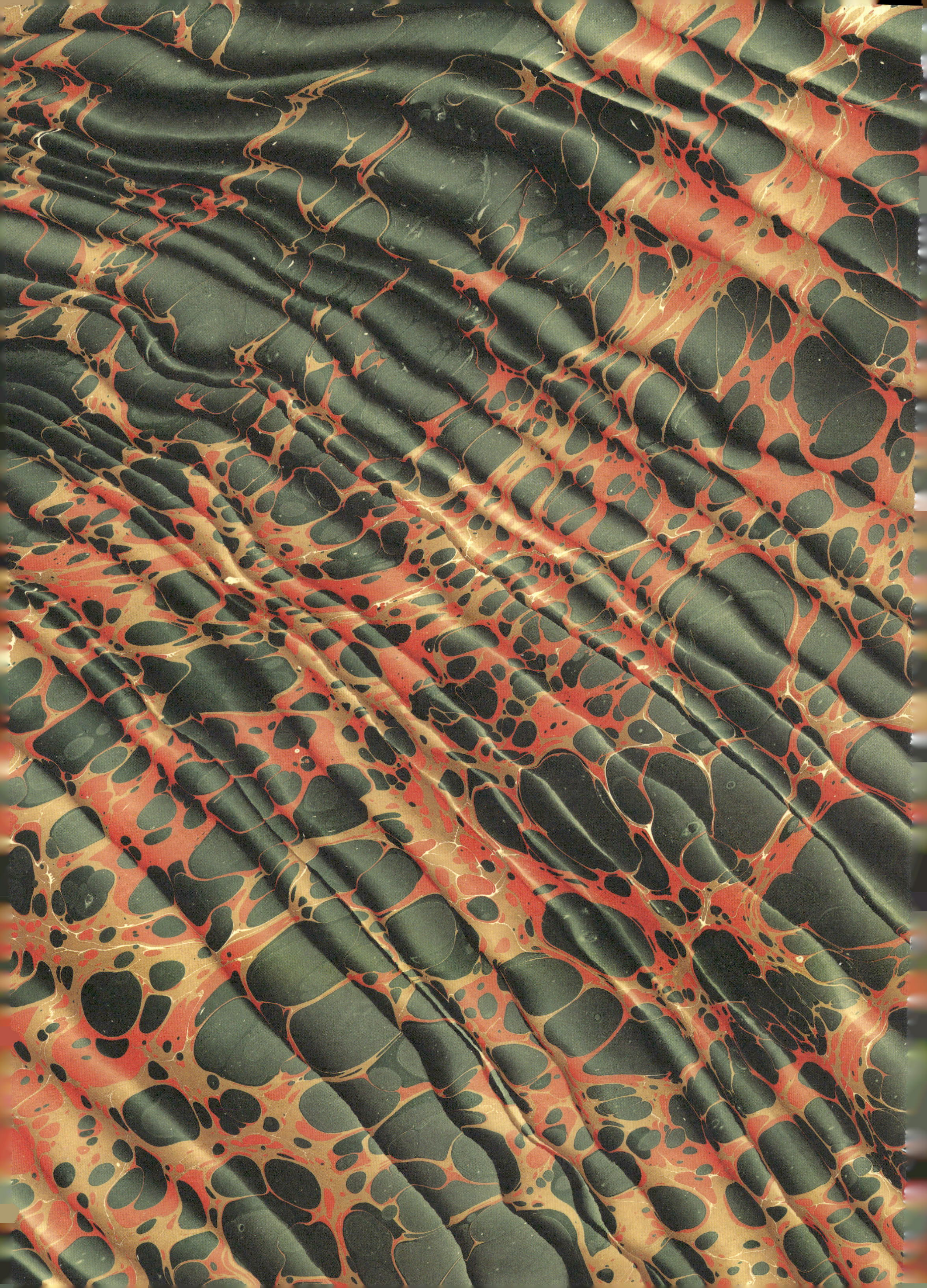